The Left's War Against the Poor

The Left's War Against the Poor

Rethinking the Politics of Poverty

John Pepple

authorHOUSE®

AuthorHouse™
1663 Liberty Drive
Bloomington, IN 47403
www.authorhouse.com
Phone: 1-800-839-8640

Published by AuthorHouse 02/06/2015

ISBN: 978-1-4969-6031-3 (sc)
ISBN: 978-1-4969-6030-6 (e)

Library of Congress Control Number: 2014922596

CONTENTS

ACKNOWLEDGMENTS

I want to thank Rebecca Abbott for reading a draft of this book and offering me many suggestions as well as saving me from some pathetic blunders. Naturally, all blunders herein are my own fault. I also want to thank my wife Sarah Blick for both emotional and financial support, support that was absolutely necessary in order for this book to see the light of day.

Let me add that many of the points made in this book I have filched from people on the right, whether conservative or libertarian. I generally haven't acknowledged the source for any of these points since I found the same point being made again and again by many different people, and I had no idea who had first said it. Accordingly, my citations are on the spare side, and I apologize if I have ignored whoever it was who first made a particular point.

INTRODUCTION

The left is waging a war against the poor. Indeed, for the last fifty years it has been waging this wretched war, a war that leftists somehow are not able to see. I myself participated in this war for most of that time and didn't see it. All I could see was how hurtful the conservatives were to the poor, which led me to wonder why anyone who was poor would vote Republican. Only in the mid-1990s did I finally wake up and realize what we were doing. Once I came to that realization, once I saw that we had been waging a war against the poor, I groaned when I thought about how we on the left had ushered in a series of Republican presidents whom we hated. We had ushered them in because we had transformed the left back in the 1960s, but we hadn't noticed that many poor people felt left behind and didn't like the transformations we were making. We dismissed them as dupes of Republican propaganda, or else as too racist to realize that the transformations we made were necessary. If I could go back in the past and do things differently, the first thing I would do would be to listen to the poor people who were complaining about what we were doing. Since that is impossible, I can do nothing other than what I'm doing in this book: informing leftists that they have made a big mistake and that it needs rectifying.

I know that all leftists will react the same way when they hear this kind of talk. They will say I am confused and that it is not the left that is waging a war against the poor, but the right. The right wages a war against the poor by supporting the rich against the poor and corporations against the workers, by opposing welfare and unemployment benefits, and in countless other ways. But the fact that the left doesn't do any of these particular things doesn't mean that the left isn't waging a war against the poor. It just means that the left is waging a war against the poor in its own way, which is perhaps why leftists cannot see this war. That is, the left is trained to see a war against the poor as consisting of the items just mentioned, such as opposing welfare; but the left's war against the poor is quite different from the right's war against the poor. One of the purposes of this book is to make clear to leftists their own way of waging war against the poor.

This particular war goes back to the 1960s, but when I began to look critically at the left twenty years ago, I found that the left had been making mistakes not just during the last fifty years, but during the last one hundred fifty to two hundred years. One big mistake was to think that capitalism was a problem and that therefore systems that opposed and replaced capitalism were the solution. Unfortunately, many tens of millions were murdered as a result of our pursuit of these systems, a fact that hasn't done us much good in persuading others that we have truth and justice on our side. My reasons for believing that capitalism is not a problem I will relate soon enough; they are the result of my experiences in academia, a segment of society in which all the problems of capitalism emerge, even though it is dominated by leftists. My basic point, though, is that the left made a mistake in opposing capitalism.

Why did the left make this mistake and why did it wage a war against the poor for the last fifty years? One broad answer is that the left was too uncritical of itself. Leftists love to be critical of conservatives and of capitalist economies, but they are much less interested in being critical of themselves and of non-capitalist economies. Obviously, this is an inconsistent procedure. But I also found a narrower answer, an answer that explained very well the war against the poor of the last fifty years. My answer is that leftism is dominated by rich people, and so would be better described as Rich People's Leftism.[1] Because of this, the fact that new policies were hurting the poor was invisible to the people making these policies. That is to say, leftism has been mostly under the control of the rich during its two-hundred-year history, and the analyses and policies that were conceived by the rich were more for their benefit than for the benefit of the poor. That has been especially true during the past fifty years. It will seem strange to many to say that systems of thought that verbally attack the rich, and which have even inspired physical attacks on the rich, should nevertheless be described as under the control of the rich; but that is what I found. In the beginning rich people basically controlled the left because they alone had the leisure time and the education to think about the plight of the exploited workers and to consider why they were so exploited. The answers they came up with were adopted by poorer people later on because those answers seemed, at least initially, congenial to the poor. As for the attacks on the rich, I found that the verbal ones were for show, while the actual physical attacks were mostly attacks on rich conservatives and not on rich leftists. However, while the answers provided by rich leftists may delight the poor by seeming to be anti-rich, I will argue that they did little or no good for the poor, but were greatly to the benefit of the rich people who went along with those answers. We need something better for the poor than what they have prescribed.

This brings me to the outline of this book. In the first part, I will argue that the left over the past fifty years has been waging a war against the poor. In the second part, I will argue that capitalism is not the problem that the left thinks it is. In the third and final part, I will argue that leftism is mostly what deserves to be called Rich People's Leftism, and I will describe what a leftism conceived and controlled by the poor, Poor People's Leftism, would look like. The basic difference is that Rich People's Leftism wants (or says it wants) redistribution of wealth, while Poor People's Leftism wants job creation.

Perhaps the first task of this book is to define who I mean when I talk about the rich and the poor. I admit that I will be using these words in various ways throughout this book, but let me say that perhaps the most basic way to distinguish the two groups is to say that anyone in the top half economically is rich and anyone in the bottom half is poor. This ignores the middle class,[2] of course, but I like this definition because it includes the lower middle class among the poor, which leftists are generally reluctant to allow. Being lower middle class means being rich enough to avoid the desperate situation of those at the bottom, but poor enough to miss many of life's pleasures. It means being too rich to get financial aid for college on the basis of need, but too poor to go to anything but the local state university. It means being too rich to get any kind of assistance, but too poor and too weak to fight against the higher taxes that seem inevitable when leftists manage to raise taxes on the rich. It means seeing people below you get entitlements and seeing people above you get great jobs, while you get neither.

To return to the definitions of rich and poor, I will sometimes be talking about the working poor, sometimes about poor whites, and sometimes about anyone in the bottom half or at least the bottom third. I don't see this varying referent as a defect, since the left should not be waging a war against anyone who is poor by any of these definitions. One of my points of contention against the left these days is that they tend to see the poor in certain terms: the poor are black or Latino rather than white, but if they are white, they are single mothers. Clearly, this leaves out a lot of poor whites, for example, those who mine coal in West Virginia or who are working class in a rural area or a small town. One of the biggest mistakes the left made during the last fifty years was turning its back on poor whites. But while I say that the left has ignored poor whites, I also say that the left has not always helped poor blacks (a point that has been made many times by conservatives). To sum up, the poor encompasses a lot more people than the left seems to think, and supporting some of the poor while dismissing others as not poor is dishonest and plainly stupid.

Another point to make clear is that while I will be talking mostly about leftists, many of the points I make can be made against liberals as well. Believing that a war against the poor must include (for example) being against welfare, believing that redistributions are the best way to help the poor, and believing that capitalism can never work for the poor are all beliefs held by everyone who is left-of-center. Nevertheless, I am not going to spend any time distinguishing between the beliefs of liberals and leftists. Since there is broad agreement among members of both groups for the points I am arguing against, it is not necessary.

The next point to consider is this: I am well aware that many on the left will think I have turned conservative, and some will think I have always been conservative. For this latter group, I suggest they take a look at my letter against Arthur Laffer published in the business section of *The New York Times* some years back.[3] For the former group, let me point out that people who are waging a war against the poor are hardly in a position to insist that I am the one who is conservative. As for the arguments I will be advancing in the second and third parts of this book, my concern in those parts is nothing other than this: *How can we best help the poor?* The fact that the answers I give don't conform to what some rich people declared a hundred fifty or two hundred years ago doesn't bother me. Their ideas have been tried and found wanting, and if leftists want to continue to cling to them when there are better ways of achieving our goal, then that is to their discredit and not mine. Let me also point out that some of what I am saying casts doubt on the sincerity of what leftists promote. I'm not talking here about leftists who are poor or lower middle class. No, I'm talking about those leftists who come from wealth, who talk about raising taxes on the rich, but who can't themselves be bothered to do much for the poor except by waiting for their own taxes to be raised. One suggestion I am going to make in the third part of this book is that instead of complaining about the need for higher taxes on the rich, wealthy leftists should step forward and donate to local charities or directly to the poor in their region. Such a practice has many things in its favor over aid via the government because when the government gets its hands on money, it often spends it in ways that do not benefit the poor. That money can even benefit rich leftists instead! It is much better to give to the poor directly.

Next, I want to explain who I am. I come from a lower-middle-class background. My parents were white collar workers, it is true, but they were employed as little more than low-level clerks. Both had gone to college, but my father didn't get his degree until I was ten. I acknowledge that as time went on, our family became wealthier to the point where I would say that we were perhaps middle middle class, but that didn't happen until long after I reached adulthood. My parents expected me to go to college, and I did, and I even went to grad school, during which time I spent several years in poverty. The result of those years together with the years I spent in the lower middle class in my childhood made enough of an impression on me that I naturally gravitated to the left, despite my parents' more conservative leanings. I supported the left simply because I believed that the left had done a lot for people from my background. I had a few disagreements with other leftists (which I talked about in my last two books[4]), but what separated me permanently from my fellow leftists was the way I was treated in academia. I will say more about this later. For now let me observe that despite the fact that most professors these days are left-of-center, they do very little for those academics who come from modest backgrounds—perhaps because they themselves often come from wealth. It was an eye-opening experience watching them treat me and other poor people shabbily, and it forced me to realize that the left was not exactly what I had been led to believe it was; it was not exactly helping the poor as much as it could be. Let me add that I have been mostly unemployed for the last twenty years. While my situation is not characterized by the desperation of young people today, who are both unemployed and have massive amounts of debt from college loans, it has been quite frustrating. I say this to point out that my preference for job creation rather than wealth redistribution is not an idea conjured up in an idyllic ivory tower that would be imposed on poor people against their will, but comes from a couple decades of actual experience with (as the British say) being redundant. It is something I want for myself.

Very little in this book is new and original. Many of the ideas expressed herein I have found in conservative venues. In fact, they are common coin among conservatives, so common that it was hard for me to determine who originally had the ideas, so the number of endnotes acknowledging their contributions is minimal. The problem for leftists is they are either unaware of these ideas, or look at them askance because of their source, or hear about them when they are ripped out of their original context. My contribution, beyond that of arguing for a leftism of the poor, is of collecting all these points in one place.

Let me now turn to the first part of this book, the discussion about the left's war against the poor that began about fifty years ago.

PART I:
THE LEFT'S RECENT WAR
AGAINST THE POOR

CHAPTER 1
THE FIVE INCOME TAXES

Before I give evidence that the left has been waging a war against the poor, I want to make an analogy. Imagine that there was not one, but five separate income taxes. Of these, one was the original income tax from the early part of the twentieth century, while the other four were new ones instituted in the 1960s by the Democrats. Imagine also that the following policies were in place. With respect to the original income tax, the Democrats demanded that it be high but also that it be progressive. In other words, they believed that the poor—and here I am including everyone in the bottom half as poor—should pay a smaller percentage of their income than the rich. However, with respect to the other four income taxes, the Democrats were indifferent. If those taxes happened to be regressive rather than progressive, they were not troubled.

The Republicans had a different policy. With respect to the original income tax, they weren't interested in whether it was progressive or not. They simply wanted the rates reduced. As for the other four income taxes, they wanted them *eliminated*.

Now, whose policies do you think the poor would prefer? Any Democrat who thinks that the poor would prefer their policies over those of the Republicans has blinders on. The poor don't like those extra four taxes, especially because those taxes tend to be regressive. The Democrats heartlessly say, "Well, you just have to pay them. They're needed." Meanwhile, the Republicans are saying, "We don't like those taxes either, and we want them eliminated."

Even worse, the Democrats' policy of having the original tax be high, the idea being that the money will be redistributed back to the poor, doesn't sit well with many poor people because (1) whatever they receive from a redistribution is gobbled up by paying the other four taxes, and (2) they believe that much of that money goes to people other than themselves anyway. Accordingly, they are stuck with high, mostly regressive taxes, and they don't like them at all. The Republicans swoop in and say, "We want to cut your tax rates." And many poor people love it.

From the late 1960s down to today, this has been the situation that Democrats have faced, and most of them have not understood it. This has had severe electoral consequences for the Democrats since at one time they regularly won presidential elections, whereas since the 1970s, their record has been much less impressive.

Since the 2008 election, what I am saying may not seem very important. There was a lot of talk after that election of a realignment in American politics, in which the Democrats would gain a lot of power and the Republicans would lose. I didn't believe this because I live in a lower-middle-class neighborhood, and I could see nothing there that would suggest any such realignment. It didn't surprise me at all when the Republicans came roaring back in 2010. Confidence returned to the Democrats with the 2012 election, but it may be a little misplaced. President Obama won re-election with fewer votes than he received in 2008, which isn't suggestive of a realignment. Anyway, the election of 2014 was another big win for the Republicans, a win that gave them control of the Senate and many state legislatures and governorships. Accordingly, I'm going to assume that any realignment is something that might happen twenty or thirty years from now, but is not happening right now, and so the Democrats are back to figuring out how to get more poor voters on their side.

Let me consider some other reasons leftists might be inclined to dismiss what I am saying. Many Democrats imagine the poor will always favor their policies. This is an article of faith among the Democrats to such a degree that perhaps not even using the analogy of the five income taxes will get through to them. In the minds of such ideologues, the left is the poor person's natural ally. That was carved in stone ages ago and can never be overthrown, nor can any amount of empirical evidence ever show them that some poor people now have different attitudes. But I say that poor people will generally go to whichever party or group they think will help them more. If they are desperate—and poor people often are—they will follow (whether knowingly or unknowingly) the adage, "Any port in a storm." Their attitude will be, "So what if I've been voting for the Democrats for half a century? I need help now, and while the Democrats are not willing to provide it, the Republicans are." Any Democrat who clings to the idea that the poor will always see the Democrats as their ally will never understand the election of various Republicans over the last half century, and they might as well save time and stop reading this book now.

A slightly less deluded Democrat may, when considering the extra taxes I am talking about, dismiss them as unimportant. He or she may say, "The Republicans hurt the poor so much through their other policies that these regressive taxes you talk about don't mean anything." But that isn't the way the poor see it. Their attitude is, "You should not be hurting us at all." The fact that they perceive the Democrats as hurting them makes them feel betrayed. When everything is toted up, it might be true that Republicans hurt the poor more than Democrats did, but I wouldn't bet on it. I believe that poor people, especially the working poor, have sound instincts and that they know better than Democratic theorists what their situation is and who is helping them more. But let's say they are wrong. It is nevertheless true that the workers believe that the Democrats betrayed them, and people who feel betrayed are not necessarily going to think rationally about the matter. They will just vote for the Republicans to get back at the Democrats.

Another response of the Democrats may be to blame the regressive nature of those new taxes on the Republicans. This response, however, doesn't seem especially intelligent. It was Democrats who wanted those extra taxes, not Republicans. The Republicans simply want them eliminated. Democrats may claim that the new taxes our country ended up with were a compromise between the Democrats and the Republicans, that the Democrats wanted them to be progressive but had to settle for them being regressive if they wanted to have them at all. However, I know of no historical evidence for such a claim. As far as I can tell, the Democrats never even considered the possibility that their new taxes were regressive. Their rhetoric would have been vastly different during the last fifty years if they had. No one who knew they were instituting regressive taxes would have also talked about "fairness" as much as the Democrats have these last few decades, so this explanation has to be jettisoned. The Democrats alone are to blame for the regressive nature of these new taxes.

Now of course if the Democrats were to make these new taxes progressive, poor people might change their minds. They would then feel those taxes were less of a burden or not a burden at all, and they would stop seeing the Democrats as their enemy. But so far the Democrats aren't demanding such a policy, and there seems little chance that they will. Accordingly, the schism between the poor and the Democrats will likely continue. The Democrats' only hope for dissolving this schism is to wish that the Republicans will make enough missteps for the poor to abandon them and go back to the Democrats. But such a tack will never cause the poor to go back wholeheartedly. Instead, they will go back grudgingly and will abandon the Democrats again as soon as the Republicans look more viable. The only tack that will work is to *stop imposing regressive taxes*.

In making my analogy and drawing my conclusions, I am going against the views of Garrison Keillor in his book *Homegrown Democrat*,[1] for Keillor believes that the Democrats want to help people. Likewise, I am going against what Thomas Frank says in his book *What's the Matter with Kansas?*[2] Frank imagines that the poor are reacting to social policies rather than economic policies, but I have to disagree. Many policies that the Democrats instituted several decades ago have economic consequences for the poor that the Democrats somehow cannot see. Of course, some poor people abandoned the Democrats because of a single social issue (abortion, for example), and it may be impossible to woo such voters back. But most, I believe, left because of economic rather than social policies.

Let me note that, while the left has been hurting all poor people, it has generally been poor whites who have reacted by going over to the Republicans. The situation is quite different for poor blacks because the support they get from the Democrats is so huge that they are willing to overlook these extra taxes. But for poor whites, it is a different matter, and for poor white males, it is a very different matter. Poor white males don't receive any special support from the Democrats, and so they have basically left the party. Many poor white women have joined them, either because they are resentful on behalf of the men in their lives or because they see the support that Democrats have offered women as something that goes to upper class and middle class women rather than to themselves.

I know that many Democrats will be shocked at what I am saying and will want to reject it. The Democrats' illusion is that they are the party that helps the little guy, but I am saying that is not true. What their party does instead is to help some little guys while ignoring other little guys; maybe it even goes so far as to help some little guys at the *expense* of other little guys. Or it helps the little guy in some ways, while hurting him in other ways. The result has been that a large number of little guys have left the party. A few, generally the older ones, have stayed. But many others have either dropped out of politics altogether, or they split their vote, or having felt betrayed, they vote Republican.

The Democrats' explanation for the behavior of these people never puts the blame where it lies, namely on their own policies. Instead, Democrats believe that these people have been bamboozled by right-wing propaganda, or else that they are too racist or sexist to accept the new policies, or (the latest explanation noted above, from Frank) that they are influenced by social policies rather than economics. All of these explanations miss the stunning reality of the last fifty years, which is that the Democrats are no longer the wholehearted friends of the poor. Democrats will sometimes favor policies that help the poor, but just as often they will favor policies in which the poor get the shaft. Or they will favor some of the poor, but not others. Whatever the case, it is bad news for the Democrats, either because they lose elections or because they win them by smaller margins than they otherwise would.

Moreover, the reactions of the poor who have been hurt by the Democrats leads to certain consequences that Democrats haven't liked. To begin with, there is the decline of the word "liberal." For many poor people who used to like liberals, the word now has an odious connotation. Second, Democrats love to talk about social injustice and how they are helping overcome this problem and how the Republicans aren't. They often get angry when this plea falls on deaf ears. But it falls on deaf ears for many people who have drifted away from the Democrats over the last fifty years because (1) they feel that they themselves have been victims of social injustice, (2) they believe that the Democrats and not the Republicans are responsible for the social injustice that they have experienced, and (3) they can see that their suffering doesn't matter to the Democrats. No one should be surprised when such people are unmoved by talk from the Democrats about social injustice. No one should be surprised when they just tune out.

Let me close by repeating what I said in the Introduction: perhaps leftists think they couldn't possibly be waging a war against the poor because that war would take a certain form, such as pushing to end welfare, exploiting the workers, and so forth. But there are many ways to hurt the poor. Conservatives don't have a monopoly on those ways, as I shall elucidate in the next few chapters.

CHAPTER 2

THE ENVIRONMENT OR THE POOR: WHICH HAS GREATER PRIORITY FOR LEFTISTS?

Today my wife and I have a comfortable middle class existence, but twenty years ago we were quite poor. I was mostly unemployed, and my wife was struggling to finish her doctoral thesis. We were living in Minnesota, and two things happened to us that highlighted the good and the bad of leftist politics.

Minnesota has a special tax refund for renters known colloquially as rent credit. The idea behind the rent credit refund is that renters are paying property taxes indirectly through their rent, but that property taxes are regressive, so they deserve to pay less. The rent credit program allows them a refund. Since my wife and I were poor, and since we were paying comparatively high rent, we got a fat refund from the state.

That was leftist politics at its best. Here it is at its worst.

Everyone in the Twin Cities was at that time required to have their car inspected every year to ensure that it wasn't polluting too much. One year our car failed, and we had to have it "repaired." The repair cost us over a hundred dollars. Given our income, that was a huge bite. That was leftist politics at its worst: it was punishing the poor for being too poor to have a new car.

It is amazing that no one on the left seems to have realized that a well-meaning environmental program like this one actually hurts the poor. In fact, it was a triple whammy against the poor because (1) the poor are more likely than the rich to have older cars that will fail the test; (2) the money required to repair the car represents a greater percentage of a poor person's income than a rich person's income; and (3) the poor are much less likely to have a second vehicle to use while their first vehicle is being repaired. The last item may be a minor annoyance, but the first two are substantial.

It Is Virtually Impossible To Have Two Issues as Your Top Priority

Let me note that this example I have given is hardly unique, and I will give more examples later. For now, I will point out that (1) the policy that caused us trouble was an environmental policy; (2) environmentalism has overwhelmed leftist politics ever since the 1960s; and (3) leftists, whether they know it or not, *prefer to help the environment rather than the poor*. In other words, one cannot have both helping the poor *and* helping the environment as one's top priority; one must choose one or the other. Most leftists have chosen helping the environment over helping the poor, yet they imagine that helping the poor is still their top priority.

What happens when one tries to have two priorities? At some point one has to make a decision. Sooner or later an issue emerges in which one can either help the environment and hurt the poor, or help the poor and hurt the environment. Which does one choose if one is trying to help both? There are no easy answers here, but there are several options. One could try to help the environment while crafting a policy so the poor wouldn't be hurt; but this may mean having a less than ideal environmental policy or else a lower likelihood of its being implemented. Or one could carefully weigh the pros and cons for each decision and make whichever choice entails the least amount of hurt. Or one could set up in advance a randomizing procedure like flipping a coin so that, as conflicts emerged, the choice made would depend on that procedure and not on anything else. In that case, neither side—the environmentalists on one side and the poor on the other—would always be the winner. In practice, however, the left over the last few decades has always chosen helping the environment over helping the poor. In spite of a theoretical commitment to helping the poor, the poor have been left behind by environmentalism.

How Did We Get Here?

Hardly anyone on the left thinks about this choice. Generally, liberals and leftists seem to think that helping the environment means helping the leftist cause and that then there is no more to think about because everyone, including the poor, will be helped. But helping the environment generally means making sacrifices, and often the poor will have to make greater sacrifices than the rich. How did leftists get into such a predicament?

Environmentalism is something comparatively new for the left. It started in the 1960s, but was unknown before then. No one associates environmentalism with those on the far left like Marx, Lenin, Mao, or Stalin. Nor do they associate environmentalism with liberals like FDR (who, to the extent that he pushed for environmental policies, made helping the poor his greater priority).

The 1960s, perhaps not coincidentally, was a great time economically for our country. The Great Depression of the 1930s, through which my parents' generation grew up and whose return they worried about at the end of World War II, had been left far behind. The American economy sparkled. Because of that economic heaven, leftists began turning their attention to things that no one during the Depression would have considered worrying about. During the Depression, the idea of worrying that too many birds were dying of the pesticide DDT would have been dismissed as completely unimportant, especially given that one-quarter of the workforce was unemployed. That unemployment rate was worrisome, not the plight of birds.

But in better economic times, the mindset changed, and one product of that wealthy era was environmentalism. The people who promoted it seldom thought about how their actions affected the poor, for often they themselves were not poor and so were unaffected. They attacked modern society, particularly corporations, and in attacking corporations they were not unlike the socialists. But the socialists attacked corporations with the idea that they would take them over and help the workers. They attacked corporations with the idea that those working there would not only continue to have their jobs, but would be treated better. The environmentalists attacked corporations for polluting the environment, and if a corporation went out of business or was forced to relocate in some part of the world where environmentalists weren't so rabid, the environmentalists didn't mind. As for the people who lost their jobs, the environmentalists, unlike the socialists, didn't seem to care much about such people and had no plan to help them.

But even worse was that environmentalists began attacking ordinary people for the pollution they caused. Since this included poor people, it was something completely new for the left, for they had never attacked poor people before. But now we all find ourselves admonished constantly over the tiniest of things that need to be done in order to preserve the environment, to save the earth, and so on; and if the poor have to pay more, either absolutely or proportionately, that is just too bad. The needs of the poor have been completely lost sight of.

Looking back on the 1960s, I find it surprising that I, with my lower middle class background, didn't pick up on the many signals that the Democrats were beginning to turn away from people like me and were beginning to focus on the concerns of the upper middle class and the wealthy. While it is true that racism, a big concern of the 1960s, was not a personal concern for wealthy white people, for other issues it was different. Feminism, gay liberation, and environmentalism were all personal concerns of the wealthier of our leftists. For poorer women, the idea of having a job wasn't necessarily liberating, since they were often forced to look for a job to make ends meet anyway, and having a career as opposed to a job was and probably still is out of reach. So feminism didn't have as much appeal for lower-class women as it did for their wealthier sisters. Likewise, lower-class gays probably have as many problems just finding work as they do with their sexual identity, so those for whom this identity is all-important are those who are relatively secure financially. Environmentalism fits the same mold. If you aren't worried about the plight of the workers when you close down a polluting factory, it is probably because you don't work there and have a much better job; you can afford not to care about those workers.

Think about what the rise of environmentalism did to old-time leftism. It did its best to destroy it. For well over a century, society had seen a horrible and continuing clash between the workers and the bosses. That clash had been so terrible and so appalling and so one-sided that it led to the construction of economic systems that we still hear about today: communism and socialism. No one talked about either of these in, say, the seventeenth century. It was the horrible plight of the workers in the Industrial Revolution that gave rise to such talk. Much of twentieth-century history was dominated by the rise of communism. The Soviet Union lasted from 1917 to 1991, a good percentage of the last century, and its very existence was overwhelming for much of the world, as well as for the American left beginning in the 1930s and continuing to the 1960s and beyond.

But the 1960s brought something new: environmentalism. Suddenly, after more than a century of bitter conflict, workers and bosses found themselves ... united. They found themselves, to their surprise, working together in a fight against environmentalists. I distinctly remember the first time I became aware of this. It was in the early 1970s. There had been a long court battle in northern Minnesota between iron ore mining companies, which wanted to use a new process to extract ore from the ground, and environmentalists, who were opposed because they thought the by-products of this process would pollute Lake Superior. This court case dragged on for a long

high, no matter what burdens the poor have to bear, because it will help the environment.

Another example is the logging industry. Environmentalists are against the logging industry, while blue-collar workers are in favor of it, again for the obvious reason that it provides good blue-collar jobs.

Sometimes environmentalists promote policies which, while they do not destroy blue-collar jobs, do impose what are seen as needless costs on the poor. One such instance of this was described in an article in the *Washington Post* written after the 2004 election.[2] The author, David Von Drehle, wanted to find out what people in the rest of the country could possibly have been thinking that made them vote for George Bush when it wasn't in their own self-interest to do so. He seems to have been enlightened by what he found, for he recounts the story of a town in Nebraska where, during the Clinton administration, the Environmental Protection Agency (EPA) demanded that the amount of arsenic allowed in drinking water be lowered from 50 parts-per-billion to 10. As one resident put it, "Now all over Nebraska, villages are having to build new water treatment plants to remove a naturally occurring element." This cost a lot of money—money that residents believed was wasted, since arsenic had always been in their water. Plus they now had to worry about how to dispose of it since it is considered hazardous waste. The federal government lent them money to pay for all this, but it would have made more sense just to refrain from doing it. To top it all off, Bush was on the side of the residents while the environmentalists, who claimed that Bush was trying to poison people, were in favor of the EPA's new demands.

In connection with this, one of the issues of the 1994 election, which was also a disaster for the Democrats, was the idea of unfunded mandates. Environmentalists are fond of demanding new regulations with each new threat that is perceived, but often these regulations cost money for local governments to implement; that money is often not available. The mayor of Columbus, Ohio, at that time, Gregory S. Lashutka, wrote an essay in the *Wall Street Journal* highlighting this problem.[3] He pointed out that he and other city officials decided to request all of the new rules established in one month, April of 1994. They were sent a huge stack of documents, so high that although Columbus is the 16th largest city in the country, they didn't have the staff to go through it all. And that was just for one month. He compared the whole business to "having your Uncle Sam take you to lunch, order your food, and then hand you the check." He mentioned that a bipartisan effort to stop this madness, to ban the enactment of unfunded mandates, was thwarted by most of the Democratic leadership. Finally, he pointed out that although these unfunded mandates from environmentalists had increased costs for everyone in Columbus, families and the elderly were hit the hardest.

Another writer with a similar perspective is Nicholas D. Kristof, who in a column analyzing the 2004 election,[4] pointed out that in his hometown in rural Oregon, the locals looked with disdain on Democrats because they "empathize with spotted owls rather than loggers." Unstated, but I hope obvious, is that this relates to jobs. Worrying about spotted owls will impose costs on the logging industry, and that ultimately means either lower wages for loggers or fewer jobs.

The problem of endangered species has given rise to a saying, one seldom heard by the environmentalists, but not unknown in Republican circles: "If you find a rare mineral on your property, you will become rich, but if you find a rare species, you will become poor." The reason is that if you find a rare species, suddenly the feds will swoop in and demand that all kinds of actions be taken to protect that species, actions that will cost you money. A few years ago, some conservative legislators tried to address this issue by demanding that the government offer compensation to property owners. Predictably, the environmentalists were angry. One of them, Rep. Nick Rahall of

West Virginia, said that the effort sets a "dangerous precedent that private individuals must be paid to comply with an environmental law. What's next? Paying citizens to wear seat belts?"[5] This must be one of the few times in history when the right has been more generous with the government's money than the left, but no one on the left seemed to notice. I suppose that leftists will maintain that all property owners are rich and so don't need any government handouts. This is just plain naïve and shows ignorance of rural areas. An obvious leftist solution would be to give a handout that is inversely proportional to the property owner's wealth. Those in the bottom half would get help while the rest could pay for it on their own. However, as far as I know, no environmentalist has ever proposed such a policy.

I could raise many other issues that illustrate the problem of the interaction between environmentalism and class, such as toilets that don't work well, windmills off of Cape Cod that were objected to by wealthy leftists living nearby, and bedbug infestations that cost a lot of money to control because the EPA won't let people use a cheap pesticide, but my point is simple: leftists who push for environmental action on some issue rarely think of how the poor are affected. When corporations hurt the poor, leftists are quick to condemn them, but when environmentalists do the same, they are quiet. Moreover, leftists see corporations as evil and imagine that imposing some cost on them will hurt the corporate bosses, though in fact the people most likely to be hurt will be those at the bottom of the corporation. People at the bottom will lose their jobs because the costs are so high the corporation will go out of business. Or it will relocate to some Third World country that doesn't have such high costs. Or the corporation will begin replacing its workers with machines. Whatever the scenario, the outlook is seldom very good for workers at the bottom.

Environmentalism as a Regressive Tax

For many environmental policies, the costs imposed on the poor amount to a regressive tax. The example with which I began this chapter is a perfect illustration. Annual car inspections seldom hurt the rich, because they have the money to buy new cars frequently, and new cars seldom fail an annual inspection.

Another example is that of higher gas prices, which also obviously hurt the poor more than the rich. Higher gas prices take a bigger bite, percentage-wise, out of the pockets of the poor than out of the pockets of the rich. Perhaps leftists imagine that the truly poor don't even have cars and just use mass transit, but this isn't the case. Many poor people live in towns or rural areas where mass transit isn't available, so they must rely on cars, and even in cities poor people use cars. In fact, they use cars even when they don't own them. During the period of my life mentioned at the beginning of this chapter, I often saw people poorer than me taking taxis home from the grocery store where I shopped. Presumably, neither walking nor using mass transit with several bags of groceries was feasible, so they had to resort to taking a cab; and taking a cab means helping to pay for the driver's fuel. (Taking a cab in this situation is a terrible solution because cabs are so expensive, partly because cities often pose restrictions on the number of cabs, causing prices to rise. Using cabs is akin to having to use a check-cashing agency, yet while the left complains bitterly about poor people having to use such agencies, they say nothing about their having to use cabs.) Finally, rising gas prices affect not just individual car owners, but mass transit as well; so even when the poor use mass transit, they are affected by rising fuel costs.

Likewise, refraining from drilling for oil hurts the poor, not just by higher gas prices, but by everything affected by higher gas prices, including food. In addition, it means a lost opportunity for good jobs. During good times, this may not mean much, but during a recession it means a lot. Getting even a few people employed means that funds to help the unemployed can be given in larger amounts to those who remain unemployed.

Similarly, preferring to help spotted owls rather than loggers means hurting the people who make their living as loggers, because it is unlikely that those at the top of the logging industry will be hurt. And attempts to hurt them will probably backfire, since those at the top may relocate to a more business-friendly location or give less pay to their workers. They will also encourage their workers to vote against environmentalists, which the workers are probably doing anyway.

Nor does punishing property owners who find a rare species on their property inevitably hurt the rich, since in rural areas the property owners are not necessarily rich.

The town in Nebraska that now needs to purify its water to a greater extent and then to deal with the resulting residue will have greater costs because of environmentalists. While the poor may not be affected more than others, there is no guarantee of this. The town will have to raise the money somehow, and to do this it will have to raise taxes. Even if the very poor manage to escape the ill effects of these higher taxes, it is by no means certain that lower-middle-class residents will. And even if the tax falls entirely on the upper half, things that could have been done in that town can no longer be done, and it is likely that the absence of those things will affect the poor. More generally, this whole policy goes against one of the ideas of environmentalism, which is conserving natural resources. Of what benefit is it to squander our resources on such nonsense? That money is basically being thrown away.

What happens when the rich are hurt by green policies? We've seen what happens. When a wind farm was proposed off of Cape Cod, the rich squawked, and the idea was dropped. The reason they squawked wasn't that it was dangerous or noisy or anything like that. It was merely unsightly. But when you're rich, you can get away with that kind of behavior. The fact that it was generally rich Democrats complaining shows how easy it is to make the poor pay for green policies and how clueless most on the left are about this.

While leftists regard environmentalism as an unalloyed good, that is not the way that all see it. Unfortunately for the Democrats, some of the dissenters are people at the bottom whose votes they need. These are the people being hurt by the green policies, and they don't like it. Instead of just putting up with it, which is what leftists expect of them, they react by voting Republican, or splitting their votes, or not voting at all. This is bad news for the Democrats, and has been so for some time, as it has been for the other regressive taxes I will be discussing in the next few chapters.

Global Warming

The issue of global warming is so sizable and important that it needs its own separate section. In fact, it needs two sections, one of which deals with the facts on global warming, which I believe have been wildly exaggerated (I will reserve that for Part III—though let me note if there is no such warming, we will have wasted a huge amount of resources that could have been used to help the poor). Meanwhile, I simply want to talk about how this issue affects the poor.

Environmentalists believe that in order to combat global warming, massive changes must be made in our society, but they seldom think about how the poor will be impacted by those changes, except maybe for those poor people who live in the Third World. They are willing to give them a break, but not the poor in the First World. In the First World, the poor will simply have to suffer.

To begin with, environmentalists tell us the problem is caused by our use of fossil fuels, and so we need to reduce our use of fossil fuels. There are two broad categories that need to be discussed: fuel for vehicles and fuel for electricity for our homes and businesses. Significantly, environmentalists want the prices of both gas and electricity to go up, and higher prices for gas and electricity won't help the poor.

Let me start with the topic of fuel for vehicles. Because having so many vehicles for individuals increases the amount of gas used, environmentalists like to promote mass transit as a way to use less gas, but promoting mass transit puts a burden on the poor. Poor people don't necessarily like mass transit, and they get cars when they can afford them. An article a few years ago in the *Los Angeles Times*, for example, talked about a poor woman who had bought a car because she was tired of taking a *two-hour* bus ride to her job.[6] That ride was of course only one way, and the time would be doubled for the return trip. The reason her bus ride took so long is that buses seldom go exactly where one wants them to go at the time one wants to go there. Perhaps environmentalists who love mass transit are thinking of Europe where mass transit works moderately well. I enjoy taking trains in Europe or the Tube in London, but here in America mass transit doesn't work very well, except in the densely-packed East Coast corridor from Boston down to Washington, D.C. Elsewhere, they are inconvenient and a bother, and the fares are always going up, plus the riders never have any control over the schedules and the routes. The environmentalists, though, seem to think it would be best if the poor used mass transit all the time, nor are they bothered by the fact that it is not the poor but rather wealthier people who get to decide on schedules and routes.

But the most important point is that the elites who promote mass transit seldom use it themselves. They think it's a great idea … for other people. The point I am making repeatedly is that leftist policies often come from wealthy elites and that those policies inadvertently hurt the poor when they should be helping them. The rich environmentalists will have cars, but the poor won't.

Another point is that environmentalists may love mass transit, but they are thinking of people living in cities. However, not all people live in cities. I now live in a small town that has no mass transit. For that matter, not all cities are good for mass transit. I grew up in Minneapolis, whose mass transit system I always hated. I've seen good mass transit in Europe, on our East Coast, and in Rio de Janeiro, for example, but such places are densely packed compared with Minneapolis. Mass transit works well in such cities, but it doesn't work very well elsewhere.

And what does packing people into cities do? It raises the cost of housing, thus hurting the poor in another way. The high cost of a closet-sized apartment in New York is legendary, while those of us living elsewhere can enjoy much more spacious housing. We can own a house without too much trouble.

As for mass transit between cities, environmentalists naturally want us to use trains rather than planes. As I said, I enjoy being in Europe where I can travel between cities by train. It used to be possible to do this here in the U.S., but as the trains, buses, and trollies have disappeared, that has become virtually impossible. Would it make sense to bring them back? First, America is much bigger than Europe. A trip from London to Edinburgh, spanning much of Britain, takes four and a half hours to cover a distance of 330 miles. But at that same speed in the U.S. it would take over thirty hours to get from New York to Los Angeles. Yes, there are trains that can go faster, but flying is more convenient on such a large continent.

Next, I've heard people in Britain who are occasionally forced to take the train complain about how expensive it is. The people in question were middle-class people, so one can just imagine how much of a bite it is for the poor.

Finally, it would take a great expenditure of time and money to get a system of trains and buses to cover all the places that people want to go. Even during their heyday, trains and buses didn't go everywhere. My mother has told me of trying to get to a small town in northern Wisconsin in the late 1920s and early 1930s using trains and buses, but she had to use a mail truck for the last leg of the journey. Such a network would not work as well as our system of roads for cars because inevitably people want to go places where trains and buses would not find it worthwhile to go.

As for travel by air, making it as expensive as possible so as to discourage it basically means that the rich, but not the rest of us, will get to travel by air. One of the amazing things about our era is the way that it is so easy for ordinary people to travel across the Atlantic or the Pacific to visit some other country. When I was a child, this simply didn't happen. No adults I knew did this sort of thing. If they had visited countries overseas, it was when they were serving in the armed forces or as missionaries sent by their churches. To do it as part of a vacation meant either spending an enormous amount of money to fly or spending an enormous amount of time on an ocean liner. In other words, one had to be rich to do it. Today, many ordinary people can and do travel overseas. Restricting air travel just means that elites will get to do it, and the rest of us won't.

Accordingly, rich celebrities who fly in private jets to an event whose purpose is to urge everyone to save the earth from global warming are implicitly sending the message that there are two classes: an upper class that doesn't need to make sacrifices, except by buying carbon credits, and a lower class that does. (After all, these people could use telecommunication devices to connect with each other so they would not need to leave home to have their conference; the fact that they insist on flying to these meetings is a big clue about how committed they are to changing the world.) As for carbon credits, the historian Victor Davis Hanson has cynically compared them to the buying of indulgences in the medieval period.[7]

Then there are the bicycle enthusiasts who think we should all be riding bikes all the time whenever we want to go anywhere. However, bikes have some limitations. They are best for transporting a person a comparatively short distance. When I had a job as a computer programmer, I would sometimes ride my bike to work. Instead of getting there in ten minutes, it would take half an hour, which wasn't so bad. But I lived rather close to my job, unlike others who lived quite far away. For them, riding a bike to work was out of the question because it would take most of the day to get there. Added to that was the fact that I picked pleasant days to ride. I cannot imagine riding when it was well below zero (Fahrenheit) or when it was stormy.

The biggest disadvantage to bikes is that they are no good for hauling big and heavy things. A significant portion of our economy is concerned with that very task, and doing it on a bike is quite difficult. Consider a simple task: moving an item of furniture across town. It might be a sofa or a dining-room table or a dresser. How is this supposed to be done on a bike? Likewise, how does one haul the elderly around? I've never heard any answer to this.

While vehicles are generally used for transportation or hauling things around, sometimes they are used for other things, like plowing a field. How well will bicycles do in terms of plowing a field? I have no direct experience with this activity, but I know that before the era of automobiles, people used horses for that task. Using a bike, then, seems out of the question, though no doubt it could be done if enough modifications were made in the bike's design and if a bunch of people were involved. But who in fact would be stuck doing this task? Almost certainly poor people.

This brings up another possibility, though. As far as I know, no environmentalist has suggested that we return to using horses for our transportation needs. But suppose we were to do this. Most of us have no experience with horses, and in addition, horses are expensive in terms of upkeep. Only the rich will be able to afford them, which means the rest of us will find ourselves very restricted in terms of travel.

This brings us back to oil. We could be drilling for more of our own oil which would bring down the cost of gas, thus helping the poor, but why aren't we? Because environmentalists are thwarting us. (Such people often imagine that they have no political power, but they are wrong.) We could have cheaper oil, but environmentalists don't want us to drill in certain areas. So the price of oil goes up, and this hurts the poor.

With respect to the other use of fossil fuels, generating electricity for use in our homes, stores, and workplaces, it seems that for virtually every sort of alternative power source one can think of, some environmentalist somewhere doesn't like it. Even wind power (which can be harmful to birds) and solar power (which if located in the obvious place, a desert, would ruin a pristine natural habitat) are objected to by some environmentalists. In fact, such people seem to be at war with our era and want us to return to life as it was two or three centuries ago, or maybe to a hunter-gatherer society.

With respect to hunter-gatherer societies, I believe that the environmentalists who admire them think they are egalitarian. However, it has been a long time since I believed people who have said that something or other was egalitarian because I've always found by experience that they were wrong, that there were inequalities they simply weren't noticing. Accordingly, whatever anthropologists or anyone else might say about hunter-gatherer societies, it is likely they are less egalitarian than imagined and that those who think they are egalitarian just aren't looking in the right places to perceive the inequalities. Anyway, I believe it is now generally acknowledged by anthropologists that such societies are more violent than was formerly believed and that those living in them had to work harder than was formerly believed. The fact that few such societies are still around seems to be proof that people found better ways to live.

For those environmentalists who merely want us to return to life as it was two hundred years ago, let me remind them of a few things. There were no weather satellites back then warning us of bad weather in the form of hurricanes and tornadoes, nor was there the great medical knowledge we now have, with new medicines being developed all the time. Is this what they want?

More important, they forget what a grind it was for many people. It involved backbreaking labor for many people because work that is now done by machine was done by human muscle. On a tour of Admiral Nelson's ship *Victory* in Portsmouth harbor in England, for example, I was shocked to learn that it took 600 men to raise its anchor. Today, that is done by a machine with the push of a button. Digging ditches, hauling things that were big and heavy, scrubbing pots endlessly (as scullery maids were forced to do)—all of this would return to the lives of the poor.

Many people in those eras were servants. Servants were required because keeping up even an ordinary house required so much work that the average family couldn't do it very easily. Today, we have many labor saving devices to help us. Even in my own lifetime, it has become easier. I remember as a small child what it was like for my mother to wash clothes and what a huge affair it was. First, she washed them with a washing machine (and I'm sure she was very thankful for that device), but then she had to put them through a wringer—one at a time!—and then into a tub of rinse water. She would wring them out again and put them into a second tub of rinse water. After that, she wrung them out one last time before hanging them on a clothesline. But she still wasn't done because then she had to do a lot of ironing. Today, it is much easier. One throws the laundry in the washing machine, transfers them when they're done to the dryer, and puts them away when they're dry.

Here's another thing to ponder. My mother could get water simply by turning a spigot, but that hasn't always been true. I recently heard of an elderly woman who was asked what the biggest change in her lifetime was, and she said, "Running water." Not cars or planes or radios or televisions or computers, but something simple: running water. If one doesn't have running water, then it will have to be fetched, and that is hard work. (I remember doing it at camp when I was a boy.) Who will do it? Once again, it will be the poor.

But let me get back to alternative energy sources. For those environmentalists who have no problem with wind and solar power and who think of it as a panacea, at this time it doesn't look viable. Such sources cannot produce more than a small fraction of our energy needs, and in addition they cannot be counted on to be available at all times. Accordingly, relying on them and banishing all other sources would mean going back a century or more, and so we return to a world of servants and back-breaking labor for many; or if not that, then very high prices for electricity, which of course would hurt the poor. In addition, anyone who thinks that such sources will be a great provider of green jobs will be very disappointed; such jobs just aren't materializing.

Just as we could be drilling for more oil, we could solve a lot of our energy needs by building many nuclear power plants. We could then generate enormous amounts of electricity, so enormous that we could switch to electric cars, thus avoiding problems of global warming and being dependent for our energy needs on foreign countries that hate us. So why don't we do this? Because the environmentalists won't allow it. And why is that? Because nuclear power plants are perceived as dangerous and because their fuel is difficult to dispose of. Keep in mind that environmentalists here in America regard Europe as greener than the U.S., although Sweden produces half of its electricity by nuclear power, while for France the figure is 80%. Also keep in mind that not using nuclear power means being dependent on oil from countries in the Middle East, and often that means going to war to keep the oil flowing. Since it is poor people here in America who end up in the armed forces, they are the ones who will likely make sacrifices so that wealthier "environmentalists" can jet to important conferences in which they ponder how to reduce our fuel needs. It is just another way that poor people suffer for the greens.

The best thing about our era is how much easier the lives of the poor, and of women, have become simply because of all the labor-saving devices available for nearly everyone. Returning to an era when many of our everyday tasks were done by people the hard way will mean that some people will be stuck doing those tasks. It's a good bet that the most vocal environmentalists, who are generally rich, will *not* be the ones stuck doing that kind of work.

For those who think if we had a socialist economy, then hard work would be distributed equitably, all I can say is that that hasn't been true in socialist countries, except in China during the Cultural Revolution. During that episode, rich elites would get sent off to distant farms where they had to work hard, but that was an anomaly in socialist history unlikely to be repeated.

In addition to all these annoying points, environmentalists are very inconsistent. Environmentalists think we should live closer to city centers so we could use mass transit, and of course the more people who live in an area, the better mass transit works. This would mean a tremendous reduction in the fossil fuels we use, which would help the earth. But then shouldn't we also encourage people to live in geographical regions with moderate climates and to avoid those with extreme climates? My home state of Minnesota is bitterly cold in the winter and hot in the summer. By comparison, Ohio, where I now live, is cold in the winter, but not bitterly cold, and is no hotter in the summer than Minnesota is. What that means is that those who live in Minnesota will use more fossil fuel just staying warm in the winter than those of us in Ohio do, which means that living in Minnesota just doesn't seem like a green choice compared with living in Ohio. But don't hold your breath waiting for environmentalists to say this. They are anxious for people to make certain changes in their lifestyles (giving up their cars for mass transit and moving closer to city centers), but not very anxious for them to make other choices (moving out of extreme climates to more moderate ones).

Let me conclude with this. The large-scale solutions needed to fight global warming will be felt more harshly by the poor than the rich. It's as simple as that. Let me add that there is a surprising sort of equivalence between the left and the right: the right doesn't care about disruptions in society and the loss of jobs as a result of globalization, while the left doesn't care about disruptions in society and the loss of jobs as a result of fighting global warming. Environmentalists want a different world, but because their primary concern is the environment, the uncertain plight of the poor in the new world they want to create doesn't mean much to them. The poor would be more wretched than they are today, both in terms of the work they would have to do and in terms of their status in society, because most would be servants.

Is this the best we can do for the poor?

CHAPTER 3
BEING SOFT ON CRIME

Virtually every leftist is soft on crime, and this is generally resented by the working class—at least the whites. It is resented because being soft on crime hurts the poor. (Because blacks have an uneasy relationship with the police, they have been much less likely to acknowledge the damage that being soft on crime does to the poor. And the left has followed their lead.) Historically, it has also hurt the Democrats, though few will admit that. From 1932 to the 1960s, the Democrats basically had one focus, helping the workers, and with that one focus they won a lot of elections; up through 1964, they won seven out of nine presidential elections. But beginning in the 1960s, the Democrats began to change, and with it the Democrats' fortunes changed as well. Since 1968, they have lost seven out of twelve presidential elections. And the first problem that emerged as the Democrats changed their focus was crime. Yes, despite the Democrats' overwhelming win in 1964, the Republicans were back with a vengeance by 1968, and the reason for this was crime. The Republicans ran law and order campaigns, and the voters ate it up.

I admit that at the time, I misunderstood it. I thought that "law and order" was just a disguised way of saying something racist. I fell in with the usual leftist view that the concern with crime was just a concern about something that didn't really exist. It wasn't until much later that I realized the voters who were worried about crime had legitimate concerns. Yet, I had hints early on. In college in the early 1970s, a bunch of us were sitting around and talking about how much we hated the police, whom we called "pigs," when a woman who came from a much poorer background than that of the rest of us piped up to say that in her neighborhood they *liked* the police. I know that many Democrats, when they learn this woman was white, will say she was therefore privileged compared with poor blacks, and so she should be ignored. But there is a basic counter-response that poor whites have to that response, and it devastated the Democrats back then. Poor whites said, in effect, "If you think my concerns are unimportant, then I assume you think my vote is unimportant, too." And they began giving their votes to other candidates. These little people reacted by voting against the Democrats; and the Democrats reacted not by listening to these people, but by belittling their concerns and calling them racist. The little people ignored them and went right on voting against the Democrats. The Republicans were delighted because they were suddenly winning elections and winning the votes of people who had never voted Republican before, simply because they were running law and order campaigns.

Leftists think that being soft on crime is part of being a leftist, that it is somehow helping the little people, but I am going to argue against that. More to the point, it is resented by a wide swath of voters important for Democratic victories: the white working class.

First, being soft on crime hurts the poor, but not the wealthy or the middle class (and so it counts as a regressive tax). Maybe when the Democrats first began promoting these policies, they believed that being soft on crime would either have no ill effects or else would have effects distributed throughout society. But they were wrong. Crime is focused in the poor neighborhoods, and that means that being soft on crime is unfair to the poor. It is the poor who suffer from such policies, not the wealthier leftists who make them and support them. Wealthier people have more resources to avoid crime than poorer people do, because they can move out of crime-infested neighborhoods to live where criminals are unlikely to bother going; at the higher ends, they can afford to install security systems in their homes or even to live in gated communities. Poorer people depend upon politicians to protect them. Though poorer people up until the 1960s had a natural inclination to vote for the Democrats, when the Democrats turned against them by being soft on crime, they turned on the Democrats by voting Republican. So, while most criminals are poor people, it is also true that most poor people dislike criminals.

There are other reasons why crime is unfair to the poor. When a poor neighborhood becomes crime-infested, the (comparatively) wealthier people in that neighborhood will leave, while those who are poorer must stay and put up with it. When poor people have property stolen, they have to work longer hours to make up the loss, compared with wealthier people who can replace stolen goods more easily. (I am thinking of televisions and computers. Naturally, expensive jewelry burgled from a rich person's home could be a big loss, but a burglar from the ghetto would probably ignore that kind of thing and go for the consumer goods.) Finally, when poorer people are victims of a burglar, they are more vulnerable because so many of their assets are in their homes or apartments. A wealthier person's assets are often squirreled away in bank accounts or stocks and bonds that are not easily stolen by a house burglar.

The plain fact of the matter is that being soft on crime is a policy that hurts the poor more than the rich. Beginning in the 1960s, being soft on crime was the first of the new regressive taxes on the poor.

Even worse is that the criminal-justice system provides more protection to criminals than to any victim who attempts to fight back, which most people think is outrageous. That is, when a potential victim confronts a burglar in his or her home and shoots the miscreant, the victim is liable to prosecution; and it seems that the victim is *more* liable to prosecution than the burglar, even though it was the burglar who initially broke the law.

Even when one is not a victim of a crime, if one lives in a crime-infested neighborhood, then one must *worry* about crime. Intellectual resources that could be used more productively in figuring out how to escape from poverty are instead spent ensuring that one is not the victim of a crime. If one is lucky enough to own a house, one will see one's property values go down; accordingly, even though one hasn't been a victim of a crime, one is a victim of criminal activity nonetheless. If one rents a house or an apartment, the landlord may decide there isn't much point in keeping up the property since the whole neighborhood is going downhill anyway, and so one must live in a hovel. The poor also have to pay more at the local stores because those establishments now need to spend more money on security and so must raise their prices. If they don't bother with heavier security, they must still raise prices to cover the cost of items that are stolen. Some businesses simply close and are not replaced, leaving the poor to cope as best they can. As the general tone of the neighborhood goes down, young people who lack the life experiences to know any better begin to regard certain behaviors as normal which they otherwise would have regarded as beyond the pale. Children grow up with warped ideas and become unable to make the transition from lower class to middle class because they behave in inappropriate ways and use inappropriate language at inappropriate times. People scribble graffiti on bare walls; and no matter what leftists might think, the existence of graffiti sends a signal to criminals that the people in that neighborhood don't care about their surroundings and so aren't very vigilant. Fires are more frequent either because of criminal activity or because people no longer care about where they live and so get careless.

The list goes on and on.

I lived in a poor neighborhood for four years while I was a graduate student, and I observed how the people there lived. In particular, I was surprised by how many more fires there were in that neighborhood compared with other neighborhoods I had lived in. Across the street from where I lived, a halfway house experienced a fire in which three people were killed. The cause was arson and was no doubt related to the background of some of the residents.

As for inappropriate behavior, I saw it all the time. To give merely one example, I was once jogging through a park where a softball game was in progress. A dog belonging to one of the spectators began following and bothering me. Every few yards, I turned around to glare at it. Finally, I aimed a kick at it, at which point the owner, a teenage girl, suddenly came to life. "Don't kick my dog!" she shouted. I can't imagine a middle-class dog owner acting that way. Very few from the middle class would allow their dog to harass someone in that way.

As I said, when neighborhoods become crime-infested, children grow up thinking that inappropriate behavior is normal. Then they find it impossible to leave the neighborhood.

Leftists may respond to my ideas about inappropriate behavior by thinking what an old fuddy-duddy I am and that the proper response is to get society to accept such behavior rather than to make poor people change their behavior. My reply to them is, "Good luck with that project." It is much simpler to get people out of poverty by teaching them manners than by urging that the rest of society accept their lack of manners. The latter is another entire cause in itself, and will require just as many leftist resources, if not more, to deal with than getting people out of poverty. Why bother? Why not take the simple route and just teach poor people manners? Or look at it this way. Why hold people who are in poverty hostage to your ridiculous ideas about how to get them out? Just do it the simple way.

The arrival of the Internet has allowed many people to talk about their lives in ways that would not be approved of by the liberals who run our media and schools, which means that their opinions are seldom heard in such venues. Poor whites can now get into one of the many discussions on the Internet and tell their side of the story, and what they say makes leftists uncomfortable. For them the 1960s wasn't the fun and games it was for many leftists (especially those leftists who came from wealthy backgrounds), but was instead a time when their fortunes were in decline. Their neighborhoods were being devastated, and their favorite politicians were suddenly uninterested in their opinions, yet leftists talk as though they are horrible people who for no obvious reason began supporting the Republicans. Any reasonably complete history of the 1960s needs to tell the story of poor whites from their perspective and not from that of some other person's perspective.

So far, I have been talking about how being soft on crime hurts poor whites and how they react. I also think this policy hurts poor blacks, though they don't respond the same way that poor whites do. The reason for the different reaction is simple: poor blacks think that the Democrats are doing it for them, so they don't protest. But even if both wealthy white Democrats and poor blacks think it is important to be soft on crime, they are wrong. Yes, blacks think that the police and courts are incurably racist. But poor blacks suffer from the same things as poor whites when their neighborhoods become crime-infested. And assuming that society is indeed to some extent racist, they will have a harder time overcoming the resulting problems than poor whites do.

To put it succinctly, poor blacks may benefit as blacks from the Democrats' policies, but they do not benefit as poor people.

I would argue that blacks actually suffer more than whites. Inner-city blacks have become their own worst enemies as a result of the left's softness on crime. Such a policy positively encourages blacks to take up crime; and if they aren't positively encouraged, neither are they discouraged. When older or conservative blacks come along telling hard truths to the black community, they are disparaged. Moreover, blacks are often the victims of crimes by other blacks, even when unintentional, as happens to those who inadvertently get in the way during a gang shootout.

Another problem for blacks is that the nearest role models for inner-city blacks are often thugs rather than respectable people, so that even those inner-city blacks who don't become thugs may have thug-like behavior. This behavior reinforces negative stereotypes that work against blacks, including those who aren't poor. In addition, being soft on crime pits poor blacks against poor whites when they should be working together. Most important, being soft on crime promotes an anti-intellectual atmosphere that is extremely harmful to inner-city blacks and, quite possibly, to other American blacks. I've known many blacks who were foreign students here, having come from Africa or the Caribbean, and they were in general more studious and interested in learning than the American blacks I knew. They had such fine qualities because they had grown up far away from the crime-loving, anti-learning atmosphere that the left began encouraging a few decades ago in the inner cities here in the U.S. The blacks from other countries were also able to take advantage of affirmative action programs that American blacks could not, because the foreigners were highly educated while the American blacks were not.

Many leftists will be angry with what I said about stereotypes, which they view as terrible and immoral. There is something to be said for such a view. On the other hand, when people feel threatened, they naturally turn to stereotypes to protect themselves. It's impossible to know everyone in the world, to know how they will react and what sort of people they are, so stereotypes can be a way of shunting around this problem. Nor do leftists rail against stereotypes in all situations. Today, for example, leftists commonly assume that people who are against global warming are somehow in the pay of the oil companies, which is first of all a stereotype, and secondly one that isn't close to being true. Yet no one on the left seems to notice that this assumption is stereotyping, which they generally condemn.

As a further example, when a serial rapist is operating in a neighborhood, all women living or working there have to worry about that, so they take precautions when dealing with strange men. They stereotype men based on whatever vague descriptions of the rapist are available, even though that hurts those men who fit the description but are innocent. Do leftists complain about this stereotyping on the part of women? Of course not. In this instance, stereotyping is considered acceptable. But there is really no difference between this situation and the first. Whites who worry about being the victim of a crime are going to stereotype blacks, because blacks are more likely to be engaged in crime. The way to deal with this problem is not to bash whites for using stereotypes, but to insist that blacks give up crime, which doesn't help them and usually hurts them. Once that problem is solved, leftists can turn their attention to the stereotyping problem, if it is even still around.

Not only does being soft on crime hurt the poor, which often leads them to vote against leftist candidates and ultimately decreases the political power of the left, but it raises new problems for the left, all of which are self-inflicted. One of these problems is that as crime rates go up, people become afraid and buy guns, which the left hates. Another problem is that of poor black children being killed by stray bullets as a result of gang activity. I cannot recall a single child in the 1950s and 60s who was killed in this way, but it is frequent these days. Every time it happens, leftists typically talk about how terrible it is and how something must be done; but they never want to eliminate the root cause that led to it, namely their being soft on crime and their encouragement of the glorification of criminal gangs in our popular culture.

Another self-inflicted problem is the incarceration rates of blacks. According to the left, that shows how racist our society is. According to the rest of the population, it shows what happens when society is soft on crime. The clincher here is that leftists typically ignore the victims of these criminals, who are often other blacks or poor whites. Either way, this policy ends up being less progressive than leftists thought it might be.

Inner-city blacks are likely to end up in prison because they have been dealing drugs; but why are they dealing drugs in the first place? They began drug dealing partly as a result of a decision made in the late 1960s by inner-city blacks to eschew doing well in school because of the notion that scholastic achievement was "acting white" (though "acting Asian" would be more accurate). When you haven't done well in school, there aren't many good jobs available to you, and selling drugs is one obvious choice.

Another self-inflicted problem for leftists is having to deal with the revival of the death penalty, which was caused by a reaction against the left's own policies. When Democrats first began being soft on crime, support for the death penalty in the 1950s and 60s had been waning. But then crime spiraled out of control, and the Democrats did nothing to help. The Democrats in fact *wanted* the police to be handicapped in catching criminals and the courts to be handicapped in convicting or sentencing criminals. Instead of criminals being sentenced to what ordinary people thought were appropriate sentences, they were getting off lightly. Sometimes, they weren't even sentenced. If they were sentenced, they could get off early on parole. Ordinary people did not like that at all. To them, leftists seemed to be saying, "Not only do we expect you to put up with crime, we expect you to feel guilty for the way you think about criminals." Given that the people making these policies were unlikely to be victims of violent crimes themselves, such an attitude was inexcusably callous. Ordinary people reacted by bringing back the death penalty. They reasoned that at least with the death penalty in place, some of the criminals could be put away permanently with no chance of ever committing a crime again. Of course, leftists fought back, and the first result of their fighting back was that instead of being executed fairly soon after their sentence was handed down, prisoners remained on death row for years. But while this was a defeat for ordinary people, they could console themselves that at least the miscreant was locked away for a longer time than if he had gotten "life" (that is, life in prison but with a high probability of parole after a couple decades).

Leftists also fought back to eliminate the death penalty, but in this fight they have been less successful, probably because of the tactics they used. Again and again, leftists focused on how unjust the death penalty was and how awful it was that a supposedly enlightened country like the United States would have it. Comparisons were (and still are) made to Europe, where it isn't present (although it seems a majority in Europe want it there, too; it's just that European elites have enough power to prevent them from getting their way). None of that meant anything to those voters who were worried about crime, nor should it have. After all, China executes many more people than America does, so why not make the comparison with them? Again, it was as though the left was telling people, "You are scumbags for wanting people killed. You just aren't very enlightened." But from the ordinary person's perspective it isn't enlightened to be concerned about vicious criminals while being unconcerned about their victims. The victims, or in many cases their surviving families, were simply forgotten. (I once wrote a book review for the *Columbus Dispatch* in which the author of a book about the death penalty didn't even bother to mention the name of one such victim.[1] He merely described him as a police officer.) Naturally, the left's campaign against the death penalty has not been very successful.

In retrospect, the obvious course of action for the left was not to inflict massive amounts of guilt on those who wanted the death penalty. It was to get the crime rate down. It was to make people feel safe enough so they could feel comfortable in eliminating the death penalty. Once they started to feel safe again, they were likely to feel that the death penalty was no longer necessary, particularly if "life in prison" really means life. Recall what I said above: when I was a child in the 1950s and early 1960s, support for the death penalty was decreasing (or at any rate not increasing). We can get back to the enlightenment of that era, but only if the crime rates go down.

In saying all this, I do not mean to cast aspersions on the efforts of those leftists who are trying to get the innocent out of jail. Obviously, being hard on crime does not mean locking up just anyone. At the same time, however, their efforts are directed in certain directions and not in other directions. Certain people who are incarcerated are helped, and others are not.

A famous example of one who was not helped is Gerald Amirault, who remained in a Massachusetts prison for years on bogus sex abuse charges that were part of the sexual witch-hunting of the 1980s. Why did leftists not try to get him out? Why did they leave him to rot in prison? Instead of the left, it was the right that worked to get him released, specifically Dorothy Rabinowitz, who wrote many a column in the *Wall Street Journal* about his plight.[2] The reason for the left's apathy was pretty simple: Gerald Amirault was seen as a typical member of a privileged class, while leftists prefer to devote themselves to those who are already victims of society. However, if you want ordinary people to come around to your way of thinking, you need to include the Gerald Amiraults because ordinary people are more likely to identify with him than with the people on whom leftists usually focus.

Other names could be mentioned, but I will not bother because my point is that those leftists worried about innocent people in jail aren't as idealistic as they imagine. They choose certain people to help while ignoring others. And they seldom pay attention to the innocent victims of crimes.

For more than a century, and perhaps for two centuries, leftists have tended to hold a romantic conception of crime and criminals. They think of criminals as rebels against the evil capitalist system, while their crimes are society's fault, and therefore the system should go easy on them. Indeed, they often think criminals should be lauded for their efforts, so we should regard many criminals in prison as political prisoners. Some leftists go so far as to argue that we ought to eliminate prisons. Almost no one in the middle or on the right argues for that.

If leftists think anything about how that affects the poor, they imagine it helps the poor. That is a mistake for many reasons, as I've just argued. Moreover, the people who are victimized, the people who end up in prison, and the people who get killed from the violence are not the theorists; the theorists get to pontificate in their ivory towers in nearly complete safety. It is the poor who get the shaft.

But there are more reasons it is a mistake. First, capitalism isn't the great evil that leftists think it is. I'll say more about that in Part II. Second, even if it were a great evil, the leftist defense of criminals would apply only to those who are thieves. It would not apply to those who are murderers, kidnappers, or rapists (unless their victims are wealthy, which often enough is not the case).

Third, the criminals who are allegedly rebelling against the system typically never rebel against those who are at the top, but against those who, like themselves, are near the bottom. Consider their likely victims, convenience store workers. Convenience store workers are far from being captains of industry or power elites, but instead are usually poorly paid souls doing grunt work. So why pick on them? For those who think the convenience store workers are people who just happen to be there when a crime is committed, that the crooks bear no animosity towards the workers they are stealing from and that it is really the owners they are mad at, the truth is rather different. As many people know by now from watching videos of actual crimes being committed, criminals do not treat convenience store clerks with the respect one might anticipate from those who are angry at the owners. They are quite willing to use violence on these workers or anyone else who gets in their way. No, these crooks are best seen not as rebels against an unjust system, but rather as bullies encouraged by the naiveté of leftists to avoid squelching their bullying tendencies. Nor is there any evidence that indicates these criminals have well-developed political philosophies about capitalism and socialism. They are just thugs. They would probably be taking more than their share in an egalitarian system, just as they do in a capitalist system.

But suppose that criminals really are rebels against the system rather than odious bullies. Why support them, given that supporting them hurts the poor so much? Are there any benefits for the poor in such a policy? The only possible benefit that a soft-on-crime policy has on the poor generally is in terms of a future revolution. That is, if enough crimes were committed, the social order would break down enough so that a socialist revolution would occur, and then the poor could be helped. But there would be a lot of suffering on the way to that revolution, and there is no guarantee the revolution would be a socialist one. It might be one like the Iranian revolution, which ended up in a reactionary theocracy. Or we might end up with warlords, none of whom liked socialism. Finally, it is a leftist myth that the poor are helped in a socialist economy, as I shall argue in Part II.

Another belief of leftists that is unhelpful to the poor is that it is impossible to deal with crime without dealing with its root causes, which they believe are poverty and racism; so we can do nothing until those are dealt with. But crime comes in waves, while poverty and racism do not, or if they do, they do not correspond to the waves of crime. For example, as the 1960s wore on, crime began increasing, yet racism was probably decreasing during that period. (I heard an older black woman who grew up in Harlem claim she never had any fear about walking home late at night in the 1930s, but obviously that wouldn't be true today.) In Britain, soccer hooliganism took root because of the new attitudes of the 1960s. Liberals and leftists said that the problem couldn't be dealt with unless one dealt with the underlying root cause (poverty), yet when the government began issuing ten-year sentences for the hooligans, it largely disappeared.[3] New York City had severe crime beginning in the 1960s, yet it was dealt with in the 1990s directly, not through root causes. The Nazi movement was not dealt with by examining its root causes; it was dealt with by attacking it directly in World War II. That was effectively the end of Nazism as a mass movement, and we investigated the root causes later.

And just as there are different theories on the root causes of Nazism, so there are different theories on the root causes of crime. The left's insistence that poverty and racism are the cause isn't the only theory out there. Crime could partly be the result of softness-on-crime policies that allow criminals to thrive and encourage naive young people to take up crime when they should have been thinking along other lines. Talking about root causes of crime is just a distraction.

Another unhelpful belief of the left is that society is really to blame for crime and so we shouldn't blame the criminal or incarcerate him. But there are many reasons for rejecting that belief. People make their own decisions, for which society is not to blame, and the person who decides to commit a crime has made the decision on their own without being forced. We might decide that society was to blame if the criminal was so poor that he or she was starving, but that is rarely the case these days when poor people here in America are if anything overweight and not starving. The only way that society would be to blame is if it strongly encouraged people to take up criminal activity, but while the left has tendencies in this direction, the rest of society doesn't, and the criminal-justice system is present to incarcerate those who take up crime. What the left is thinking is that the capitalist system is to blame for the maldistribution of wealth and the criminal was merely attempting to redress this unfairness. But as I have already suggested, such criminals would probably be taking more than their share even in an egalitarian system; there just isn't any reason to think that criminals are somehow attacking capitalism per se when they commit crimes, and so there is no reason to think that society is to blame.

Likewise, claiming that criminals were abused when young and so must be excused has to be rejected as well; plenty of people who were abused when young do not take up criminal activity. Nor does it help to say that these criminals simply cannot help committing crimes. Many poor people avoid committing crimes, but even if it were true that these criminals cannot help themselves, one could also apply it to other segments of society. I with my lower-middle-class background simply cannot help but being against crime.

Another unhelpful belief is to get angry at the system when the average thief spends time in jail while people at the top can get away scot-free. There are two cases to be considered here, the person who is the head of a big corporation who has actually broken the law, and the person in a similar position who has not. When a corporate head has broken the law and still somehow manages to avoid going to jail, it is usually because of politics. It surprises leftists when I say that they are not alone in wanting such people put in jail, that libertarians want them in jail, too. The most recent example is that of the bankers who nearly ruined the world's financial system, but who were nevertheless bailed out by our government instead of going to jail. It seems worthless to tell leftists that that occurred at a time when the president and both houses of Congress were dominated by the Democrats; somehow, they still think that it is the right that is to blame for them not being in jail. Obviously, that shows that leftists have a skewed sense of when someone is to blame.

The other case is that of the corporate head who has not broken the law. According to leftists, such a person has nevertheless acquired their wealth in an immoral way and so ought to be in jail. I am going to deal with that later on (in Chapter 14), but for now I am simply going to say that encouraging poor people to take up a life or crime (or at least failing to discourage them from doing that) when it is likely that they, and not corporate heads, will go to jail for theft not only doesn't help the poor, but is reprehensible in its own way. Why aren't these people in jail themselves? Instead of pushing for corporate leaders to be put in jail because they are capitalists and so supposedly exploited people at the bottom, why don't we take those who encouraged people at the bottom to take up a life of crime *and put them in jail?* There is a nasty little joke about stock brokers who lose their client's money that can be adapted here. The joke is that the broker made money, and the firm made money, and two out of three ain't bad. Likewise, we could say that the low-level, idealistic aid workers helping out in the inner city stayed out of jail, and the ivory-tower theorists pushing for those at the bottom to take up a life of crime stayed out of jail, and two out of three ain't bad. If you're going to complain about people getting off scot-free, why not include those who encourage people at the bottom to take up a life of crime?

Being soft on crime doesn't help the poor, and policies encouraging crime among the poor are in effect a regressive tax.

CHAPTER 4
PUSHING FOR THE DECLINE OF OUR SCHOOLS

When I graduated from high school in the late 1960s, American public schools were adequate. They weren't as good as our private schools, nor were they perhaps as good as the better public schools in Europe, but they were adequate. My basic complaint was that city schools were not as good as suburban schools. The reason seemed to be that tax money was actually going from the city to the suburbs, which meant less money for city schools, where poorer students went, than for suburban schools, where wealthier students went. But beyond that, they were adequate. Even if they weren't as good as the best public schools in Europe, our system wasn't as bad as the European system in which people were put onto separate tracks too early in life. (I do not approve of this tracking because people I knew in high school who would have been shunted to a vocational track in Europe came alive when they got to college. They suddenly plunged into their studies and went on to become doctors and lawyers, or got M.A.'s or Ph.D.'s.) Unfortunately, since that time the Democrats tinkered with schools until they became much less than adequate.

Inadequate schools have inspired the rise of the voucher movement, and although leftists think of the voucher movement as a bunch of religious nuts, this isn't true because many inner-city blacks want vouchers. No one talked about vouchers back in the 1960s, and few people home-schooled their children. Today, both these ideas are common. Although many people are unhappy with the way our schools perform and are looking for alternatives, they find themselves thwarted by the Democrats, who made many changes to the schools and then refuse either to unmake them or to allow for vouchers.

It should be obvious who will be hurt most by changes to the public schools that make them less than adequate: the poor. Poor people could use a good education to get out of poverty, but they can't get out of poverty if they don't get a good education. The inner-city blacks who want vouchers, despite their loyalty to the Democrats, can see that there are big problems with our schools and that they aren't being helped by what has happened to the schools. Look at it this way. People who are wealthy enough and who dislike the public schools put their children into private schools. If they can't afford private schools, they can still afford private tutors. Poor people cannot afford either of these options. They are just stuck with the public schools.

What went wrong? Probably the biggest change happened in the 1970s, when it became virtually impossible to impose discipline on students in public schools without risking a lawsuit. As conservative commentator Daniel Henninger observed, many good principals responded to new policies like this one with a policy of their own: Why bother? Why bother trying to impose discipline if all you're going to get out of it is a lawsuit?[1]

I went to a public school and used to be a strong supporter of public schools. What changed my mind was reading the remark of a teacher who said that leftists seemed more interested in protecting the bullies and thugs in the classroom than their helpless victims. That teacher's remark was made before the Columbine tragedy, and after that tragedy the schools did begin to pay a little more attention to bullying. But I suspect that discipline is still a major problem for the schools.

For example, every now and then one hears about and even gets to see the out-of-control behavior of young children in school. I first noticed this behavior perhaps ten years ago on a televised newscast about a six-year-old girl who threw a tantrum in the classroom, with the result that the police were called. That was so extreme it was on national television. None of the teachers or administrators dared touch the girl because they knew a lawsuit would occur, and they knew that they could lose the suit and their jobs. In the days when our schools were adequate, that problem would have never made it onto national television because it would have been dealt with by the teacher in the classroom. But leftists are more interested in that out-of-control girl's rights than in making sure that learning takes place in our schools.

A second problem is the idea that we ought to be teaching our students something other than dry facts. Instead, this line of thought maintains, we ought to be teaching them concepts, or how to learn, or how to be critical. In theory, that sounds great, but in practice, it doesn't work very well. One needs a lot of facts in order to make some sense of the world. Once that foundation is established, one can move on to learning concepts, learning how to learn, being critical, and so on. In order to learn a foreign language, for example, one must learn a lot of dry facts; there just is no escaping that. The same goes for geography, history, and many other subjects.

As far as teaching critical thinking is concerned, much of it basically teaches people to be critical of conservatives but not of leftists. Such thinking prevented me from seeing what we on the left were doing to the poor, that we were waging a war against them. The teaching of critical thinking is often nothing but propaganda. But let us suppose for the sake of argument that it is not propaganda. How exactly does teaching critical thinking help one get a job? Jobs that require critical thinking generally go to rich people and not poor people, so the emphasis on this type of thinking often does the poor no good. I'll say more about that below.

Another bad idea promoted these days is the idea that learning should be fun; and if it isn't, the teacher is to blame. But learning cannot always be made fun, and if students are given the idea that it should be, they won't develop the self-discipline that will enable them to persist in learning when, even though it is not fun, it is in their interest to do so.

Another problem is the loss of standards, particularly the idea that since it is so terrible for a student to fail and that since the student's failure is probably the school's fault anyway, no student should ever get a failing grade. The result is that a lot of people who could have learned a great deal more get passed along from one grade to the next with no one really demanding much of them. They graduate from high school and try to get jobs, but in the world of business, people have higher standards. Either such graduates aren't hired or businesses must spend a lot of time training them, and of course the cost of that training gets passed on to the customer. Since the customer has already paid for this training via taxes for the public schools, the customer is thus charged twice for the same item. Of course the poor are hurt the most by a double charge like that.

Moreover, if the graduates decide to go to college instead of trying to get a job, they will be forced to take remedial classes until they are ready for the real college classes. Not too long ago, the following news was reported: "Nearly 80 percent of New York City high school graduates need to relearn basic skills before they can enter the City University's community college system."[2] Even if the percentage were much lower—say, 20 or 30 percent—it would still be terrible. It would be terrible because those students will have to spend even more money on college than they ordinarily would, because they will have to stay in college longer before they can graduate. That is, if they are required to take remedial classes when they get to college before they can take the real classes, then they won't have finished their requirements at the end of four years, so they will have to spend even more time and rack up even more in student loans (which I will discuss in the next chapter).

Along with the loss of standards is a cynical rise among students in the belief that cheating is justifiable. The simple response to them is: Would you drive across a bridge designed and built by cheaters, or would you entrust your health to doctors and nurses who cheated their way through school?

Another problem is the rise of the self-esteem movement. Back when I was in school, no one worried much about the students' self-esteem. It was unconsciously assumed that any student who achieved something would have higher self-esteem than those who didn't achieve anything, and that that was the way it should be. The idea that self-esteem *precedes* achievement would have been thought utter rubbish. As some conservative commentators have noted, our students aren't very good at math compared with students in other countries, but they have higher self-esteem about it than those students do. Most people can see there is a problem here.

Then there are the new approaches in certain subjects. In reading, the idea that one should learn to pronounce syllables and to sound out a word has been replaced by the whole word approach, in which the student is supposed to recognize an entire word. Parents have objected to that, and the response of educators is to ignore them because they assume that the objectors are fundamentalist Christians, as though they alone would have problems with the new approach. In math, it is assumed that learning the multiplication table is boring, so why spend one's time in such a tedious fashion? There is some sense to this assumption because with the rise of calculators, there is less need to do a lot of tedious figuring. But what happens if there is no calculator at hand or one suspects it is broken or one makes a mistake in punching in the numbers? Mostly, though, the ways that students are taught to do multiplication and division are baffling to most who learned the old-fashioned way, nor do students seem to get much out of these newer and more creative methods.

Finally, the last problem the schools face is politicization. Leftist politics dominate, and what leftists want taught in school will be taught, and what conservatives want taught won't be taught. Every leftist would be screaming about this situation if it were reversed. For example, leftists want teachers to be concerned about social injustice, but how the right defines that and how the left defines it are light-years apart. While people on the left talk about racism and sexism, people on the right talk in completely different ways. They talk, for example, about how government interferes with business. They talk about a person struggling to get out of poverty, who starts his or her own business but is forced to close it down because of a pointless regulation. Or they talk about how Christians are disparaged in the mainstream media. How many on the left would tolerate it, if that were all that was taught in our schools about social injustice? Even more important is that many among the white working class feel that they have experienced social injustice and that they have experienced it at the hands of the very people who wish to teach about social injustice; yet those doing the teaching are completely clueless that that is how their students feel. Finally, what about being accused of racism when one in fact is not a racist, or sexism when one is not in fact sexist? Aren't these examples of social injustice, too? There needs to be a broader sense among educators concerning what counts as social injustice.

Another problem with politicization is that new situations are arising all the time (for example, the terrorist attack of 9/11) that ought to be debated from a neutral perspective; instead, leftist teachers simply make pronouncements. (I've personally seen this politicization only at the college level and not at lower levels. Anecdotal evidence suggests the same thing holds true elsewhere.) Leftists may respond by saying that the schools were politicized back when I was in school, and that they were politicized to the right. But that has nothing to do with the idea that events and topics like 9/11 should be debated, while the fact remains that the schools were adequate and widely respected back then, but are inadequate and not widely respected now. Take your pick.

My main point is this: *The poor depend on public schools to get them out of poverty.* When those schools do not perform, the poor have a much harder time making their escape. The fact that not just poor whites but even poor blacks want vouchers shows how bad the situation is. Naturally, the wealthy leftists who invent these policies are not bothered by the havoc they wreak, because they can send their kids to private schools to escape the chaos. But their use of private schools is proof of what I am saying, that the left is betraying the poor.

Teaching Students to Be Rebels

Another aspect of the situation is that not only have leftists urged that teachers teach in certain ways (emphasizing critical thinking and the learning of concepts rather than rote memorization), they have urged students to adopt certain attitudes, too. Since the 1960s, they have urged students to be rebels, to resist conformity, to demand that what is taught be relevant and entertaining, and so on. They have urged all of these attitudes because they took the cynical view that our schools were designed to do nothing other than churn out mindless and obedient workers for our factories and other places of employment. All of that sounds great in theory, and anyone who rejects it will sound horribly stuffy and Victorian, but reject it I must. To speak plainly, such thinking works against the poor. It may work for those who are wealthy (and then again it may not) but "the cold it gives the wealthy is pneumonia for the poor." The brutal fact is that such thinking makes the poor unfit for the workplace. (I cringe when I think of the bad attitudes I had at many jobs.) When the poor are unfit for the workplace, employers look to machines to do those jobs; or else they look to foreigners, either by hiring immigrants or by moving their factories to other countries. They may hire illegal immigrants because illegal immigrants do the jobs that Americans don't want to do. Yet, Americans at the bottom used to do that kind of work. Why would they have stopped? Isn't it just because of the bad work attitudes that had been instilled in them by leftists?

To say all this in other words, according to leftists, schools were originally designed by conservative elites to prepare the poor for dull-as-dishwater, mindless jobs and to force conformist thinking upon them so they would be ready and willing at a moment's notice to be shipped off to war in some distant place. Consequently, liberals and leftists decided to remake our schools. They introduced critical thinking, and they said they wanted our students to be rebels.

The key question, though, is, what sort of jobs are there for people from the bottom who think critically? There is almost nothing for them. Some have argued that there are already too many college graduates for the number of jobs requiring a college education,[3] but as far as I know, no one on the left has dealt with the problem of which among those who have a college education will be chosen for such jobs in order to ensure that those jobs are distributed throughout all classes in an equitable manner. Leftist elites think that those jobs should go to those with the best credentials, which means those chosen will have gone to elite schools, which further means they will probably be wealthy. That is bad news for poor people who have learned to think critically but have not gone to the best schools.

More generally, how many employers are going to hire someone from the bottom who is a rebel? People at the bottom have very few job opportunities as it is, and schooling them in this way just makes things harder for them, so why do it? It is easier for upper class people educated in this way to change their lives around, if they suddenly decide that that sort of education and attitude was all a mistake. They can rely on their parents' resources to help in getting some decent schooling and to turn things around. I am reminded of a cartoon in *The New Yorker* in the 1970s showing an executive in a huge office whose secretary comes in and says, "Mr. Bradshaw, your son is here. He's given up living in the teepee and wants to join the firm."[4] That is what things are like at the top; one can usually make a change without serious consequences.

But at the bottom, it is a different story. By the time one emerges from one's rebellion, one may have developed an addiction to drugs, have a criminal record, have numerous children whom one must support, and have no parental resources to fall back on since one's parents are poor. Even worse, one will have received a high school education that is often worthless. If one went on to college and majored in something useless like American Studies, one may have racked up a huge amount in college loans that will take years to pay off, and the degree will do little towards getting a job that would help do it. As I've learned the hard way, jobs for people with those kinds of degrees tend to go to people from wealthier backgrounds. And as I've also learned the hard way, leftists don't actually care about this sort of class discrimination and continue to urge people to major in a course of study that is useless for those at the bottom.

Am I saying that teenagers from poor families should not engage in any rebellion? No, but they should be careful to choose forms of rebellion that are easily reversed. Wearing unusual clothes and doing strange things with one's hair are harmless since these practices can easily be reversed by wearing clothes and having hairstyles that are more mainstream. But committing crimes, getting addicted to drugs, and other practices basically destroy a poor person's life, at least as far as getting out of poverty is concerned.

Busing

Probably nothing showed the white working class that the left was waging war against them so much as the issue of busing. The idea behind busing was desegregation, and the idea behind desegregation was that racism festered because of segregation; so to help destroy racism, desegregation was necessary, and as part of desegregation, busing was necessary.

At first glance, this idea may seem rather benign, but the devil is in the details. Instead of being scattered randomly throughout big metropolitan areas, blacks were generally clustered in the interior, so ideally they and white children throughout the metropolitan area would have been intermixed, with no one getting out of the situation. Instead, busing was confined to cities (rather than cities *and* their suburbs), and it was restricted to public schools. The result was that it tended to fall on the white working class instead of wealthier whites, and naturally the white working class did not like it at all. The leftists who were wealthy talked, of course, as though busing were something important, but they acted so that their own children escaped it. That is the pattern repeated many times in the left's betrayal of the white working class: impose a draconian measure on poor whites that is deemed necessary for social justice, but ensure that you yourself escape its consequences.

Christopher Lasch in the last chapter of his book *The True and Only Heaven* makes similar observations. In Boston, the people making the busing policy were all from the suburbs,[5] so they themselves weren't subject to it. Anyone who resisted was automatically considered a racist. Sadly, some of the poor whites accepted this label as accurate, though they had the good sense to respond with indifference when confronted with it. But the reality was that these policies were made by others and imposed on them; they were imposed in such a way that the policy resembled a regressive tax; and those making the policy were able to escape having it imposed on themselves. Would poor whites have resisted so vehemently if the burden had fallen mostly on wealthy whites? Almost certainly not. But it is likely that the people who then would have been resisting, and thus being called racist, would have been those wealthy whites. The unfairness to poor whites of the details of desegregation utterly escaped the notice of the "limousine liberals," for whom the resistance to busing was proof of the resistors' racism, which in turn was proof that racism was an evil that would take harsh measures to eliminate.

A similar sort of mentality has confronted us with the problem of immigration. As Jonah Goldberg has written:

> Now, the offense some take to the seeming underside
> of Mexican immigration might seem uncharitable,
> snobbish or bigoted to *Post* reporters, senators and

editors at the *Times*, but such people tend to live in buildings or communities that protect themselves from poor working class Mexican Americans, and every other kind of poor American to boot (except as the help). Not a lot of Mexican immigrants are going to park on John Kerry's lawn or get approved by Maureen Dowd's condo board.[6]

The idea here is that though immigrants may cause problems when they move into a neighborhood, those who control our media rarely want to report such problems (except from the immigrants' point of view). The people who experience such problems are unimportant, of no account, probably racist, and so on—never mind that these were the people who fueled Democratic presidential victories from 1932 to 1964.

The poor suffer from not having good schools, and the schools are not good because of leftist tinkering. Tinkering with our schools is just one more way in which the left wages war against the poor, and in this instance, not just poor whites, but poor blacks are affected, also. It amounts to a regressive tax because it is the poor who suffer, while those who are wealthier escape the consequences either by sending their children to private schools or hiring tutors to help their children.

The poor deserve better.

CHAPTER 5

MAKING COLLEGE UNAFFORDABLE

When I was young, going to college was something one did for the better kinds of jobs. There were plenty of jobs available for those who just had a high school diploma, however. Those who planned to do blue-collar work might go to a trade school for a couple years, or they learned a trade (such as plumbing) from their fathers or while serving in the armed forces. Those who did go to college found that college was generally affordable, and even if people couldn't afford it outright, they could pay for it with a part-time job or a full-time summer job. Even when I was in graduate school and became a teaching assistant in the mid-1970s, I found I could save enough money during the school year so that I didn't have to work in the summer, despite my only working half-time (and getting considerably less than half the pay of a professor).

But a few years later, I noticed that people who were working as half-time teaching assistants had to get a second job to make ends meet, and they had to work during the summer as well. Soon, most students had to take out loans to get through college, though it is true enough that that started in a small way. My wife, for example, who started college in 1982, had accumulated about $27,000 in loans by the time she got her Ph.D. in 1994. These were a burden on us, but we were fortunate when we inherited enough money to pay off the remaining principle. By the early 2000s, however, my wife and I were astonished to hear that a woman we knew had over $100,000 in loans. How could anyone pay off such a staggering sum? Today, however, that amount of debt has become common enough. More and more we are hearing about young people who have taken out huge loans, and as a result of the current recession, have very little chance of paying them off.

What happened? According to the left, the states began to cut subsidies to higher education, so tuition went up and students were forced to pay more than previously. This factor, sadly, is only part of the reason tuition has been going up so rapidly. But let us assume for a moment it is the primary factor. Isn't it possible the states did that in response to increasing politicization in the college classroom? If so, then the left has no one to blame but itself for the cut in subsidies. Likewise, what about individual contributions? I remember commercials on television back in the 1960s urging viewers to give to the college of their choice, but I haven't seen such a commercial in a long time. What happened? As our colleges became more and more leftist, a lot of people on the right and even in the middle stopped contributing. They probably wrote letters filled with blistering complaints that forced the people sponsoring those ads to give up on them because they were no longer worth the money.

If cutbacks in subsidies from state legislatures were the only factor contributing to the horrible rise in tuition over the last few decades, then private colleges, which don't get such subsidies, would not be raising their tuition; but they are doing so as well. Unfortunately, there are three other factors involved in the rise of tuition, and all of them involve the left.

The first is administrative bloat. The number of administrators seems to increase all the time, and tuition must rise to accommodate the increased number of those being paid. Many of these administrators are in new positions which are the result of government regulations *instituted by liberals and leftists.* All the affirmative-action monitors, environmental-compliance overseers, and diversity officers drive up the cost of tuition. Although they were hired as part of a liberal agenda—and such an agenda is generally about fairness—the people whom this agenda ignored were the students from poorer backgrounds who would have a harder time paying for the ever-rising tuition. In other words, fairness for some has meant unfairness for others.

The second factor is that as student loans became common with lots of federal money available, tuition naturally rose to take advantage of the situation. Had no federal money been available, if just ordinary banks made these loans, loan officers at those banks would have been reluctant to continue giving out loans as tuition rose so rapidly (faster than the rate of inflation). They would have begun asking questions about the ability of students to repay such loans. I know that some, remembering how bankers acted during the housing crisis, may question this account; but in connection with the housing crisis, bankers assumed that home prices would keep rising, so it made some sort of sense to sell to people who might not be able to afford it at the time the loan was made. Soon their house would be worth much more than they paid for it, and if they got in trouble, they could resell it. With student loans, it was different: there just wasn't a huge labor shortage that guaranteed that salaries would keep rising. It made no sense for loan officers to keep giving out student loans (unless they assumed the government would step in to bail them out, which is what economists call moral hazard). If less loan money had been available, colleges would have been faced with a choice: either make college cheaper or keep raising tuition and squeeze out the poor. Since plenty of governmental aid was available, colleges had little incentive to lower tuition.

But it was not just higher tuition and the too-easy availability of student loans that caused a problem for the poor. The third factor was caused by the fact that so many people these days find they *must* go to college in order to get a job that used to require just a high school diploma. Accordingly, rising demand to get into college allowed colleges to increase the cost. That is, the demand to get into college has gone up, while the supply of colleges has not, except in the form of a few for-profit colleges. (And how have traditional colleges, dominated these days by leftists, reacted to these for-profit colleges? They have been as hostile as possible, showing once more that they don't have the poor's interests at heart.)

How did it happen that so many find they must go to college? It happened because employers used to be allowed to give aptitude tests to prospective employees in order to weed out those who weren't likely to be able to do the job, but now they can't, and the reason they can't is because of leftists. A series of legislative and court decisions going back to 1964 has prevented companies from giving general tests for many jobs.

At one time, employers were free to test job applicants in any way they wanted. The first step along the way to disaster began in a seemingly innocuous fashion: the 1964 Civil Rights Act. This act forbade employers from refusing to hire individuals based on their "race, color, religion, sex, or national origin." While that seems harmless enough, it contained the seeds of disaster because some people insisted that employers were giving tests for the purpose of excluding minorities. Still, the problem didn't emerge until 1971 with the Griggs vs. Duke Power case.[1] The results of that case were that companies could use only the narrowest of tests that related specifically to the job in question; general ability tests were out. That was because even though discrimination might not have been intended through the use of such tests, if different races performed differently, that was enough to conclude there was discrimination anyway. Even worse was that even the narrow tests could still be challenged, and it was up to the companies using them to show that they related specifically to the jobs in question. Rather than deal with possible litigation, companies responded by demanding that employees have a college degree, thus basically outsourcing their testing to the colleges.

What this history shows is that efforts to help blacks avoid discrimination ended up hurting all of the poor. (Keep in mind that this change wasn't made in response to intentional discrimination, which might have made the change tolerable, but because different groups were faring differently on tests.) Forcing people to go to college, people who weren't required to do so in the past, hurts the poor because they are more likely than the rich to end up in jobs that don't actually require college. Going to college is accordingly a four-year waste of time for them, for they could be making money and getting established during that time instead, and a financial burden as well, for they are far from being able to pay for college without sizable loans that will take years to pay off. In addition, the larger numbers going to college mean that colleges can raise tuition, just as any business can raise prices when demand goes up. Finally, if the poorer students fail to get a job after graduation, which is a real possibility these days, they are in a nearly hopeless situation since they will have huge loans with no means of paying them off.

None of that helps the poor, no matter how much the advocates of a college education talk about its advantages. Ending up in debt is a terrible way to start one's adult life, and since one can't discharge the debt via bankruptcy (as a result of the Bankruptcy Abuse Prevention and Consumer Protection Act of 2005), these unfortunates are basically hampered for life.

It gets worse. Is a college degree actually worth what college educators say it is worth? I've seen many discussions about the advantages of a college education in terms of income, but I've never seen a single study that took into account the economic background of the people who were studied. That is, it's easy to point to the *average* benefits of a huge number of college grads, but how do these benefits differ when class background is taken into account? No one should be surprised that people from wealthy backgrounds will get higher incomes as a result of going to college, but it's not so clear to me that that is the case for poor people. Whatever average figure is calculated in these studies, one must remember it is already skewed higher since wealthier people are more likely to go to college than poorer people. Moreover, as I mentioned in the last chapter good jobs often go to those from wealthier backgrounds, so those from more modest backgrounds who go to college may find that their fortunes haven't improved very much.

Nor are the intangible benefits as good as they used to be, because of the politicization mentioned in the last chapter. Much attention is directed towards "critical thinking," but critical thinking as taught in our schools and universities generally means being critical of the right and not the left. While it is often said that our colleges focus on race, class, and gender, a more accurate description is that they focus on race, gender, sexual orientation, and the environment. Class has dropped out. Class just doesn't count for much in our colleges and universities these days, and when it is mentioned, it is done from a hopelessly out-of-date perspective. That perspective imagines that the left is the friend of the poor and refuses to acknowledge that the left has been waging a war against them for the past fifty years. The result is that the poor are either indoctrinated in ideas that don't relate to them or do them any good, or else they resist indoctrination and find that what should have been an enlightening experience was nothing but a waste of time and money.

Another annoying factor is the heavy emphasis on "diversity," by which is meant diversity in terms of gender, race, national origin, and sexual orientation, but never in terms of economic background; accordingly, poor whites who attend college never get to feel they are part of the diversity that is constantly being talked about. They are made to feel as though they are somehow a group that is over-represented, even though in many of the elite schools they are under-represented.

Still another factor is that students are made to feel guilty for what our military has done. Many poor students have a connection with the military, either because they personally served or because their parents did; yet they are made to feel guilty for what our military has done, even though the policies in question were actually instituted by richer people. A poor-friendly education would take that into account.

Possibly the worst thing that wealthy leftists do is encourage people to go into a "studies" major (such as American studies and gender studies). There are very few jobs for people who major in some "studies" area, and the few jobs that exist will go primarily to those who went to the best schools. Since such people generally come from wealthy backgrounds, choosing such a major is a monumental catastrophe for a poorer person. But college advisers seldom tell you that.

Some leftists will say that instead of making students pay for college, it should be free. What a boon for the poor that would be! But when we look at Europe, where college has been free, we see what actually happens, namely that college ends up being for the rich. After all, a "free" college education has to be paid for in some way, and since that usually involves precious tax money, there is a motive to restrict it to those who are worthy. But those found "worthy" are generally going to be those who are richer, so the poor lose out—both because they can't take advantage of it and because through their taxes they have to pay for it anyway. Some will wonder, why shouldn't college be free since primary and secondary education are free? But college costs more, since the instructors with their higher degrees have to be paid more, the laboratories are better equipped, and so on. There is little incentive among wealthy elites to allow the poor easy access to that, and as I just argued, the result will be that "free" college will help the rich and not the poor. However, I could see supporting free tuition at community colleges or trade schools, since the rich seldom go to those types of institutions.

Another suggestion is that we have low-interest loans for the poor. But that doesn't get at the problem, which is that making loans available too easily helps push tuition higher. Ideally, we should get back to what it was like when I was in college, when tuition was cheap enough that an energetic person working full-time in the summer and part-time during the school year could afford college without requiring a loan.

The high and continually rising cost of college, together with policies that force people to go to college who shouldn't have to go there, represents a tax on the poor. While these policies were made for reasons that seemed good from a leftist point of view, the effects on the poor were not taken into account.

CHAPTER 6
A MISCELLANY
OF SMALLER COMPLAINTS

In the previous chapters I listed the larger ways in which the left is waging a war against the poor. In this chapter I list a grab bag of smaller ways in which the left is also waging this war.

The first concerns a tactic rather than anything materially harmful. I'm referring to those leftists who insist on telling poor whites they are privileged with respect to blacks. That may be true, but it is a stupid thing to say. When you are trying to get poor people on your side, what you should be talking about is how lacking in privileges poor whites are with respect to rich people (and how you are going to help them), not how privileged they are with respect to some other group (and how you plan to help that other group and not them). When you're near the bottom, the last thing you want to hear, especially if it's from someone closer to the top than you are, is how some have it even worse than you. It just breeds resentment in those who hear it. When I hear that kind of rhetoric, I feel like voting Republican; but when I hear rhetoric about how lacking in privileges I am, I feel like voting Democrat. Which do you think is more effective?

Moreover, is this rhetoric even true? Is it really true that poor whites are privileged compared with blacks? Those saying this will rattle off privileges that poor whites have over blacks, but somehow they ignore affirmative action as a privilege for blacks that might counterbalance things. Look at it this way: either affirmative action is effective or it isn't. If it is effective, then it needs to be counted as a black privilege, and if it's not, then it needs to be abandoned. Some will suggest that if it's not effective, we need to work to make it effective. But it's been around for several decades now, with plenty of time to make it more effective, so this response just doesn't work. Affirmative action is a privilege that poor blacks have over poor whites.

In addition, one of the privileges that poor whites supposedly have over poor blacks is being able to go into a rich neighborhood without raising suspicion. But that isn't due to racism per se, but rather to the bad choices many blacks have made during the past few decades, choices encouraged by leftists. Once most blacks stop making those choices, that problem will disappear of its own accord.

A more annoying part of the left's war on the poor is the phrase "privileged white males." This phrase isn't exactly suited to helping the left show that they care about the poor, unless they think that all white males are rich. Since that clearly isn't true—think coal miners in West Virginia—they should revise this phrase to "privileged *rich* white males." I know that originally the phrase was meant in a relative sense: any white male compared to an otherwise similar white female or a black would be privileged. But this relative sense has disappeared from the general public's consciousness and has been replaced by an absolute sense, so that people now interpret it to mean simply that every white male is privileged compared to any white female or any black. And that simply isn't true. Consider, for example, a rich white woman who went to all the best schools and a poor white man who barely finished high school. Is he really privileged compared to her? He may be privileged with respect to gender, but she is privileged with respect to wealth. Moreover, she can take advantage of affirmative action to lessen his privilege, while he has nothing comparable with which to lessen her privilege.

Affirmative action was designed by leftists as a type of compensatory justice in which people who were discriminated against in some way in the past were helped by reverse discrimination. The intended beneficiaries of this program were blacks; but as the program was being voted on, someone slipped in another beneficiary, women, possibly with the idea that it would then be voted down. Instead, it passed. The obvious point to make about affirmative action, from the perspective of class, is that it has never been used to help poor people. Despite all the help the left has given to the poor through the decades, leftists were simply not interested in giving affirmative action to the poor. They still aren't. I had to fill out many affirmative-action forms when applying for jobs in academia, and while I was required to check off my race and gender, I was never allowed to list my economic background. That is what leftists call social justice. That is what they call fairness.

In recent years, in conversations with other leftists, I have begun raising the idea of adding economic background to affirmative action, for the simple reason that in academia (and maybe other segments of society), one's economic background may work against one. How have they responded? With, at best, tepid enthusiasm. That leads me to say what I've said elsewhere but which bears repeating as often as possible: the right doesn't like making changes in society, while the left doesn't like making changes in its agenda. The left's agenda right now is devoted to using affirmative action to help women and blacks, but not the poor. And they believe that shouldn't be changed.

In the bad old days, professors in the humanities were generally rich white men, with a few white men from more modest backgrounds who had also been hired. Today, it is quite different. As a result of affirmative action, professors are generally a mixture of races and ethnic groups that includes both men and women. But most of these people are still rich, and the ones who are missing are the poorer white males who used to be there. (Job ads that say, "Women and minorities are encouraged to apply," might just as well say, "Poor white males need not bother to apply.") In other words, two steps forward (for women and minorities) and one step back (for poorer white males). It never occurred to the proponents of affirmative action to wonder who was going to be displaced when all these women and minorities started arriving. Rich white males? Of course not. The victims were poor white males. Nothing in the hiring mechanism insured they would stay around, so it was the poor white males who got the shaft and not the rich white males. That is social justice, according to the left. That is fairness. Of course, in addition to poorer white males, we ought to have more poorer people in general, but right now poorer white males have no legal help for getting in, while poorer women and minorities can at least appeal to affirmative action.

Another part of the left's war against the poor is to single out for attack those corporations that offer the poor inexpensive goods. Two in particular are Walmart and McDonald's, the former because leftists think they exploit their workers and the latter because leftists think the food being sold isn't very healthy. But let's say Walmart exploits its workers; Walmart is also giving many poor people a good deal on products they need to buy, and that isn't a bad thing. Compare it to trial lawyers, whom leftists love: trial lawyers help a few individuals (who may or may not be poor), thus making products more expensive for everyone. Walmart at worst hurts a few poor people while helping many more. You the reader should be able to decide which is better to do.

Speaking of unhealthy food, I want to consider that topic in connection with the left's war on the poor. Healthy food is expensive, and for many of us, not very enjoyable to eat. Today, poor people in America are seldom starving and are indeed often overweight, yet leftists think their being overweight is terrible. When they can, they ban certain types of food that poor people are likely to consume to excess, with the rationale that what they are doing is good for the poor. Naturally, they don't see that as part of a class war in which they (the rich) are hurting their enemies (the poor), but that is what it amounts to. I ask, Why not let poor people, who miss out on so much in life that rich people get to enjoy, have their pleasures unmolested by richer people's hectoring? Yes, it may shorten their lives, but their lives might well be relatively shorter anyway for many other reasons (such as working in dangerous occupations). Forcing poor people to eat and drink what leftists think they should be eating and drinking is yet another part of the left's war on the poor.

Many current policies from leftists that are intended to help the poor often backfire. Rent control is one of the policies leftists tout as helpful for the poor, but most of us who live in cities or towns that don't have rent control can see that it does hardly anything for the poor, except maybe for a few poor people who were lucky enough to be in such a city when the controls were first enacted. For everyone moving in later, housing is difficult to find except at prices that are out of sight. Another policy, one that isn't even intended to help the poor but which leftists push anyway, is to restrict development in a given city. That sounds great from an environmental perspective, but it hurts the poor because it drives housing costs sky high.

Another example concerning housing is the way that leftists wanted to force banks to give home mortgages to poorer people so the poor could buy a house, just like richer people. At first, that seemed like a great idea, but it turned out these poorer people couldn't really afford the houses they were buying, except when offered ridiculously low terms for the first two years of their mortgage. Most people finally saw that was a bad idea when home prices suddenly went way down because then many poor people were stuck with a mortgage they couldn't afford. They couldn't sell the house to pay off the mortgage because their mortgage was "underwater"; that is, the amount of equity they had in the house was far less than the amount required to pay off the mortgage. Yet they couldn't not pay it unless they were willing to have their credit rating go down, which would hurt them in finding a place to rent (or even getting a job). So, many stayed in houses in an impossible situation, unable to move to find jobs elsewhere in the country where new jobs were being created. Without this leftist push for home ownership, poor people would have been renting an apartment or a house, and if the rent had gone up, they would have found a cheaper rental. If they had wanted to move to another part of the country for a job, they would have been stuck with at worst a year-long lease that they had to break. Poor people would have had a much easier time if they had simply been renting.

Another example of helping the poor that doesn't work very well is that of unions that are hard to break into. When my wife was in high school, she wanted to have a career in theater, not as an actor or a director but as a scene painter. After some investigation, however, she found that it would be nearly impossible to get into the scene painters' union unless she were willing to live in poverty for many years prior to being accepted. Once accepted, she would have received high wages, but there was no guarantee of acceptance. The union rules favored those already in the profession, but not those younger aspirants who wanted to be in it.

Another issue relating to unions concerns the high pay that people in state governments, who are members of unions of public employees, get for doing fairly ordinary jobs. What's more, the people whom leftists expect to pay for those high salaries are themselves ordinary people in the private sector *who don't get all the perks that those people get.* That is pushed in the name of "fairness," though many ordinary people in the private sector, even those who are otherwise liberal, have big problems with it. After all, *they* don't get the protection from being fired and the high pensions that the people in the government do.

The very concept of a union for government employees is a problematic one, given the history of unions and governments. Unions were formed to fight against private employers whom employees thought weren't giving them enough of the profits. Certainly during my lifetime, leftists have always supported unions (with one disastrous exception I will mention in Part II), but they have also always supported the idea that governments are on the side of the workers. Accordingly, there shouldn't be any need for a government union since the government is supposedly on the side of the workers already. (In addition, the government is not a profit-seeking entity, so there are no profits to share in a fairer way.) The idea of a government union was resisted for a long time, but finally in the 1970s it became a reality, and now we are feeling its horrible effects. In an ordinary union, there are strong pressures to keep the demands of the unions in check, since management will see the company go bankrupt or their own salaries diminish if they give in too much. But with a government manager, the pressure is less because a government manager will always assume that taxes can be raised to cover the increase in wages, particularly in states like California where the idea of raising taxes is thought of as progressive. Yet at some point the taxes and corresponding wages get so high that ordinary people in the private sector start to rebel; even when they don't rebel, the wages and benefits are so high that the state cannot afford them.

Another aspect of the war against the poor is that leftists think that raising taxes on the rich is the equitable solution for the problem of inequality, for it helps the poor and punishes the rich for being too wealthy and too stingy. But often taxes on the lower middle class and the lower class are not lowered, but instead are actually raised whenever taxes on the rich are raised. Then the leftists lose such voters; and even when they don't lose them, they impose on their supporters a completely avoidable burden. The process I suspect works like this. Leftists demand higher taxes on the rich, but the rich have many ways to avoid such taxes, so there is a shortfall in expected revenues. Accordingly, these same leftists demand higher taxes on other people, and each successive group that is victimized tries to shove those taxes onto someone else. Since the wealthy are very adept at avoiding such taxes, they in effect shove the taxes onto the upper middle class. The upper middle class, while not quite so adept as the wealthy, can still force a bigger burden onto the middle of the middle class, which in turn can force a bigger burden onto the lower middle class, which in turn can force a bigger burden onto the upper levels of the lower class. Unfortunately, that's as far as it goes, because that group cannot force a bigger burden onto anyone poorer because of the stiff support that the very poor have from leftists. So they are stuck paying higher taxes than they should.

Here is an example of what I mean. Let's say a single person, a waitress, made $20,000 in 2013 (a situation that might describe many young people today). Let's say she had no income from interest or business, plus she had no credits or deductions of any kind. She simply earned $20,000 in wages, salaries, and tips. What does she owe the federal government? Her federal tax is $1,085. That may not sound like much, but when you are making only $20,000, it is a lot. With such a small income, you need every penny. Even if you have calculated your budget correctly, any unexpected expense (for example, a medical bill or rising transportation costs) can devastate you. Why not, then, reduce the tax on such a person to, say, $200? The cry is always for higher taxes on the rich, but never for lower taxes on the poor.

In addition, our waitress with her small salary is unlikely to make much in the way of interest on a bank account, especially given the low interest rates these days, but what she does make will be taxed. But if she were to have stocks from which she earned dividends, which is even less likely, those dividends would not be taxed. She could earn $46,250 entirely on dividends and not be taxed at all. Why not, then, eliminate the taxes on interest for the poor? Again, the big push by the left is always for higher taxes on the rich, never lower taxes on the poor.

The high tax on people of modest income was what California's controversial Proposition 13 in the 1970s was all about. That proposition pushed for relief from the high taxes on the lower-middle class homeowners who were losing their homes because of rising property taxes. As such, it was something leftists should actually have been in favor of, but instead they dismissed the push to lower those taxes as something coming from the right, which therefore made it suspect. It was a big mistake (and I plead guilty for misunderstanding that for two decades).

Next, I want to mention the various attempts by leftists to help poor people by regulating parts of the economy. These are well-intentioned, but they usually backfire. For example, suppose shoddy wiring causes a house to burn down thereby killing its occupants, who were poor. Leftists scream that we must have regulation; we must have wiring codes that will prevent these tragedies. What they don't say is exactly how these codes will be paid for. Once codes are in place, then we need government inspectors who will check things and demand changes if wiring isn't up to code. Their salaries need to be paid. Housing prices for poor people will go up as their housing is made more expensive in order to meet the new codes. It all sounds good in theory, but as the conservative Thomas Sowell has said on many occasions, there aren't solutions; there are only trade-offs. We are trading the lower-cost but more dangerous housing for safer but more expensive housing. Moreover, the house with bad wiring *might* catch fire, but the house with up-to-code wiring will *definitely* be more expensive. If enough regulations are passed in a region, the poor can find themselves priced out of homes altogether (after which the left complains about the lack of affordable housing). And that is something that those looking out for the poor should not want.

There are many examples like this. A column from a few years ago by John C. Goodman is filled with many of them.[1] As Goodman puts it, people in the middle class (and of course the upper class) expect that markets will satisfy their needs, but those in poverty have a very different experience. Cheap housing ("small, prefabricated homes for zero lot developments") would help them, but regulations often prevent such housing from being built, so the poor pay higher prices for housing. And of course, the demands to have everything up to code increase the costs as well. Poor people could get reasonably good and inexpensive health care, but regulations can demand that only an M.D. offer any help. Walk-in clinics in shopping malls help the poor, but they too are heavily regulated. Child-care is expensive because of the regulations, so that a friendly neighbor has a hard time offering to take care of the kids in the neighborhood. The regulations go on and on. They may have been put in place to help the poor (though Goodman assumes they were put in place to help special interests), but they do not help the poor.

These, then, are the various ways in which leftists wage war on the poor. Some of the poor may be helped in some of these ventures, but my point is that most of the poor are not helped and are even harmed. We may also note that these ventures were done with good intentions, but of what use are good intentions if poor people end up getting hurt in the long run?

Leftists need to do better.

CHAPTER 7
CONCLUSIONS CONCERNING THE LEFT'S WAR AGAINST THE POOR

It is time to reach some general conclusions about what I have been saying in the last few chapters.

1. **It is possible for the left to wage a war against the poor, and it has been doing so for the last fifty years.** Leftists think they know what a war against the poor looks like: it consists of what the right is doing to the poor. Since the left doesn't act the way the right does, leftists conclude that they aren't waging a war against the poor and actually are poor people's best friend. They are then amazed when many poor people decide to vote Republican.

How does the right hurt the poor? The right supports corporations that exploit the poor in their jobs or abandon them by relocating their factories overseas. The right supports the fat cat bankers of Wall Street, who rarely do anything for the little guy. The right is against raising taxes on the rich; the right in fact wants loopholes for the rich. The right never wants progressive change. The right hates welfare. The right wants a smaller government that will leave the little guy defenseless. And so on.

What I've been pointing out in the last few chapters is that the war the right is waging against the poor isn't the only way to wage a war against the poor, and that the left has been waging a war against the poor in its own way for decades. Many poor people have responded by either refraining from voting, splitting their votes between the two major parties, or going over to the Republicans. In the view of leftists, that can't really be happening because they "own" those voters. As a result, leftists have spun a variety of explanations for this phenomenon: the Republicans are using clever propaganda, or these people are really racist and sexist and can't quite bring themselves to accept progressive change, or they are voting on social issues rather than economic issues. But there's plenty of evidence to indicate that poor people didn't and don't like the war I've been talking about. The left's current preference to put environmental issues above issues of poor people is often enough to cause the affected poor people to switch parties.

2. **No ideology "owns" the poor.** Leftists think they have permanent "ownership" of poor people's support because they are supportive of poor people, while those on the right are not. But as I've been arguing, leftists aren't as supportive as they think they are. Anyway, no one "owns" the poor because the poor can't afford to be as ideological as wealthier people. The poor will naturally gravitate to whichever party is helping them or, alternately, hurting them the least. Once leftists started hurting the poor back in the 1960s, the poor responded by going elsewhere.

3. **The growing inequality in our society has been made worse by leftists.** Leftists in recent years have been saying as often as possible that inequality is growing in America and that we need to do something about it. What they haven't wanted to admit is that this growing inequality has been made even worse for those at the bottom because of the hidden costs they themselves have imposed on the poor.

4. **Changing demographics may help the leftists, except where it counts: with their image**. Many aspects of the war I have been talking about affects poor whites more than it affects other groups. Will changing demographics help the left? To some extent. As poor whites become a smaller portion of American society, the left's war against them will mean less in terms of lost votes; but at the same time, the left cannot claim to be the champion of the poor when it is waging a war against some of them. Since some aspects of the war against the poor affect all poor people and not just poor

whites, the left's goals will always be at odds with its message. The left wants to help the poor, but when it ruins the schools for all poor people, it isn't doing much for them, unless the goal is to keep them poor so as to retain their votes, and that would mean the left is simply using the poor for its own ends and not really helping them.

5. **Government is not necessarily the solution**. Many poor people now see the government as a problem rather than a solution. They vote for candidates who will lessen their taxes because they see taxes being used against them rather than for them. It's as simple as that.

6. **Leftists have never thought about the losers of the Sixties**. If the winners were blacks and rich leftists (especially women and homosexuals), who were the losers? Here I'm talking not about those who deserved to lose (such as racists in the South), but rather those who lost even though they did *not* deserve it. The losers include the poor whites who lost because their neighborhoods were deteriorating (and let me hasten to add they were deteriorating not because blacks were moving in, but because crime was spiraling out of control). In addition, lower-class white males lost more than lower-class white females did. In 1960, lower-class white males were basically the focus of the left. Yes, the left also paid attention to women and blacks who were workers, but it was tacitly understood that white males were the heart of the working class and so deserved the most attention. However, by 1980, a mere twenty years later, lower class white males were thought of as so privileged that leftists basically regarded them as Rockefellers.

Next on the losers list would be lower-class white females, unless they were single mothers. If they were single mothers, the left doted on them, but not otherwise. Notice that lower-class white females cannot take advantage of recent advances for women to the same degree that wealthier women can, for they were always expected to work. A few new opportunities have opened up for them, but it's not as though most of them are likely to become doctors, lawyers, or engineers. No, they can now work not only as a maid or on an assembly line, but also doing things like carpentry; that is what the left has done for them.

The left never really thought about who would be pushed down when it tried to raise up blacks and women and other groups. If they thought that the people pushed down would be those at the top, it turns out that that did not happen. What happened was that different groups at the bottom to some extent changed places.

7. **Diversity does not include poor whites**. All the talk about diversity these days excludes poor whites. When diversity is talked about, poor whites are not included in what is meant by this word. In some contexts, of course, that doesn't matter since there will be many poor whites present. In low-level jobs, plenty of poor whites are present so we don't need to worry about whether they are included there or not, but in other sorts of jobs, that isn't true. Academia was dominated by rich white males for a long time, with a few poorer white males included beginning in the 1960s. But with affirmative action, poorer white males have been excluded to make room for women and blacks. Poorer white females are also likely excluded, simply because academia has always preferred the rich, so the result has been diversity in terms of race and gender but not class.

8. **Leftists have not prevented inner city blacks from engaging in self-destructive behavior.** During the 1960s, it seemed very important to ensure that blacks had educational opportunities equal to those of whites, but then inner-city blacks decided that doing well in school was "acting white," which was to be avoided. My impression here is that in the late 1960s, just as white America had decided to accept blacks, inner-city blacks decided they would reject white America's values. This is perfectly natural behavior; rejecting someone who for so long has rejected you is very understandable. But at this point the left should have stepped in and said, "We aren't going to support you on this stance. It is self-destructive and will hurt no one but yourselves." For those who think it doesn't hurt blacks,

consider this. My wife is a professor of art history, and when searches are done for open positions in her department, the administrators cry out for black candidates, but in fact there are none. The pool of educated blacks is just too small to fill those jobs. The people who could have filled them rejected the idea of getting a good education because they thought of it as "acting white" (though "acting Asian" might be more accurate). Even when they managed to reject this self-destructive behavior, they may have been persuaded by leftists that society is so racist that they would not have a chance at such jobs, so they went into other lines of work. So, those jobs go to white candidates or else to the occasional foreign black who comes along. The left, by not stepping in, has allowed inner city blacks to be self-destructive.

9. **The left's war against the poor was waged primarily by rich rather than poor leftists**. That is a conclusion I will expand upon in Part III, but for now let me just say it is hard to imagine that this war would have been waged if poor leftists had been in control of the left. When workers lose their jobs because of environmental activists, those workers typically have no voice in what happens; but if they had had a voice, they would have curtailed the power of the environmentalists. When schools began deteriorating in the poorer sections of big cities, poor people would have demanded changes for the better, but they had no voice to do that. Instead, when those at the bottom say things that rich leftists don't like, they get marginalized. Their messages don't get through; they are considered racist if white or sell-outs if black; and the media never covers their plight, except from the angle that makes them into the bad guys.

The big four focuses for leftists these days are race, gender, sexual orientation, and the environment. Class issues are way down the list. When they are dwelt upon, it is from the standpoint of a vanished world, a world that existed before the 1960s. Class issues of today (like reining in the environmentalists so they won't hurt the poor) simply aren't on the radar of any contemporary leftists who talk about class.

Let me conclude with a story that illustrates how feeble the left is these days about class issues. Two women in academia attended academic conferences and found themselves excluded, though in different ways. One, a graduate student, found that her adviser had invited all his male students out to dinner; she as a female was excluded. The other, an expert in the culture of a foreign country, found herself excluded from a panel discussion. She had spent considerable time in that foreign country and had furthermore helped each of the members of the panel discussion as they had come to study in that country. They were now all professors, but why was she excluded from the panel? It was because she had gone to an ordinary Midwestern university, while they had gone to elite schools. In academia, there is an easy equation between going to an elite school and being considered good versus going to a less-than-elite school and being considered not very good. But for those of us who came out of lower-middle-class backgrounds, as both I and this woman did, ordinary state universities are where we went to school, while the rich went to the elite schools.

The conclusion of this story is that, although the left these days complains about exclusion, and while leftists can easily see that the first woman's exclusion (which was based on gender) was wrong, they just can't manage to see that the second woman's exclusion was also wrong. That is because the second woman's exclusion was based on class, but leftists just aren't very good with class-related incidents these days, especially, but not exclusively, when they happen in academia.

PART II:
CAPITALISM IS NOT
THE PROBLEM

CHAPTER 8

THE EVILS OF CAPITALISM CAN ARISE EVEN WHEN CAPITALISM IS ABSENT

The basic argument of this chapter is simple. I claim that the evils allegedly caused by capitalism can arise even when capitalism is absent. If so, then those evils aren't unique to capitalism; and if they aren't unique to capitalism, it is entirely possible that they have nothing to do with capitalism and everything to do with the human condition; and if that is the case, then trying to destroy capitalism is pointless. In the next two chapters, I will show that attempts to destroy capitalism don't work very well and certainly don't help the poor. As we deal with human limitations, it turns out that trying to thwart them in the heavy-handed ways that leftists have dreamed about and have occasionally managed to achieve just reveals new problems. It's like squeezing a balloon: if you succeed in squeezing most of it, another part will pop out in a greater way than it did before.

To show that the evils of capitalism can arise in capitalism's absence, I'm going to talk about a particular segment of society in which capitalism is largely absent, namely academia. I say that academia is both outside the clutches of capitalism and that the evils within it are identical to the evils of capitalism, despite the fact that most professors today hate capitalism. I spent many years in academia, and what I observed there, especially in the humanities, I found quite surprising and even shocking. My illusions about socialism were shattered in academia. In fact, I went into academia supporting socialism and came out supporting capitalism.

Let me begin by saying that academia is outside the capitalist system to the extent that that is possible within a capitalist economy. Academia is part of the non-profit sector (in recent years some for-profit schools have sprung up, but they are looked down upon by most academics), and it is run in ways that people in the business world would find strange. Professors aren't usually hired because they will be a big hit, thus drawing more customers (that is, students) to the school. Instead, they are hired because they are good academics, people who will please their fellow professors, but not necessarily their students. Likewise, articles submitted to journals aren't accepted because they are interesting—most are boring—or because they will attract a huge audience and make the journal rich and famous. They are accepted for other reasons.

Here I am talking about the schools and journals at the top. Those lower down may have to operate in ways that are more concerned with satisfying the needs of students and readers, respectively. But the closer to the top one gets, the less concern there is for the paying customers.

Naturally, it is also true that almost nothing within a capitalist society can be truly considered as outside of the capitalist system. Colleges and universities, after all, charge tuition, pay salaries and wages to the people working within them, and compete with one another. There are even complaints from leftist professors that corporate America has been taking over academia in recent years. But none of this is relevant to what I am talking about because even if academia were part of the capitalist system, it is occupied by a vast legion of leftist professors who could easily deal with the problems I am going to describe, but who have steadfastly refused to do so.

What exactly are these problems? I am going to list the problems in academia that currently exist, but let me note that I am mostly talking about the humanities and not the sciences (though some of what I say may apply to them, too) and that while some of these problems are temporary, others have been with us for a long time:

1. **There is massive unemployment in academia.** This has been the norm since at least the early 1970s, and the problem shows no signs of abating. It is true that in the late 1980s, it seemed as though the problem was going to disappear. It seemed as though there would be a shortage of professors in the 1990s, and there were plenty of newspaper articles talking about this would-be shortage.[1] These articles encouraged young people to go through graduate school in the hopes of getting one of those coveted jobs. Instead, though, the professor shortage never materialized, which made the job situation even worse, because there were even more people looking for jobs than there would have been without those predictions.

2. **There is exploitation.** Because of the jobs crisis, many would-be professors must settle for less than full-time, permanent work, and such people are generally exploited. It is beyond the scope of this book to talk in detail about the exploitation of these people, who are generally called "adjuncts," but that they are exploited is well-known in academia (though seldom talked about by those at the top). They typically get less money for each class that they teach than tenured or tenure-track professors do, they get no benefits, they have to beg to renew their contracts every year, they often must work at two or three different institutions to make a living wage, and so on. Notice that I am talking about exploitation not of the staff people (a separate problem), but of would-be professors.

3. **There is a vicious hierarchy.** Academia contains several hierarchies, some of which I admit are benign. It makes sense that older faculty members will have a higher rank (assuming they have been doing things worthy of promotion), simply because they are older and more experienced, though I confess to being surprised when someone I knew teaching at a community college pointed out that everyone teaching there was at the same rank: instructor. Isn't that more egalitarian than the situation in four-year institutions in

which there are assistant professors, associate professors, and full professors? Yet there is no movement among "egalitarians" in the four-year institutions to get rid of the different ranks.

As I said, the hierarchy of the different ranks may be one that is benign, but there are other hierarchies more vicious than that one. The one mentioned above between tenured, full-time faculty and untenured, part-time adjuncts is one such hierarchy, but there is another one even more vicious, one that has permeated academia for centuries: the hierarchy between those associated with elite schools and those associated with non-elite schools. This hierarchy is similar to either an aristocracy or a caste system (depending on the field) in that people at the bottom, the non-elites, find it nearly impossible to rise to the top. This is in contrast to capitalism, in which some at the bottom do manage to rise to the top, and many others manage to rise from poverty to the middle class.

That academia has a vicious hierarchy will be disputed by those at the top (as well as outsiders who are their champions, such as *The New York Times*). These people will indignantly claim that academia is a meritocracy, and maybe even more meritocratic than capitalism is. (Some have even said it is egalitarian.) But why should leftists listen to those who are at the top only? Don't those of us at the bottom get a say? I will say more about meritocracy in the next point below, but for now I say that academia is a vicious hierarchy because of the limited upward mobility it permits. People who start at the bottom stay at the bottom, because academia is very much credentials-driven; it is very much an institution that permits people to be at the top only if they have gone to the right schools, which means that getting into the wrong grad school can affect one's entire academic career.

Capitalism, no matter how much it is disparaged by leftists, does not work like this, for it allows people to advance based on their merit. There are plenty of stories of poor people who started out at the bottom of some large corporation and ended up at the top. Others have started companies in their garages that have become very profitable. A friend of mine worked at a software company in a fairly low-level position, and he believes he was about to be fired (or close to it, anyway) when he landed a job at a different company that appreciated his talents more than the first did. They sent him to Germany to start up a subsidiary for them, and in less than five years he had made a million dollars. It is true that upward mobility isn't guaranteed and that there are many factors (such as racism or sexism) that can prevent a person from rising, but none of those factors are inherent in capitalism the way that credentialism seems to be inherent in academia. Capitalism, after all, is based on profits, and the company that eschews a talented person because of their race or gender or some other extraneous factor is simply allowing other companies to hire them instead.

4. **The rich get richer and the poor poorer.** I mean this in two senses. First, there is the sense that concerns the wealth within academia. Wealth within academia refers to actual wealth, such as grants of money or well-paying jobs that require comparatively little teaching, but also to honors that can be used to more easily attain that wealth, such as getting many books and articles published. (Admittedly, this wealth is almost nothing compared with the wealth of the richest people in our country, but on the other hand, it is quite substantial compared with what adjuncts get. Today's tenured academics generally live a comfortable, middle class lifestyle with generous benefits.) Who are the people who typically get big grants? Why, they are the people who have already gotten big grants. Similarly, who are the people who typically have articles published in prestigious journals? They are the people who have already had such articles published. A person who has never gotten a grant or never gotten anything published is very unlikely to get a big grant or an article published in a prestigious journal, *unless* he or she happens to have gone to an elite graduate school. Going to an elite school is the way to begin to get big grants or to get one's articles published. The rest of us dream of such things, and most of us fail. We get jobs at

he will perform at age 22 or 25, which is what matters to the average fan of professional sports. If player B turns out to be as good a player as player A, no fan is going to exclude player B because of the bad coaches he had or the bad teams he played on in the past. That is a true meritocracy.

But that is not how academia works. The dominant factor governing success in academia is where one went to school, with those going to lesser schools having less chance of getting a job and those going to more elite schools having a greater chance. Since the more elite schools are vastly more expensive than the less elite ones, they are in effect schools for the rich, which means that success in academia tilts very heavily toward those who have the right class background.

Let me give a parallel example from outside academia, namely the editorial pages of *The New York Times*. Who gets chosen as a regular columnist for such a lofty position? A look at the biographies in Wikipedia of the current columnists shows that many went to elite schools and that those who didn't go to elite schools almost all went to Eastern schools. In other words, you don't work your way up to the position of columnist for *The New York Times* from the bottom. You don't start out at a community college, transfer to the local university, begin a career writing for a small-town newspaper, and move to a larger newspaper after a few years, gradually working your way up to *The New York Times*. No. You have to start near the top to be a columnist with that newspaper. You can be the most brilliant columnist ever, and *The New York Times* won't look at you because you have the wrong credentials (and probably the wrong class background). A few years ago when *The Times* decided to choose a conservative columnist, whom did they choose? The very brilliant and witty Mark Steyn? Of course not, because Mark Steyn doesn't have the right credentials. As far as I can tell, not only did he not go to an elite college, he didn't go to college at all. So, the spot went to someone safe, William Kristol, who had gone to the right schools.

What this means is that a wide swath of the population would find that the columnists at *The New York Times* are like a breed apart and are people with whom they have little in common. For example, among the students in my high school class, I believe only one went to a truly elite school (not, as it turns out, one that is represented at *The Times*). Many of my classmates didn't even go to college, several of us went to the local university, and some went to private schools that still weren't quite part of the elite. There is a shocking lack of diversity, in terms of school background (and, ultimately, class background), at *The Times*, but this doesn't seem to bother any of its leftist columnists nor any of its leftist readers, even though they frequently chastise the Republicans and their institutions for not being diverse enough and for "not looking like America."

To return to academia, when the poor make it to the top, it's because they managed to do well on tests that allowed them to get into an elite school (generally on a scholarship). In other words, success for the poor hinges on how well they do on standardized tests that they take when they are young adults. If they do poorly on those tests, then they are *forever excluded* from reaching the top, no matter what intellectual successes they might achieve later in life. Already this seems like a brainless and unjust way of handling things, but I want to ask first, what are these tests like? Do they guarantee that talented poor people who take them will do well on them? The first problem is whether poor people will even take them, since often poor people have bad guidance when it comes to academic matters. Assuming they take the test, it's likely they won't be as prepared for it as richer people are. Richer people go to better schools, they can hire tutors, they can retake the test multiple times without worrying about the cost, and so on. The poor are therefore at a disadvantage even before they sit down to take the test.

Another problem is whether these tests test the right thing. After all, the most important ability in academia is not so much having general intellectual ability or a lot of knowledge in one's field, but the ability to generate new ideas so as to make important advances, and there is some doubt about whether these tests test for that. For example, psychology professor Robert J. Sternberg (formerly at Yale) noticed something odd about two graduate students he knew, one of whom had great grades and did fabulously well on standardized tests, the other of whom had good (but not great) grades who did only modestly well on those tests. The first student did wonderfully well in the first year of graduate school, but just never had anything new to say and struggled after that year, while the second, who ought to have done worse in grad school, in fact did better because she was so creative.[2] These tests simply do not test one's creativity and ability to generate new ideas, and so those poor people who are likely to get into a graduate program in an elite school aren't necessarily those who deserve to be let in.[3]

Consider, then, someone from a modest background who starts at the local community college. She is going to a community college because she had bad counselors, got mediocre grades in elementary and secondary schools, or didn't do well on standardized tests. (For many, this will seem a wholly unlikely background from which to become a professor, but in fact I knew several people like this in my high school who became inspired in college and began getting the As they could not get in high school. Some went on to get advanced degrees, and others could have done so.) She then goes on to the local university to complete an undergraduate degree, and finally goes to other similar universities to get graduate degrees. If these universities are ordinary rather than elite universities, she will likely end up teaching at a community college (if she is lucky enough to get a permanent job). She will never advance, no matter how brilliant she is, or if she does advance, she might manage to work up to a university of lesser rank than the one she graduated from; she simply will never get to the best schools with the best pay and the best likelihood of getting good grants.

This is the way the hierarchy works in academia. The poor, especially if they don't get into an elite school, are not treated well in academia. Accordingly, despite the insistence of those at the top who think it is a meritocracy, it is not a meritocracy, and there is little likelihood it will ever be a meritocracy. Similarly, despite the beliefs of the many leftists in academia who think they are kind to the poor, they are not in fact very kind to the poor since they are doing nothing to help smart but poor people thrive in academia.

Let me describe my own experiences. I come from a lower-middle-class background and went to the local university (the University of Minnesota) where I got both a B.S. in mathematics and a Ph.D. in philosophy. I knew there was a hierarchy in academia, but I also thought that, since academia was a realm of the intellect, the quality of one's ideas was what counted the most, and I knew I could generate plenty of good ideas, so I didn't worry. In addition, I thought I would be treated fairly in academia, compared with the corporate world, and that even if I were to be treated unfairly, my fellow leftists would support me. I was wrong on all these counts. Academia turned out to be hierarchical in terms of where one went to school and not in terms of the quality of one's ideas, it was not a place where I was treated fairly, and my fellow leftists didn't rally to my cause. In short, I bumped up against the class ceiling in academia.

As I said earlier, I think of academia as either a caste system or an aristocracy. To the extent that I think of it as a caste system, I admit it is not a rigid caste system, since a few individuals who come from modest backgrounds and who went to lower-ranked graduate schools managed to get further than one might expect (because they happened to go into a field that was desperate for people at the time they graduated, for example). So perhaps the term aristocracy is better, though my perception is that the people at the top *want* it to be a caste system. But whether it is a caste system or an aristocracy and whether it is rigid or somewhat flexible, academia is a hierarchical system in which there are Brahmins and untouchables.

A good example of a Brahmin in academia was Linus Pauling, who managed to get a scientific article published in a journal despite its containing an elementary mistake in chemistry.[4] At the other end of the spectrum are the untouchables, except that in academia we are not untouchables so much as unpublishables. If we were to submit an article with an elementary mistake in it, it would be rejected instantly, but even very good articles will generally be rejected, simply because the editor doesn't want the journal they edit to be tainted by publishing an article by someone with poor credentials.

I am an unpublishable (or nearly so). Everything I sent for publication was rejected. It didn't matter how much clever argumentation or how many original insights I included in my articles or who had vetted the article before I submitted it. They were rejected anyway. At first, my articles were only average, and the rejection letters actually had some valid (although I thought minor) criticisms. As I got older and more experienced, my articles got better and better, but instead of getting acceptances, I was still getting rejections. The only difference was that the rejections became more and more pathetic. They began having the appearance of desperation, of the reviewers struggling to seize upon something, anything, in my articles as a reason for rejection. Tiny flaws in my articles that could be corrected in minutes were touted by the reviewers as grave and serious objections that ruined everything I was saying. They could get away with such outrageous behavior because they had power and I didn't. There was never any downside for editors or referees in rejecting any article of mine because I was at the bottom and had no power to raise a fuss. The only thing I ever got published was published through the back door (by winning a contest). And despite the belief of the editors of every journal in my field that the sun would stop shining and cockroaches would take over the earth if an article of mine were to be published, the sun continues to shine and cockroaches have somehow been kept in abeyance.

Why were my articles rejected? Not because they were bad. No, they were rejected because of my lowly status, because I went to the University of Minnesota rather than to Harvard. I know that most academics and graduate students hearing this will immediately conclude that my articles were not very good and that I am in denial, but in fact I did get enough feedback from people at the top to know that was not true. For those who still think I am in denial, let me note that as a result of all my rejections I began asking every professor about the system, and it turned out everyone had a story of a rejection that didn't seem fair. The best is a story I came upon about Albert Einstein getting a rejection letter, long after he had made his name, and how angry he was about it.[5]

Let me also note that it was only a matter of time before someone like me came along to challenge the system. By that I mean that I was taught by leftists that I ought to rebel against the Establishment and to hate the rich. Once I realized that the people judging my work were very likely to be richer than me, what conclusion did leftists expect me to reach? Did they really expect me to slink quietly away? Here is another point: I ask those assuming that I am in denial who are also leftist and who are committed to listening to those of us at the bottom, what is this supposed to mean? What is "listening to those at the bottom" supposed to mean if you automatically accept the judgment of those at the top and never the judgment of those at the bottom? Those who assume I must be no good because I never got anything published are assuredly *not* listening to people at the bottom. Anyway, the plight of the adjuncts reinforces my interpretation of what happened to me. If my story were the only story about injustice in academia, it could be legitimately dismissed as the ravings of someone in denial, of someone who had no broader perspective on reality. Instead, the plight of the adjuncts should remind the skeptics that there are thousands of people who have been poorly treated in academia. They have been poorly treated in a segment of society in which, because it is dominated by caring leftists, ought to be a segment in which *no one* is poorly treated.

Let me conclude this section with a final anecdote about the hierarchy in academia. My wife is several years younger than I, and since she benefitted from things I learned along the way, she has become modestly successful in academia. Once it became possible to run a journal online, she began one herself so that her field would have more venues for publication for younger scholars (and also because, after hearing my tales of how editors treated unknowns, she wanted to do better). After her journal had been in existence for a few years, she was at a conference where she was introduced to the editor of the top journal in her field. The woman was not expecting this introduction, and after repeating my wife's name with surprise and disdain, she turned and walked away. The onlookers were stunned at the bad manners she displayed, but I wasn't a bit surprised. Her elitist behavior perfectly illustrates the existence of the hierarchy, and the hierarchy guarantees that those from modest backgrounds will usually not thrive.

5. **Among those at the top there is, if not greed, at least stinginess.** People at the top resist any sort of reform of academic publishing or of the hierarchy that would make things better for poor people, which looks very much like stinginess from where I sit. If these people were conservatives and were generally against reforms, they would be acting consistently with their primary political beliefs. But they are generally liberals and leftists who like the idea of reform for the sake of the poor, so what else can this be but stinginess? At one point, I wrote letters to every academic who had recently written a book espousing socialism and asked if they were willing to extend their socialist principles to academia. Only one person answered and that person was honest enough to say that he wasn't willing to do it. But a true socialist should be willing to have those principles imposed everywhere. (One of the ironies of the views of leftist academics is that they are strongly committed to academic freedom, which ought to be a libertarian's concern, and not at all committed to academic equality, which ought to be their own concern.) Established academics, leftists or otherwise, always claim that they are against any reforms because

all sorts of objections would be raised against it. But the fact that such a solution has never even been proposed is a sign of stinginess in leftist academics.

These, then, are five big problems in academia today. They all occur within a segment of society in which capitalism is largely absent. Yet they are among the same problems that critics of capitalism have complained about for two centuries: unemployment, exploitation, a hierarchy, the rich getting richer and the poor poorer, and greed at the top. While academia cannot be accused of other problems of capitalism, such as imperialism or environmental problems, the point is they can be accused of some of them; and the ones they can be accused of were the ones that were initially noticed as part of the Industrial Revolution. This is astonishing. What is more, these problems have occurred during a period in which leftists have been dominant. (For a long time, leftists absolutely rejected the claim that they dominated academia, despite the protestations of conservatives, until surveys were published in the 1990s proving it conclusively.) Nor have they been discussed much by those within academia who are obviously liberal or leftist. It is apparently so much easier for those within academia to complain about conditions *outside* of academia than to do something about conditions within it. Accordingly, denunciations of American foreign policy come from nearly every academic, but concerning pressing problems within academia there is little or no action. Likewise, it is so much easier to demand that *others* make big changes and give up privileges. It is much harder when the person to blame is yourself; it is much harder when the big changes have to be made by you.

Some leftists will respond by saying that the five problems in academia that I mentioned were not the result of leftists; leftists simply inherited them. But while leftists may not be held to blame for the origin of these problems, leftists have done little or nothing to improve things. Indeed, the main reason I am writing this book is that I watched the socialists and Marxists in academia do virtually nothing about these problems. On occasion they did genuine harm. Here is one such instance. As I mentioned earlier, it seemed in the late 1980s that the bad job situation was going to subside and there would be a shortage of professors in the 1990s. Instead, there was a shortage of jobs, and all the young people who had been encouraged to go into academia were suddenly looking into the abyss. Matters were so desperate that graduate students at Yale who worked as teaching assistants formed a union, and at one point in 1995 they went on strike and withheld grades until things were done to help them. Here is how one brutally honest leftist academic, Cary Nelson, described what happened next:

> Sara Suleri, a brilliant postcolonial critic... urged disciplinary action against one of her teaching assistants.... Nancy Cott, a widely admired labor historian, spoke out against the union, and David Brion David, a distinguished historian of slavery, sought college guards to bar his union-identified teaching assistant from entering the room where undergraduate final exams would be given.[6]

Anyone who thinks about this incident for more than three seconds will realize how strange it was and how it shows that many things we believe about the left are simply wrong. When confronted with a situation that capitalists are often confronted with (a strike by labor), these leftists handled it in exactly the same way that capitalists do. In fact, what has been the leftist solution to the oversupply of Ph.D.'s in academia? It has been to do nothing; in other words, the solution that is preferred by academic leftists is nothing other than to use the free market, despite their alleged hatred of market solutions.

Now I want to consider other examples in which the problems of capitalism emerged, even though capitalism was not present.

1.   One leftist blogger (I can't remember who it was) complained about the small amount of pay she was receiving for blogging, compared with wealthier leftist bloggers. "Couldn't they throw some money my way?" she groused. And why not? Since leftists believe in redistribution, why shouldn't they be willing to do it when they are in charge and have the money to do so? The idea promulgated by leftists that this world would be wonderful without conservatives is nonsense, the reason being that there are situations in which leftists have full control and yet refrain from making changes. Academia is close to that situation, and the set of leftist bloggers is exactly that situation. There are no conservatives preventing wealthier leftist bloggers from donating money voluntarily to the poorer ones.

2.   For that matter, let us be like mathematicians and consider the set of all leftists. As it turns out, some leftists are poor, but others are quite rich. Why not, then, have a redistribution from the richer leftists to the poorer leftists? Answering this question honestly goes a long way toward seeing what leftism—which I prefer to call Rich People's Leftism—is all about. It's more about criticizing rich conservatives than it is about helping the poor.

3.   Critics of capitalism seldom talk about what preceded capitalism. From what they say, one might get the impression that capitalism was imposed upon an egalitarian society. It wasn't. The society it was imposed upon was already hierarchical, and in some ways more viciously so than capitalistic society became. Capitalism allows for upward mobility, which the previous society did not. Listen to the diatribe against the navy expressed by Sir Walter Eliot in Jane Austen's *Persuasion*, complaining that the navy is "the means of bringing persons of obscure birth into undue distinction, and raising men to honours which their fathers and grandfathers never dreamt of."[7] This is the system that preceded capitalism and which in fact persisted as capitalism began to displace it. That aristocratic

system loomed so large in my mind when I was learning history that at first I found Marxist rhetoric bewildering. "The bourgeoisie and not the aristocrats, who make such a big deal about birth, are the problem?" I asked myself. It took a long time for me to digest this, and it has taken me even longer to un-digest it, to realize how wrong the Marxists were.

Under the aristocratic system, many people had been exploited. They were exploited as servants, or as tenant farmers who were subjected to high rents by their landlords, or as sailors impressed into the navy. When they were not actually exploited, they could be thwarted, as the subject of the book by Simon Winchester, *The Map that Changed the World*, was thwarted.[8] William Smith was quite talented and is known as the father of English geology, but according to Winchester he was thwarted by aristocrats who couldn't accept the possibility that anyone other than an aristocrat could be talented.

Exploitation and treating the common people as unimportant was the status quo for many centuries. The arrival of capitalism was nothing particularly new in this respect. What was new, however, was the arrival of modern feelings about fairness. These feelings did a great deal to form the U.S. Constitution and America's subsequent history. And fortunately, as I shall argue later in this part of the book, the path that America pursued was not that of equalizing the wealth, but rather that of equalizing power and opportunities.

4. Slavery has been around for millennia and has existed in many parts of the world, but capitalism has existed for only a few centuries, despite the fervent wish of capitalism's critics to blame capitalism (or the West) for slavery.

5. Women have been treated as second-class citizens in virtually every pre-modern society, even though capitalism has not been around for that long. In fact, in the late 1960s and early 1970s there was a struggle among feminists between those who were primarily socialists, who thought of women's problems as just another example of capitalist exploitation, and those who insisted that women's

problems had nothing to do with capitalism *per se.* The latter group won, and they were of course perfectly right since women's problems preceded the arrival of capitalism. Moreover, although the average woman may have been treated better under communism than under capitalism, it's not as if communist countries allowed women at the very top. The leader of every communist country has been male.

By now my point should be clear and persuasive: the alleged sins of capitalism occurred even when capitalism wasn't present. They have even occurred when liberals and leftists dominate. For most people, that should be enough to at least suspend judgment on capitalism.

CHAPTER 9

ELIMINATING CAPITALISM DOESN'T NECESSARILY HELP THE POOR

In this chapter, I consider what happened when capitalism was dealt with head on. That is, I consider how workers fared under communism. The chief consequences of communism were these:

1. The poor remained poor.
2. The middle class became poor.
3. The rich who were against the new regime were either executed or forced to flee.
4. The rich who managed to ingratiate themselves with those in power remained rich.

That the poor and the former middle class were poor in the communist countries is well known. If these countries had been filled with highly prosperous poor people who were richer than the middle classes elsewhere, there would have been enormous pressure (not just from Communists, but from most people) in all other countries to move to the same system. Instead, the effects were widely known (despite a large number of lies being reported about the situation), and there was enormous pressure here in America and elsewhere from the middle classes, from rich conservatives, and even from many in the working class *not* to move to such a system, to avoid moving to such a system.

This avoidance can also be seen from immigration into and out of countries. Today, we in America have many immigrants from Latin America, but Cuba has very few; instead, the occasional Cuban athlete escapes when traveling abroad (often here to America). It may be objected that Cuba is hard to get to for poor Latinos, since it requires crossing the sea, while the U.S. is comparatively easy for them. But in response, note that there is little movement to Venezuela, either. Keep in mind that Venezuela is trying to become a second Cuba, and it would be easier to get to, and it also uses the same language as the immigrants; yet Latinos still prefer coming here. Besides, whatever value this excuse might have had in the past is worthless today when so many immigrants from Africa manage to cross the sea to get to Europe. Accordingly, people in Latin America could do the same: they could move to Cuba. But they don't.

Moreover, the communist countries never achieved a classless society. There were plenty of people at the top, and as far as I can tell, these were people whose ancestors had been at the top under the czars. Hedrick Smith, a *New York Times* reporter who wrote a book on the Russians, reports on this situation: "Workers' children expected to finish high school and become taxi drivers, policemen or factory workers and intellectuals' children expected to go to college."[1] So much for the alleged classless society.

Why did the communist countries wind up with classes despite wanting to eliminate them? Richard Pipes explains that in order to run a society without a market, many decisions must be made by the government (instead of by individual buyers and sellers as in a free-market economy) and that this required a large bureaucracy.[2] Once entrenched, the people in this bureaucracy used their power to gain special privileges.

This explanation is part of it, but not the whole. What is missing is that the lower class was never granted any power in this system; it was the rich leftists who had power and got to run things. Had Communists and socialists ever thought about how power (and not just wealth) was supposed to be divided up in the classless society, the whole enterprise might have been done in a more humane and satisfying way. Instead, ruthless and power-hungry people emerged and took over. The results were horrible and did nothing to help the poor.

In addition to the hierarchy between the bureaucracy and the average Russian, there was also a hierarchy in terms of town and country. Smith quotes several Russians who talked about this. One woman said she was surprised at how narrow the gap in living standards was between city and rural life here in America compared with the Soviet Union.[3] Another woman observed that rural schools in the Soviet Union were quite inferior to urban schools,[4] and Smith inferred that that meant rural children probably had a much smaller chance of getting into a university. Moreover, because the Soviet Union discouraged internal travel, people were unlikely to be able to move to better themselves, whereas in the United States, people can move and travel freely whenever they like.

Sadly, then, a classless society, a society without hierarchies, never emerged. David Ramsay Steele has something pertinent to say about this situation:

> Intellectually, Fascists differed from Communists in that they had to a large extent thought out what they would do, and they then proceeded to do it, whereas Communists were like hypnotic subjects, doing one thing and rationalizing it in terms of a completely different and altogether impossible thing.... Fascists proclaimed the end of democracy. Communists abolished democracy and called their dictatorship democracy. Fascists argued that equality was impossible and hierarchy ineluctable. Communists imposed a new hierarchy, shot anyone who advocated actual equality, but never ceased to babble on about the equalitarian future they were "building." Fascists did with their eyes open what Communists did with

their eyes shut. This is the truth concealed in the conventional formula that Communists were well-intentioned and Fascists evil-intentioned.[5]

My point here isn't to defend fascism, but rather to put communism in perspective. It didn't create a classless society, and good intentions just aren't enough. Must one expect that hierarchies will automatically emerge, as the fascists believed? Answering that question is beyond the scope of this book, but I will say I have little faith, after what I saw in academia, that leftists are as devoted to egalitarian principles as they say they are, or that they will attack all hierarchies.

The one advantage of the communists' system is that the workers were not exploited on the job. (The joke was that the workers pretended to work and the system pretended to pay them.) But they were still at the bottom, and there were enough other costs in the system to make it generally unpalatable. A big problem with the workers' paradises was that they suffered so many shortages. Accordingly, although the workers weren't exploited on the job, they ended up in long lines trying to buy an extremely limited number of goods, so their time was exploited. Exploitation is basically theft, so the communist system simply changed the sort of theft involved from money to time.

Is this what the poor actually wanted?

CHAPTER 10
ELIMINATING CAPITALISM CAUSES ITS OWN PROBLEMS

Eliminating capitalism causes its own problems, all of which are well known. Some of these are the result of the lack of markets, and some are the result of the unbridled power of those at the top.

The lack of markets is dealt with in communist countries by central planning committees, made up mostly of rich people; but as many libertarians have argued, these committees cannot possibly deal with all the decisions about prices that must be made in a society. Sometimes a merchant must change prices hourly as a consequence of changing conditions. No central committee could make changes that fast. The results for the communist countries were surpluses of a few goods and shortages of all the others, with each of these conditions lasting a long time.

That accounts for the long lines in stores in communist countries, as well as the fact that most people lived in poverty. That is, even if the average worker had had lots of money, which he or she didn't, there was not very much to buy with it, so the workers lived in impoverished circumstances. The poor remained poor, and the exploitation of the workers' labor under capitalism was replaced by the exploitation of the workers' time under communism.

Was this what the workers wanted? Of course not. Hedrick Smith in his book *The Russians* tells of some Russians who were allowed to leave the Soviet Union and go touring in Western Europe. There were a few Westerners on the tour, and when they reached Italy, the Westerners trooped off to Pompeii and other tourist sites, while the Russians went shopping.[1] Why? Because they had so few opportunities to shop in their own country.

What the poor want (often enough) is to be rich. What Communists and socialists give them is merely the absence of exploitation. But the absence of exploitation is not everything in life, and most workers want more than that. Twice in Smith's book, ordinary Russians were quoted as saying, under certain circumstances, that communism had been achieved. And what were these circumstances? They were circumstances that we in the West are all used to, a well-stocked store containing affordable items.[2] Communism in their minds was achieved not merely by an absence of exploitation or ownership of the means of production by the state, but by a well-stocked store. The lack of markets didn't help the workers very much.

The other set of problems came from the consequences of the unbridled power of those at the top, which resulted in the murder of tens of millions of people. While this has been mentioned many times by many people, it is worth talking about again because it was so horrible.

These people were murdered because there were simply no institutional curbs on the power of those at the top. Leftist theorists never talked much about how power should be distributed in an egalitarian society because the focus was on how goods and wealth should be distributed. So when Lenin and others took over their societies, they simply ran roughshod over anyone who stood in their way. Their goal was to set up the ideal society, focused on eliminating the exploitation of the workers, nationalizing the means of production, creating a classless society, and equalizing wealth. But equalizing power was not part of it, nor was giving any power to the workers; the power went to those who were rich. The workers would not even be allowed to own the factories they worked in. Rather, the state would own them, and since the workers had no power to influence the state, they had very little say in how the factories were run. Since the factories were run in a lackadaisical way, the workers benefitted in the sense that they were not exploited (though not in the sense that it helped the entire system produce enough goods). But very little recommended the system to them beyond that. Meanwhile, huge quantities of humanity were put before firing squads or starved to death, or if they were lucky, sent off to prison in Siberia or to a distant collective farm.

People on the right rue the fact that one can mention Hitler and assume that everyone will agree we are talking about someone who was monstrous, but that the same isn't true of, say, Lenin, Stalin, and Che Guevara; and they are perfectly right. No matter how many people Che Guevara murdered, he is still thought of as a decent human being by many people in our society, the reason being that he had good motives. But those "good" motives were horribly flawed. They were flawed because the Communists never took into account the distribution of power, and the results were too horrible for words. People like Che, and the people who defend them, have given the left a bad name for many years.

Nor was it only people who were somehow privileged under the Tsars who were subject to being murdered. Communism, after all, was a system designed to help the worker, but plenty of other poor people besides the workers have existed throughout history. Peasants, for example, are generally poor, but their situation was ignored by the communists and socialists (although Mao paid much more attention to them than his predecessors had). People like Lenin felt no qualms about treating peasants badly.

Aside from the barbarity of the communist systems, the average citizen was powerless in ways that we in the West, or even in much of the Third World, would consider ridiculous and incomprehensible. Smith has an entire chapter on information and how it was withheld from the average Soviet citizen. One example that struck me was of a man from a distant province whose daughter flew to Moscow for a week to take an entrance exam at a university. After ten days, she still hadn't returned, so he flew to Moscow to find out what happened to her. The university where she was supposed to take the exam had not seen her, nor had family friends she was thinking of visiting. The police suggested he go to the airport police, where he finally learned that his daughter had been killed in an airplane crash, though he was advised to keep this information confidential. No one had heard about this crash.[3] Such a system is immoral.

What about less extreme systems? What about socialism as opposed to communism? The basic idea behind various systems of socialism is the redistribution of wealth, and as such socialism runs into some of the same problems as communism. It is true that in countries that have democracy as well as socialism, there are not the large numbers of people murdered that one finds in the communist countries, but that is hardly the result of socialism. It is the result of democracy. Those socialists who were not in favor of democracy never worried about power sharing, limits on power, separation of powers, or checks and balances, because all they were interested in was the redistribution of wealth. Redistribution of power was done by democratic theorists, theorists whom most leftists despised. Take democracy away from even the mildest of socialistic societies, and everlasting dictatorship will be the result since there is nothing in socialism *per se* that would push such a society back to something democratic. On the other hand, keeping democracy means that the voters could vote to eliminate socialism, so there is often pressure among socialists in such countries to keep democracy to a minimum, or else to control the press and schools as much as possible so that the people can be easily manipulated and vote the way socialists think they should.

One of the ironies of history is that Marxist theory was designed for advanced industrial societies, but instead of arising in such countries, it arose in countries that were not very advanced at all in industrialization and were basically feudalistic. Such countries needed redistribution of power much more than they needed redistribution of wealth, but the tragedy of history is that they got the latter (or an attempt at it) and not the former.

Not only do leftist solutions not do much for the poor, they have such severe problems on their own that they ought to be avoided. Even the mildest of socialist systems will abuse power, unless a strong democratic spirit is present to prevent such abuses.

CHAPTER 11
THE REAL PROBLEMS OF THE INDUSTRIAL REVOLUTION

The Industrial Revolution of two hundred years ago is well known for having exploited the workers. The exploitation was so severe that leftists of the time invented a variety of solutions to combat it, the most extreme being socialism and communism. Their basic ideas were that capitalism was to blame (because of the greed of the factory owners) and that redistribution of wealth was the solution. I have been saying that the problems that the workers faced back then can arise even in the absence of capitalism and so capitalism could not have been the source of those problems. However, I also want to argue in a different way that a maldistribution of wealth could not have caused the problems, either. Instead, there were other problems, two political and one non-political.

First, however, I want to consider the question: Were the workers in fact exploited? My initial reaction when reading about them was that they were not. Nor am I alone in thinking this. C.P. Snow writes:

> The industrial revolution looked very different according to whether one saw it from above or below. It looks very different today according to whether one sees it from Chelsea or from a village in Asia. To people like my grandfather, there was no question that the industrial revolution was less bad than what had gone before. The only question was, how to make it better.[1]

His grandfather had been one of the workers (though he eventually managed to become a "maintenance foreman in a tramway depot"[2]), and earlier Snow had observed that as far as his grandfather knew, his own grandfather could neither read nor write:

> My grandfather was pretty unforgiving about what society had done, or not done, to his ancestors, and did not romanticize their state. It was no fun being an agricultural labourer in the mid to late eighteenth century, in the time that we, snobs that we are, think of only as the time of the Enlightenment and Jane Austen.[3]

Keep in mind that this is someone talking about the feelings of his own grandfather, so it is not as though Snow's ideas were the result of abstract theorizing. Moreover, they still seem to be relevant, for these days when I hear about exploitation in some factory in the Third World that is owned by a multinational corporation based in America, the following pattern seems to hold. The first news reports talk about how bad the situation is, but generally subsequent reports give a somewhat different perspective. One learns that the exploitative situation, as Snow observes, only seems so to us and that in the context of the country in question, the wages are good and the workers happy to get such good jobs.[4] Naturally, like Snow's grandfather, they would like things to get even better, but having their factory closed down so that rich leftists in the First World can feel good about themselves is not what these workers want.

Notwithstanding this evidence, let me take it as a given that the workers of the Industrial Revolution were exploited. The question is why. Let me start with the political problems, one of which as I hinted in the last chapter was the maldistribution of power. Back then workers could not vote. They were not even citizens but were mere subjects who had to put up with whatever the elites in society wanted them to put up with. There was no chance for them to elect their own leaders who could have done something about their situation. They simply had to hope that someone with power would eventually notice that what they endured was inhumane and that changes needed to be made. Now that every adult citizen has the vote, conditions for the workers are enormously changed. Legislation now exists that limits the number of hours that workers can be worked, prevents young children from working, and ensures generally safe working conditions. If the workers had had the right to vote from the beginning, all of this legislation would have been put into place almost as soon as the factories began hiring.

In addition to their lack of the right to vote, the workers back then had little or no chance to get educated so they could have better opportunities or at least be able to understand their situation. Many of them went to work at an early age, worked many hours during the day, and were used until they dropped dead. Today, of course, things are very different since every child is expected to be in school until the age of sixteen. The result is a completely different environment for the lower classes compared with two hundred years ago. While there are still people in poverty, they can vote and get a good education (except when the schools are ruined), so they can collectively help change the circumstances that they were born into.

The non–political problem is an even more important factor than the political ones. For the workers of that era, the non-political problem was that *there were so many workers*. When there is a shortage of workers, the workers seldom experience exploitation. In the fourteenth century after the bubonic plague had killed so many people in Europe, for example, the sudden shortage of workers meant that many people who had been nothing but serfs were lifted out of their condition by people higher up who needed workers and were willing to hire them under freer conditions than they had ever experienced before. But that wasn't the case during the Industrial

Revolution. The population was rising rapidly, and society couldn't handle all the new workers who were suddenly appearing. When there are too many workers, wages go down and people become ripe for exploitation since they are desperate for any job.

It is easy to condemn the exploitation in the factories, but the situation could have been worse. What if there hadn't been any factories at all? What would have happened to the people? They would have been unemployed and living on the streets. Is this really a better situation? Of course not.

Leftists, naturally, will insist that not only should the workers have been employed and not living on the streets, but also that they should have been paid better. I'll take up the point of their pay in subsequent chapters. For now, let me note that the big problem was the large numbers of potential workers and the failure of society to provide good opportunities for them. Let me also note that the problem leftists want to attribute to greed and to solve with redistribution was the result of overpopulation and should be solved, to the extent that it can, with job creation.

Even worse for the left is that not only have leftists misdiagnosed the problem from two hundred years ago, *they have done just as badly as early capitalists in dealing with the same problem.* That is, the exploitation of adjuncts that I mentioned in Chapter 8 is the exact same situation of the workers of two centuries ago. There is an oversupply of adjuncts, and as should be evident, the leftists of academia have done no better in dealing with this situation than the captains of industry did back then. When leftists complain about capitalism and the exploitation of the workers, they claim they don't like market solutions, but they have been quite content to use a market solution to solve the adjunct problem.

These, then, are the factors that caused the exploitation of the workers. The political factors were their political powerlessness— their lack of the chance to vote to improve their conditions by means of having politicians on their side—and their having no chance to get an education. The non-political factor was the overpopulation that led to their being desperate enough to put up with exploitation. Greed had little to do with it; nor did capitalism, the maldistribution of wealth, the existence of private property, or any of the other alleged evils that leftists have enumerated in connection with this situation.

CHAPTER 12
HOW THE UNITED STATES OVERCAME THOSE PROBLEMS

In the last chapter I argued that a major factor involved in the exploitation of workers was the lack of political power that the workers had back then. They were not allowed to vote, nor was there a system of universal education that would have helped them break free of the clutches of exploiters. Their opportunities in life were very limited.

In this chapter, I will argue that America took a different path than that suggested by the leftists of the nineteenth century. Those leftists wanted a redistribution of wealth in the form of communism or socialism, while America went in the direction of a redistribution of power together with increased opportunities for the poor.

In Europe the type of socialism that made the biggest impact was communism, a system in which those at the top had near absolute power. The results were horrible: tens of millions of people were murdered. Even under the more democratic systems of socialism that we see today, much of the power is vested in the hands of the elites rather than in the people. For example, under the socialism that was introduced into Britain shortly after World War II, the percentage of people going to college was smaller than it was here in America at that time.[1] College was still basically the preserve of the rich, and since many of the people in government had been educated at elite schools, the poor were basically represented by people wealthier than they were and not necessarily working in their interests.

When I think about my life if I had been born into the Britain of that era, I shudder because I doubt I would have gone to college, and even if I had, I would have been surrounded by people from wealthier backgrounds than mine. As it was, there was no question that I was going to college, and my friends at college were mostly like me in being lower middle class, with some who were somewhat richer and others who were somewhat poorer than me. In other words, here in capitalist America I could have become, say, an electrical engineer or a physicist, whereas in socialist Britain I would have been only an electrician or a lab worker. This pattern may have changed in recent years, but with the introduction of the European Union, power seems to reside in a lot of elites who aren't even elected. Again, the pattern is more about redistributing wealth than distributing power equitably.

America, on the other hand, was more interested in an equitable distribution of power. For example, America had the separation of powers built right into the Constitution. So long as the Constitution is respected, there can never be the sort of absolute power that was enjoyed by the rulers of communist or fascist countries. The Constitution forbids it. Right away that was in America's favor. It leads to a saying from the right to the effect that the left is always predicting that fascism will overtake America, but it always seems to fall on Europe instead.

In addition to our Constitution, there was the slow and steady acceptance of the idea that every adult should get the vote. Of course that happened in other countries as well, but it was not something pushed for by the left, because the left was skeptical of the idea that giving workers the vote would do anything to change their condition. But as I pointed out in the last chapter, once workers get the vote, they can influence policy and change laws to work in their favor since they have such large numbers on their side compared with the capitalists. Another problem for America that leftists constantly bring up is the issue of slavery, but eliminating it was also part of the idea that every adult should get the vote, and we fought a bitter war to eliminate it. In addition, the institution of slavery predated the writing of our Constitution; it is hard to imagine anyone in late eighteenth-century America *introducing* slavery since it was so foreign to their ideas. The writers of the Constitution coped with it as best as they could, hoping it would go away on its own.

Another part of the problem for the workers of the Industrial Revolution was that they were not being educated. Being educated gives one more opportunities in life than otherwise; education opens up many worlds. One learns about life in Greece and Rome, in China and India, and so on. It also can give one the technical training to become more than just a skilled tradesman; one can become an electrical engineer instead of just an electrician. In addition, an education can give one the intellectual skills to analyze one's situation and to invent solutions. Being educated has always been an important part of American life, the idea being that uneducated people could not partake in political affairs with any competence.

What if a system of universal education had been in place during the Industrial Revolution? That would have resulted in several advantages for the working class. Not only would their children have received an education, but by taking these children out of the workforce, the wages of the remaining workers would have gone up. In addition, some of the factory workers would no doubt have been employed by the schools instead, which again meant a higher wage for those workers who remained in the factories, for as the supply (of workers) goes down, the price (for their labor in terms of wages) goes up.

As America tried to equalize power and opportunities for poor people, one very good thing that came from such an approach was the founding of many public libraries, often through the efforts of rich capitalists. I went to public libraries all the time when I was growing up, and greatly appreciate the opportunities I had to read so many books about so many things. But not all had such opportunities. Here is how science-fiction writer Sarah A. Hoyt describes the libraries of Portugal, where she spent her childhood:

> ... the libraries in Portugal are repositories of original material – some of it very old. If you want to do anything that requires primary sources you go to the public library. The entire system is the equivalent of the section of libraries here [in America] devoted to local history and documents.
>
> As in those, you can't check books out, and quite frankly, you wouldn't want to. The few fiction books in there are those considered of historical and/or literary value.
>
> There are of course other libraries, *most of those being rather small and confined and private.* Most parish houses have a lending library at least for young people. A lot of youth clubs have libraries. Schools from middle school up have libraries.[2]

We are lucky to have the libraries we have, though now with the Internet, information is much easier to obtain than formerly. But there are still many new books that one can check out from a library, as well as newspapers to read, and it is all for free.

Finally, another way that America helped the poor was simply by creating for them many good-paying jobs, which weren't available in Europe. This was why my ancestors came to America. There was little or nothing for them back in Europe, and they had heard about the wonderful opportunities here in America. Nor were those opportunities created as the result of slavery or imperialism, since slavery had been eliminated by the time most of my ancestors came (and in any case they came to the North), while the small amount of imperialism we engaged in had not really begun. Nor were we oppressing Latin America and so gaining opportunities that way. The countries of Latin America were well established (if not as countries, at least as colonies of Spain and Portugal) long before America got going. If anything, then, *they should have been oppressing us.* Moreover, we are still producing so many job opportunities that people in Latin America have been coming here for decades.

Socialism in America never took hold, which has been a great source of mystery for the left and an even greater source of condemnation by them, though to my mind it is a good thing. Poor people came here expecting opportunities to get out of poverty, and the last thing they wanted was interfering busybodies destroying those opportunities in order to "help" the poor. America took a different and better path, one that when followed with no admixture of socialist elements, did and continues to do quite well in getting people out of poverty.

It is true that because of the current economic situation, many have declared that capitalism is dying and needs to be replaced (though if there was any time when capitalism should have died, it was in the 1930s; yet it didn't die). At the time that our current distressed circumstances began (in 2008), I was just about ready to submit this book for publication; however, I did not want to talk about the current situation and to defend capitalism under such conditions, so I put off publication of this book and published two others instead. This was a wise decision since the situation has clarified now, and it is perfectly clear that the more socialistic systems of Europe are having just as many problems as capitalism in the United States, and maybe even more problems. However, the Scandinavian countries have largely avoided the problems of other European countries because they experienced a similar crisis in the 1990s, which led them to pull back to some extent from socialism.[3]

Many leftists complain that America isn't as upwardly mobile as Europe now is. It is not to the left's credit that leftists were not acknowledging the greater upward mobility of America over Europe when I was younger. But assuming that what they are saying is correct, the decline in upward mobility here in America seems less due to capitalism than to other factors.

First, elites in various fields (academia, law, and finance) have been allowed to decide that only people who have gone to the very best schools (as they themselves did) will be considered for hiring. The reason presumably is that the small number of jobs means that those hiring can afford to be choosy, and when they are choosy, they go with graduates of the elite schools. This is great if you come from a wealthy background and can easily get into such schools, but not so great for everyone else. As I like to say, in academia I was stymied by the "class" ceiling.[4] Second, with a portion of the population deciding that getting a good education means "acting white," there will be little upward mobility possible for them, and so they languish at the bottom. Finally, to some extent all schools for the poor have been destroyed by leftist tinkering, as I pointed out in Part I. There is nothing to suggest to me that, had conditions remained what they were in the 1950s, upward mobility would have declined.

This completes Part II. I have argued that capitalism is not the problem because the same problems which are allegedly due to capitalism can emerge even without capitalism. In addition, the left's preferred alternative to capitalism, communism, does little to help the poor and in any case has severe problems of its own. Finally, the problem for the exploited workers of the Industrial Revolution wasn't capitalism, but was both a lack of power and an oversupply of workers. Here in America we eschewed leftist solutions and instead helped workers get power, with the result that workers are treated much better in America today than they were in early nineteenth century Britain.

There is nothing to be ashamed of concerning capitalism in America.

PART III:
A LEFTISM BY, FOR, AND OF THE POOR

CHAPTER 13
THE LEFT IS RUN BY RICH PEOPLE

In this chapter I will argue that leftism has long been run and continues to be run by rich people, which means that their needs are put before the needs of the poor. (The needs of rich leftists are that they want to look like they are on the side of the poor, but they also want to keep their money.) In addition, I will argue that rich leftists tend to want to keep the poor poor rather than to allow them to improve their position.

The Existence of Rich Leftists

When I was young, I had no idea that rich leftists were anything but an occasional curiosity whose existence we poorer people ought to celebrate. Not until I got older did I come to realize that they are much more numerous than I had imagined and that they, and not us poorer folks, ran things. I'll get to that second point in a bit, but for now, let me point out how many prominent leftists have been rich. I don't mean they are all billionaires (or their era's equivalent). I simply mean that they were or are in the upper half of the population economically. The list includes Karl Marx, Friedrich Engels, Robert Owen, Vladimir Lenin, Fidel Castro, Leon Trotsky, Rosa Luxembourg, and many others. Today, the left in America focuses its ire on the Koch brothers, while completely ignoring the influence of rich leftists like George Soros. In France, François Hollande campaigned as a socialist who hated the rich, but once in office it was revealed that he had several residences on the Riviera. Naturally, there are some poorer leftists who have become prominent, but what is surprising is how likely a prominent leftist is to be rich, given that leftism is supposed to be a movement of the poor.

My growing realization that there were many more rich leftists than I had imagined was the result of many things, but here is one passage I read that helped:

> Robert Michels (1876-1936)...came to his belief in the inevitability of elites from a background in left-wing organizations.... He noticed how few genuine workers attended trade union meetings, how the leaders of the Left were almost invariably educated men and women from the middle or upper classes, and that it was their will and interests, rather than those of the working class, that tended to prevail.[1]

Many other passages helped me on the way to my current understanding of political realities, but this one helped more than any other. Nor need we be bothered by the fact that Michels ended up supporting the fascists, a path I wholly reject. His subsequent folly shouldn't be a reason to reject the truth of his observation.

Leftism Is Run by the Rich

I admit it will seem strange to many people to say that rich leftists run the left, which is a movement for the poor. But I say that the key word here is "for." Just because the left is for the poor doesn't mean that it is *of* the poor or *by* the poor. But let me consider some objections.

First, if the rich were controlling the left, then why would the left be so interested in raising taxes on the rich? Why would people who run a movement act in a way so contrary to their own interests?

But I say that the demand to raise taxes on the rich is nothing but "theater." People who are rich, including rich leftists, know perfectly well how easy it is for rich people to avoid paying higher taxes, if they are determined to avoid them. There are many avenues of escape, including the extremes of making less money or moving to another country. Accordingly, demanding that the rich pay higher taxes is nothing but a ploy by rich leftists to make it look as though they are on the side of the poor, when in fact they may not be.

Moreover, as conservatives have often pointed out, anyone who wants to give extra money to the government can do so voluntarily, but almost no one does. In fact, anyone who wanted to give directly to the poor could do so, but as surveys have shown, it is conservatives and not liberals and leftists who are more likely to give to charity. This is because leftists typically think that individuals acting on their own should not be helping the poor and that instead the government should be doing so; consequently, they don't give. That is a strange viewpoint. It says, "I am dedicated to helping the poor, but only if the strong arm of the law forces me to do it." What level of dedication does that show? It is obviously a lower level of dedication than that displayed by those who actually go out and give money to poor people directly and of their own free volition. In addition, it is hardly likely that rich conservatives, who don't want their taxes raised, are going to be impressed by such a low level of dedication on the part of rich leftists; if you yourself are unwilling to give *voluntarily*, why would you expect others to give *involuntarily*, under government compulsion? Yes, some liberals and leftists do give, but the point is that not enough do. (As I pointed out in Chapter 8, leftist bloggers who make a lot of money at blogging could donate some of their money to leftist bloggers who *don't* make much money, but in fact they never do.) Accordingly, even if rich leftists are dedicated to the poor, their efforts are ham-handed (and probably not what the poor need).

Finally, once the government gets that money, it can be channeled toward all sorts of people, only some of whom may be poor. Some of that money even goes to rich leftists. Liberals and leftists often complain about corporate welfare, government money that goes to corporations instead of the poor. What they don't acknowledge is the existence of welfare for the rich leftist: the many grants in academia and the arts that mostly go to liberals and leftists from wealthy backgrounds and not to poorer people. An example of welfare for the rich, whether leftist or not, is the free university educations that can be found in Europe and which liberals and leftists want in this country, too. Poorer people are less likely to go to college, even when it's free, so the main beneficiaries are rich people.

Accordingly, the demand for higher taxes on the rich is nothing but "theater." It is either for show, or else it is with the idea that having higher taxes means a bigger government and that a bigger government means more jobs and more power for rich leftists. A better sort of demand would be for rich people to give money directly to the poor in their community, but that demand is seldom made. In Chapter 19 I will argue that the role for the rich, whether leftist or not, isn't to pay higher taxes, or to urge wealthy conservatives to pay more taxes, but to give directly to the poor in their communities.

Another reason for doubting that the left is under the control of the rich is that in communist countries, rich people were forced to flee or were even executed. How could the left be run by the rich if that was allowed to happen? But the key here is which rich people suffered in these ways and also who forced those rich people to flee. The rich people who suffered were the ones at odds with the regime, but those who went along with it did fine. When one looks at the results of communism and not its rhetoric, one sees all too plainly what was going on: rich conservatives and even not-so-rich conservatives were forced to flee or were executed. The middle class dropped into poverty. The poor remained poor. But wealthy people who went along with the regime did well (with the exception of the purges during the 1930s in the Soviet Union, the Cultural Revolution in China, and the killing fields in Cambodia). They, and not the poor, were the winners. And who in fact was in control? It was the rich. No one should be under the illusion that communism was run by the poor; it was run by the rich. It is not as though the leadership and the central planning committees were composed of a rotating and randomly-chosen group of ordinary citizens (such as was in effect in ancient Athens for their councils). No, rich people were always in control. In fact, the constant push for central planning by so many leftists, not just in the past but right up to our own day, shows that the left is run by the rich, since they are the ones most likely to end up as planners.

A third reason for skepticism is that when I was young, in contrast to today, it was quite hard to see that leftism was run by the rich and not the poor. At that time, our most distinguished politicians who were left-of-center had ordinary backgrounds. Lyndon Johnson was a schoolteacher, Hubert Humphrey had been a druggist, Harry Truman hadn't even gone to college, and Walter Mondale went to law school on the G.I. Bill after having served in the army. In addition, the war on the poor that I recounted in Part I hadn't yet begun, so the focus of the left was on helping the poor and not on doing other things that inadvertently hurt them. But as I mentioned in the previous section, rich leftists have had a far larger role in helping, influencing, and controlling the left than one would initially imagine. For example, the politicians just mentioned were influenced by Franklin Delano Roosevelt's New Deal, and Roosevelt was a rich liberal. Moreover, in contrast with the period of my youth, today it seems to be a requirement of the Democrats that any of their presidential candidates should come from either Harvard or Yale if they want to be nominated. The last time the Democrats nominated someone who didn't go to an elite school was in 1984, which was three decades ago. That means, since elite schools basically attract the wealthy, that our Democratic presidents come from wealth; and even if they were poorer and somehow got into an elite school, they were required to pass muster by wealthy people in order to get nominated. When looking at what preceded and what followed the era of my earlier years, it seems painfully evident that it was an unusual interlude, a time when ordinary people with ordinary credentials could get to the national stage, but it was nothing but an interlude. Usually, rich progressives dominate the left.

These are the main points of suspicion against my claim that the left is run by the rich. Here are the points in favor.

1. The war against the poor mentioned in Part I of this book could never have started if the poor had been controlling the left. When leftists began shutting down factories because they polluted too much, the protests of the workers who lost their jobs would have been listened to, but instead they were ignored. When leftists began destroying schools used by the poor, the complaints of the poor would have been listened to, but instead they were ignored. When leftists began making changes so that colleges had to hire more administrators, which led to a steep rise in tuition, the complaints of the poor would have been listened to, but instead they were ignored. When leftists began being soft on crime, the complaints of the poor who were victims would have been listened to, but instead they were ignored. In addition, who ended up in jail for crimes? The theorists at the top? Of course not. It was poor people. Poor people were victimized by crime in one of several ways, either by being the actual victim of a crime or worrying about being a victim or by ending up in jail, while those who encouraged the poor to commit crimes were actually *paid* to dream up such policies. The war against the poor had to have been done by rich leftists, who simply didn't care what the poor thought or suffered from their policies.

2. The history of the left explains to some extent why rich people control it, for the left began at a time when poor people were not generally in a position to do much of anything for themselves, so rich people began doing it for them. Let me begin when the left as we

know it first emerged as a result of the exploitation of the workers in the Industrial Revolution. (Prior to that, the left's focus, to the extent that the left existed, was on ending the privileges of the aristocrats; the very word "leftist" emerged in the French Revolution, and ending such privileges was mostly what the French Revolution was all about.) At that time, the poor generally had neither the time nor the education to analyze their own plight and to suggest alternatives. Instead, it was richer people who emerged and began analyzing the situation and devising solutions. They were the ones who dominated and were in control. People like Marx, Engels, Owen, and others all came from comfortable backgrounds.

As the nineteenth century wore on, and the revolution predicted by Marx and others never materialized while capitalism continued to thrive—and indeed the situation of the workers even began to improve—leftists like Lenin decided that a vanguard was needed to start the revolution without relying on the poor. (The idea that since their predictions were not coming true, maybe their whole theory was wrong and ought to be abandoned seems not to have occurred to many intellectuals.) Such a move, of course, basically meant that the left was *officially marginalizing the poor*, but no one on the left thought such thoughts. In addition, once the Communists took over in Russia, much of leftism was basically run from Moscow, and since the new Soviet Union was set up by Lenin, who was from a wealthy background, leftism was run either by wealthy people or along lines set up by wealthy people. Moreover, communism, as I have been pointing out, helped the rich (at least those who supported the Party), while everyone else was miserable and powerless. It is hard to imagine that the poor, if they had controlled the left, would have put up with this system for very long, but they generally did not control it. Yes, it is true that Stalin came from a poor background (although neither of his parents had worked in a factory and so were not really considered workers by the usual leftist definition of that term), but like many another poor leftist, he simply accepted the views of the wealthier leftists about how to run things. Even more important, it is not as though he allowed power-sharing among all the poor people in the Soviet Union, and in fact his rule was almost the exact opposite.

To what extent were poor people able to change and dominate the left, or if they couldn't dominate the left, to set up their own movements that more truly represented the poor? And to what extent were the poor able to publicize the idea that socialism, communism, and the left in general were dominated by the rich and their ideas? In China, Mao included the peasants as part of communism's focus because he himself was from a peasant background. He also instituted the Cultural Revolution, which was aimed at wealthy elites in the Party, but it was a disaster and ultimately changed nothing. Likewise, in Cambodia Pol Pot killed off many wealthy elites, but it too was a disaster, and it had no effect on who had control of the left elsewhere in the world; nor did it change anyone's ideas on who controlled the left.

Here in America Samuel Gompers pushed for unions as the way to help the poor because unions consisted wholly of the proletariat; he absolutely rejected any organizations or movements that were dominated by anyone who wasn't from the proletariat, and so he rejected communism and socialism. His successor George Meany had similar policies. The two of them did as much as anyone to prevent socialism from establishing itself here in America. However, neither was able to win the larger public-relations victory: making it clear that socialism and communism were dominated by wealthy elites and their ideas.

Generally, it seems that here in America poor immigrants had come for the opportunities and so had less interest in any of the left's ideas. (Naturally, this resistance to socialism has elicited a huge amount of enmity against America among leftists.) Even those who came as socialists or communists often changed their minds when they got here, or else their children were much less radical. (For example, my brother-in-law's grandfather, who came from

Russia, was a communist, his father was a liberal, and he himself is a libertarian). An interesting comment on America from the middle of the last century comes from Whittaker Chambers' book *Witness*, in which an unnamed European observed that the poor in America supported the Democrats, the middle class supported the Republicans, and the wealthy supported the Communists.[2] Why would the wealthy do that, if in fact it meant that rich people would lose all their wealth? The point, though, is that communism did *not* mean that. As long as one supported the Party, one needn't lose all one's wealth, and one got to have control through participating in central planning. The context of this remark was that someone was surprised at how rich people were vehemently against Chambers in his battle against the communist Alger Hiss when one would expect them to be supportive. But a cynic wouldn't be surprised: Chambers, while he went to a good college, Columbia, was no match for Hiss with his Harvard law degree; and while Chambers spent part of his childhood in the middle class and part in poverty, Hiss had a pedigree of sorts, even if he grew up in "shabby gentility." It is clear with whom the rich would rather identify.

But let me get back to the larger point: were the poor in America who became communists able to wrest control from the rich or to turn the left into something that was more of and by the poor and not merely for the poor? Not at all, since Moscow was basically in charge. Moreover, it seems (from the comment in Chambers' book) that poor people were not so likely to become communists, and so it was rich people who dominated. But even if poor people had joined in large numbers—and one old communist assured me that all the workers were communists back then—it is still unlikely that they would have dominated, given that the rich had money while the poor didn't, and given the heavy-handed control of communism from Moscow.

By the time I came of age in the late 1960s, things had changed to the extent that leftists in the West could go in whatever direction they liked without worrying about what Moscow thought about things, but I have to say that I never heard anything about how Gompers and Meany had resisted communism because they didn't like its bourgeois origins. It wasn't until this century when I read a book by a conservative that I learned about their views.[3] All I knew was that there were liberals who were anti-communists and that their anti-communism seemed to spring from nothing other than their antipathy toward the anti-democratic nature of communism. Not a word was spoken to the effect that communism ought to be rejected because it had been started by the rich and not the poor.

And so I and others just fell in line with the older ideas. Those older ideas seemed helpful to the poor, so there was no point in questioning them. (I myself thought of the left as a movement that had helped people like me in the past, while conservatives had opposed people like me, so I went along with leftist rhetoric.) Attitudes of hatred against corporations and America and in favor of socialism and communism and the old Soviet Union seemed natural to adopt, even if it was corporations that were going to hire us. It just never occurred to any of us, nor did anyone ever tell us, that maybe the left's ideas were not so great for the poor, that they had been devised by rich people, that because of that maybe those ideas were more helpful for the rich than the poor, and that we ought to consider what a leftism not just for the poor but by and of the poor would be like.

As far as I know, no poor people elsewhere explicitly rejected socialism or communism because of their bourgeois origins and because of the possibility that they might not represent the poor adequately. As one conservative put it, "given the invidious class distinctions in Europe, the workers felt they needed middle-class allies, and the socialists played this role. In gratitude, the workers were willing to accept their ideology."[4] The poor in Europe, of course, didn't need to become socialists. For example, Eduard Bernstein was originally a Marxist who later switched to the milder Social Democratic Party as a result of noticing that Marx's predictions were not coming true. Parallel movements, then, did exist, but they failed to marginalize the communists or to publicize the idea that communism was an essentially bourgeois movement.

The result after about one hundred seventy-five years of leftism is that while communism is mostly dead, socialism is still very much alive. Even more important, while alternate movements for the poor exist (in the form of labor unions), the fact remains that leftism is generally known as a movement *for* the poor and not as a movement *of* the rich. The idea that communism is nothing but the last gasp of feudalism, a reactionary movement that cleverly disguised itself as progressive and pro-worker but whose main purpose was to allow the rich a chance to keep control of society as the more enlightened ideas of the eighteenth century gained credence, is seldom heard.[5]

3. Poor people like C.P. Snow's grandfather were not asked their opinion of what they thought of the Industrial Revolution. (Recall that he had said it was better than the earlier conditions, but that more needed to be done to make it better.) Nor were all of the poor even included in the left's policies at the beginning. Peasants, servants, and in fact all poor people who didn't work in factories were excluded from the thoughts of many early leftists. Today, poor whites are excluded, unless they happen to be single mothers.

4. Another reason for believing that the rich and not the poor control the left is that the basic idea of the left has always been spreading the wealth, but not spreading the power. While initially this would seem to go against my thesis, in fact it supports it because if you control the power, you control where the wealth goes. It's very easy, when you have control, to say that you are redistributing wealth to the poor when you are actually doing something else entirely.

5. Along similar lines, the left has long been leery of democracy. In the nineteenth century, they thought that communism was the proper method for helping the poor, with themselves at the top, of course. They paid lip service to rule by the proletariat, but even their name for this rule, the "dictatorship of the proletariat," shows that they didn't think much of democracy. Anyway, this rule by the

proletariat never happened, and instead there was rule by the elites. Even now, while the left has mostly made its peace with democracy, it prefers to keep control of the media and our schools, which basically means that rich leftists have an awful lot of control over election results and how poor voters will vote.

6. There is also the callous indifference shown by leftists towards freedoms that poor Americans cherish, such as freedom of speech and religion. When you're rich, these don't matter as much because having lots of money offers a lot of compensation, but when you're poor, they may be one of the few things in life that mean something to you.

7. Another reason for believing that rich people run the left is the constant emphasis on the need for big government to help the poor and to generally promote a progressive agenda. In the most extreme cases, this means central planning of the economy, but who is in fact doing that planning? It is rich leftists. (As I have already mentioned, it is not as though the central planners were chosen by lot from all citizens as part of a rotation system.) But even in economies that don't have central planning, the push for bigger government is constant and unchangeable from the left. Why? Wanting big government is more than a little strange, given what governments have done throughout history. It is not just the libertarians who want government to be reduced; that ugly stepsister of the left, the anarchist movement, wants it as well. (In fact, they go further in that they want government eliminated completely.) Anarchists are always pointing out the horrors of every government, but the mainstream of the left never listens to them. Nor are leftists undaunted by the fact that big government sometimes goes against their wishes, as when it doles out welfare to corporations or saves banks that deserve to fail and refrains from putting the banks' officers in jail. So why the emphasis on big government? Is there something for the poor it can do that local governments or even private charities can't do? No. Its real purpose is that it offers control and good jobs to rich leftists. As I have already pointed out, the left is reluctant to add

class background to affirmative action, because it means that the good government jobs, the ones that now require an elite education and lots of connections, will no longer be their preserve.

8. Yet another indication is the way the left deals with taxes. There is constant talk of how the rich must be taxed at a higher rate, while there is seldom talk of how the lower class and the lower middle class ought to be taxed at a lower rate. In addition, some of the money from taxes goes to rich people in one form or another, or at any rate, not to the poor. Big government grants in academia seldom go to poor people. When they go for medical research, that isn't necessarily a bad thing, but when they go to the humanities, it is doubtful if the poor get any benefits whatsoever. There are also tax-funded entities like National Public Radio (NPR) that are seldom used by the poor, but which they must pay for anyway. There is even talk now among leftists, since newspapers have fallen on such hard times, that *The New York Times* ought to be subsidized by the government, a proposal that once again helps the rich more than the poor, who never read it.

The New York Times, by the way, is a good example of an institution that is part of what I am calling Rich People's Leftism. I say this because to the casual reader, it *seems* to be in favor of helping the poor. It *seems* to be against helping the rich. It isn't until you realize that this is a paper not for the poor but for wealthy leftists (as is shown by the advertisements) that you realize that that first impression is wrong. They are all in favor of policies that wealthy leftists think will help the poor, and not for any policies that would encroach on the power of wealthy leftists. They do not seem to be in favor of adding class background to affirmative action, they seldom talk about the adjunct situation in academia, they prefer helping the environment to helping the poor, etc.

9. Another sign that leftism is run by the rich is that when leftists have had more control over countries, poor people in those countries seldom had opportunities to go to college. As I argued in

the last chapter, fifty years ago America did a better job of allowing the poor to go to college than did the more leftist countries of Europe, and America still does a better job than countries like Sweden and Germany.

10. Then there are leftist policies like rent control that are supposedly designed to help the poor, though in fact it is wealthier people who are helped. Everyone knows that the people most hurt by this system are poorer young people who move to big cities in order to get a start on a new career and who have no access to apartments that are under rent control and so pay sky-high prices, yet the system is still kept in place and defended.

With respect to regulations in general, the poor are never given any realistic information about how things will change once a regulation is put into place. They are told their lives will be made better, but they are seldom told how their lives will be made worse. The example I gave in Chapter 6 was of regulations demanding that electrical wiring be up to code so that the houses of the poor don't burn down, but which when implemented cause the cost of housing to rise. A contemporary example is that of demanding that banks not charge hefty fees on overdrafts, with the result that some banks began to charge fees for every check.

11. There is a constant push by leftists for foreign aid to the Third World, while there is little push to get the rich people in those countries to share their wealth with their own fellow citizens. Shouldn't that idea be the starting point for leftists?

12. Another clue is the massive amount of guilt ladled out by leftists to everyone for crimes that we personally didn't commit but that were committed in the past, such as slavery or imperialism. Who in fact committed these crimes? They were mostly committed by the rich. Yet instead of blaming those whose ancestors committed these crimes, all of society is blamed.

But many of us come from poorer backgrounds, and our ancestors had nothing to do with these crimes, so why should we share in the guilt?

The response is that we have nevertheless benefitted from their actions. To begin with, the amount one has benefitted from such actions might be extremely tiny, in which case the guilt isn't warranted. This guilt might be a respectable response if all the *disadvantages* one has experienced were also mentioned, but they almost never are these days. If you are a lower-class or lower-middle-class white male, your class background and what you suffered because of that background are never mentioned, while all the advantages you have from being white and male are brought up constantly.

Moreover, in places like Britain, people from the former colonies have been invited in to make up for Britain's past imperialism, but of course these people do not live among the rich; they live among the poor, whose costs for housing go up as the demand goes up and who suffer from whatever criminal tendencies the newcomers have.

Finally, one would think from leftist rhetoric that slavery was something done only by Americans against African blacks and that imperialism was done only by Westerners against the rest of the world. The facts are quite different. Many cultures used slaves. Even white Americans were taken into slavery on the Barbary Coast, which led to America's first military action overseas in 1805, and many black Africans were enslaved by Muslims and not Westerners. Moreover, slavery is still practiced today. An article in the *Economist* a few years ago discussed slavery in North Africa, specifically mentioning Niger (where it is estimated that 43,000 are enslaved), Mauritania, Mali, Chad, and Sudan.[6] Instead of complaining about slavery that used to exist in the West, why don't leftists do something to eliminate the slavery that exists now *outside* of the West? In addition, many different cultures have practiced imperialism; it is not just the West that did so. Despite these facts, which can be dug out of most history books, the left prefers to talk as though only America had slaves and only Westerners were imperialists.

While no one who has been enslaved would defend that institution, imperialism is a different matter. Every now and then I have run across voices from the Third World who are not bitter about Western imperialism or who even want it to return.[7] Are the voices we are hearing from the Third World truly representative? Are they not mostly those of rich people whose ancestors suffered more from imperialism than the poor people of the Third World? That is, these countries were hierarchical, and when imperialists came along, those at the top suffered loss of power and prestige, while those at the bottom suffered merely by having a different group at the top. They may have even preferred the newcomers.

Even if we dismiss these last musings, the vast majority of poor people in the West had ancestors who had nothing to do with imperialism and so should not be made to feel any guilt over it.

13. Still another indication that the rich run things is the way that rich leftists want leftist principles applied in certain areas, but not in the areas they themselves like. They complain that rich conservatives "have made enough money," but they don't make this same complaint about themselves. And while leftists often point to what they call the "obscene" profits of, say, the oil industry, they never point to the "obscenely" high endowments of elite universities, even though almost none of that money goes to help the poor.

When we have a presidential election in the U.S., some leftists are sure to point out that since America is so powerful, people outside of America deserve a voice in who gets to be our president. Yet these same people would balk at that principle being applied to institutions they favor. *The New York Times* is a powerful newspaper; does that mean that less powerful newspapers—or better yet their readers— should have a say in how it is run? Harvard is a powerful educational institution; does that mean that people at less powerful institutions should have a say in how it is run? The answer to both of these questions is, of course, no.

Another example is that leftists in America are constantly pushing us away from the use of fossil fuels, and so we have laws encouraging us to use ethanol from corn. But the poor in the Third World are affected by that decision (since it means higher food prices for them); would the left like it if those poor people had the right to overturn that decision? I suspect they would not like it.

Academia is a preserve of rich leftists who, despite their idealistic dreams about egalitarianism, don't want academia to change, even though it is viciously hierarchical. As I observed in Chapter 8, I began asking academics who were socialists if they were willing to extend their socialist principles to academia, and the answer was no (the reason being, of course, that rich leftists control academia these days and genuine socialism would ruin that system of privilege). In addition, a certain question never seems to get asked by egalitarians: What role would elite schools play in an egalitarian society? The obvious answer is, no role at all. Since rich leftists don't like that answer, they steer all talk like that back to what they want, which is egalitarian principles applied to corporate America. That is the proper use of egalitarian principles, according to them.

14. This brings me to what for me was the big clue that the rich were running the left: my experiences in academia. I saw how the poor were treated by those leftists who were at the top in academia, and it was not pretty. Those of us from modest backgrounds often got stomped on. The left didn't care. If you are a woman or a black in academia today, you will be respected or at least supported by the left. But if you are poor, you will be neither respected nor supported by the left (unless you went to an elite school). Academia, because it is so dominated by the wealthy, is a segment of society in which rich leftists can let their hair down; within academia they can show their true colors. Do they want socialism? No. Do they want the abolition of private property? No. Do they want redistributions? No. Do they

want cooperation rather than competition? No. Do they want the end of hierarchies? No. Do they want to help the poor? No. What do they want? Wealthy elites at the top.

I won't repeat what I said about this topic in Chapter 8, but let me add one point. Every elite school (with the exception of perhaps Berkeley) is a school for the rich, yet no one on the left seems bothered by this. No one wants to turn things upside down and make schools for the poor into elite schools. The conservative philosopher Keith Burgess-Jackson once remarked that one would expect liberal and leftist academics to be concerned about the fate of those who came out of places like Appalachian State, but that turned out not to be the case.[8] Progressive academics are obsessed with rankings and with congratulating those who come from the best schools (which are mostly schools for the rich), while looking down on those who come from lower-ranked schools.

I went into academia as a supporter of socialism who hated rich conservatives because I thought they weren't paying their fair share of taxes, and came out a supporter of capitalism who hates rich liberals and leftists because of their hypocrisy and because they hog all the best jobs.

Keeping the Poor Poor

Not only is the left run by rich people, but they also want to keep the poor poor; they want them to know their place. The best evidence for this is the way that people like me were treated in academia, but let me note some other examples.

Under communism the poor were helped only to the extent that they were no longer exploited, but because their lives were made miserable in other ways, there was no real improvement. They were seldom allowed to rise to positions of power, and they lived in cramped living quarters with few provisions.

Another example is the way wealthy leftists encourage the acceptance of lifestyles that they themselves would never adopt for themselves. For example, wealthy leftists champion the poor woman who has a child out of wedlock, while conservatives find the situation horrible. But those rich leftists who champion such a lifestyle would never adopt it for their own. No, such women lead careful lives, and if they do have a child out of wedlock, it is because they have become well established in their careers and so can handle the shock. Or else they give it up for adoption, or more likely, get an abortion long before it becomes a problem.

Still another example relates to the inclusion of class background as part of affirmative action. People who spend lots of money to send their children to the best schools do not want them to have to compete on level terms with people who went to ordinary schools. This is why the hierarchy persists in academia, despite academia's being filled with leftists. Academics at the top tend to come from wealthier backgrounds, and allowing those from poorer backgrounds to participate as equals would be unthinkable. Sure, they want to help the poor, but they also want the poor to know their place, at the bottom.

Nevertheless, here in America, the system is more egalitarian than in Europe. As the *Economist* noted, in America one can start out in a community college and end up with a Ph.D., but one cannot do that in many European countries.[9] This is true despite Europe's allegedly more egalitarian arrangements.

What do leftists do when it is pointed out to them what a huge and unequal impact that schools for the rich have on power and influence in America? If they are inclined to do anything about it, they push for getting more poor people into those schools. Yet, to paraphrase what Jane Austen says on the first page of *Mansfield Park* about pretty girls and the rich men they want to marry, there just aren't enough slots in those schools for all the deserving and smart poor people. Why not instead de-emphasize the importance of those schools? Anyone who is an egalitarian should be concerned about the existence of elite schools for the wealthy and their enormous power in politics and the media. Instead, we are constantly hearing from leftists about the nefarious influence of "corporate interests."

Another idea that rich liberals and leftists love is tracking. In Europe this is a big deal, while here in America it fortunately isn't so important. Tracking means that those who are deemed not very smart in high school are tracked away from college. This may seem sensible and wise, but I knew several people from my high school who didn't seem especially smart back then who nevertheless went on to college and got degrees; one such person went on to get a Ph.D. The basic implication of tracking is clear: people who come from poor backgrounds don't belong in college. To make matters even worse for the poor, these same leftists want college to be "free," which means that poor people would have to pay for schooling (via their taxes) that they would never be able to take advantage of.

Finally, it has often been noted that welfare is typically structured to keep people on it rather than to help them get off of it. The welfare recipient finds that he or she ought not to get a job because then the welfare benefits will be cut off, so it is better to stay unemployed. And so the poor remain poor. This serves the purpose of the rich leftists because they can then point to such facts as showing how horrible America is and how the rest of us should simply let them have total control.

In conclusion, leftism is run by wealthy leftists and not by poor leftists. Those wealthy leftists may want to help the poor, but they also prefer that the poor stay poor; they think the poor should stay in their place. Let us consider their motives. Do wealthy leftists really want to help the poor? Maybe some do, but others seem to have different motives for turning to the left: they didn't like their conservative relatives who made all the family's money (which seems to be true of many wealthy humanities professors), they were at odds with those in power (which seems to have been true of Lenin), they came to the left almost by accident (which seems to have been true of Castro), or they realized they could keep a lot of money and control or get good jobs by turning to the left (which seems to have been true of any number of African leaders).

Whatever the case may be, the left is at best a movement for the poor, but not by or of the poor. And since leftism is not really a movement of the poor but a movement of the rich, that means that poor people, when they consider whether to support the left or the right, should realize that what this really means is whether they want to support rich people of the left or rich people of the right. My argument for the rest of this book is that rich people of the right offer, on balance, a better deal for the poor than rich people of the left.

CHAPTER 14
AGAINST REDISTRIBUTIONS

The preferred leftist method of helping the poor is not via private charities, but via a government redistribution. I want to argue against such a method.

1. A redistribution won't work because it requires raising taxes on the rich, and the rich have many resources for fighting a raise in taxes. The tax system is very obliging to them, and even if taxes are raised, they can squirrel away money in various tax shelters to avoid the higher taxes. If they run a business, they might be able to charge higher prices, thus passing along the higher taxes to their customers. If worst comes to worst, they can simply make less money than before; if local taxes are raised, they can move to a different part of the country (as have many rich residents of Detroit), or if national taxes are raised, they can renounce their citizenship and move to a different country. The result is that those supporting a redistribution who were expecting higher tax revenues must now raise taxes on the not-so-rich, but while the not-so-rich don't have the resources of the rich, they can still deflect some of the tax increase so that government officials have to raise taxes on the middle class, then on the lower middle class, and finally on those who are moderately poor. Those people, unfortunately, cannot really deflect a tax increase onto the extremely poor, so they are stuck with higher taxes, and even though they are moderately poor, they get no benefits in return. Accordingly, what should have been to the poor's advantage ends up hurting the wealthier among the poor, while doing much less than expected for the poorest of the poor. It does much less than expected for them since the expected increase in revenue never really materializes. The money from the very rich isn't easy to collect.

2. Taking money from the rich is counterproductive in the sense that their money is better used for creating jobs. Creating jobs will be the focus of Chapter 16, so I defer this discussion until then, but let me note that generally a redistribution to the poor is nothing but a stopgap, a sort of emergency measure that doesn't really help them as much as an actual job would.

3. As mentioned in the last chapter, rich leftists who claim to want higher taxes so as to support redistributions don't really want them. It's all theater. They could give voluntarily, either to the government or directly to the poor, but they don't do so.

4. The reluctance of rich leftists to give voluntarily means that rich conservatives believe they shouldn't have to give involuntarily. They will do what they can to resist any rise in their taxes. The same is true for corporations.

5. A call to raise taxes is often not the solution to the problem. For example, the recent Occupy Wall Street movement was made up of unemployed people who had a lot of debt from college loans. They demanded that the 1% (that is, those in the upper 1% economically) have their taxes raised. Yet it was perfectly obvious what their own problem was: *they didn't have jobs.* If they had had jobs, they wouldn't have been protesting because they would have been able to make ends meet, even with their high amounts of debt. A redistribution probably wouldn't have helped them much, assuming any money had actually come their way.

6. A related point is that when the economy is humming and there are jobs aplenty, most people don't think about taxing the rich because everyone has many opportunities to advance. Since they believe they themselves might someday be rich, why would they want to tax the rich?

7. The people who *do* think about taxing the rich, even when the economy is humming, are leftists. This suggests that leftist rhetoric must be taken with a grain of salt. In recent years we've been told that inequality has been increasing compared with what it was forty

years ago. But I was alive forty years ago, and leftists were talking about taxing the rich back then, too. (Strictly speaking, what they were talking about back then was that the rich used loopholes and so were able to evade taxes too easily.)

8. As conservatives endlessly point out, redistributions have bad effects on society. People whose money has been taken via higher taxes—taxes not intended for the basic workings of the government but simply to be given to the poor—feel their money has been stolen from them. Why work hard if you can't keep what you have earned? And since the government will have to go after those who are even moderately poor in order to have enough money for a redistribution, people near, but not at, the bottom may feel they are being turned into slaves. They and everyone above them will work less and strive less. Not only will people feel their money is being stolen, they will also feel their money wasn't even very helpful to those receiving it. They will feel that it was just thrown down a rat hole, the reason being that nothing much changes with redistributions.

At the other end, people who get money from a redistribution come to think that society owes them a living. They come to have an entitlement mentality, and even though they are being given money, they will not be grateful for it and will hate their situation. They will hate it because they can see that other people have a level of wealth they will never have, and they will hate it because there is no real niche for them in society. They are basically deadwood, and generally people don't like being deadwood. These people won't strive, either, because the system is set up so that their benefits will be cut off before they are in a position to stand on their own two feet. Society goes dead in the water. That is what happened in the communist countries, which could never manage to produce very much and required help from the capitalist countries. It is what is now happening in Venezuela, where there are all kinds of shortages of basic items like toilet paper.

9. Some of the money from a redistribution will get siphoned off and go straight to rich leftists. This will happen because once the government gets its hands on some money, there is no guarantee where it will go (especially when the people at the top who are in control are generally not poor). It might go to the poor, but there is simply nothing to stop some of it from going to rich leftists. Rich leftists naturally try to hide this by getting very angry about government money that goes to rich conservatives (generally corporations), but the fact is that they themselves are often the recipients of government money. Some of the money from a redistribution will go to them because a redistribution requires a big bureaucracy, and undoubtedly many rich liberals and leftists will be part of that bureaucracy, particularly in those positions at or near the top.

Some of it will go to them in other ways. For example, the money will be given out as grants to scholars and artists (and the recipients are typically rich since the process of finding those who are worthy of such grants favors the wealthy; it's not as though grant money is distributed equally or in some random fashion). Some of it will go to them even as intangibles, such as radio or television stations that are subsidized by the government and that appeal to them, but not to poorer people. It is inevitable that a redistribution run by the government will help the rich, simply because they have so much clout. It doesn't matter if the rich people involved are on the left or not; money will still come to them from the government.

10. Not all of the poor want a redistribution. To the extent that poor people want a redistribution, it is because leftists bring up redistributions constantly and so that is what the poor hear. Yet my ancestors in northern Europe did not hear this rhetoric and what they wanted was something different. They wanted good opportunities, which they heard were available in America. In the absence of leftist rhetoric, the demand by the poor for a redistribution lessens.

11. As Margaret Thatcher observed, the problem with socialism is that sooner or later one runs out of other people's money. Once

a redistribution scheme gets going, it's hard to stop more of the same, because a redistribution is never enough for the poor. They are always going to want more, and so more resources are poured into extracting more money from the rich, but as already noted, society begins to shut down as resentments build. Besides, it's not just the rich having to cough up money, but those lower down. In addition, redistributions attract more poor people from other regions, which means there is even less money to go around for those receiving it, which compounds the problems enormously.

The current situation in the European Union illustrates how society can run out of other people's money, for not only is a heavy welfare system in place, but immigrants are pouring in from Africa and Asia. While the prescription is for "austerity," meaning cutting down on government spending, what is actually being tried is a different sort of austerity, namely raising taxes on the rich, and of course it isn't working. The Scandinavian countries faced this situation back in the 1990s, and despite a strong inclination for socialism, they cut back on government spending and have avoided the problems currently confronting the rest of Europe. As a Danish historian, Gunnar Viby Mogensen, put it, "The welfare state we have is excellent in most ways. We only have this little problem. We can't afford it."[1]

12. All of this has a bad effect in terms of the advance of technology (for many inventions are dreamed up with the idea that the inventor will become rich, but if that's not possible, why bother?). Many leftists these days seem to spurn technological advances because of possible environmental problems, but these advances have helped the poor enormously. A lot of back-breaking work is now done by machines, plus medical advances have given people greater life expectancy and a lesser amount of suffering from illnesses as well. All of this will slowly come to a halt as redistributions work their poison on society.

13. In addition, when redistributions are rampant, they encourage people to spend a lot of time in lobbying the government since the government has so much money to dole out. Obviously, lobbying

the government is much less useful to society than inventing new products.

14. Redistributions are a way to keep the poor poor. They do nothing to raise them to the level of the middle class since that would require far more money than is available, so the poor generally remain poor (or even if they are raised a little bit there is a price paid in terms of shortages or lines or crime or something else gone awry). Keeping the poor poor seems to be what rich leftists want.

15. Perhaps the biggest redistribution in America isn't even directed at the poor, but at the elderly. I'm referring to the social security system, which takes money from the young and gives it to the elderly. As most acknowledge, we have a big problem looming since there are so few young people compared with older people of my generation who will be expected to support us. Since young people are relatively poor, while the elderly often have some money stashed away, this would seem to be the exact opposite of what leftists would want, yet it is the sort of thing we ought to expect once we allow for redistributions and making the government big. Once we make the government big, then the whole system gets distorted by those who can command the best lobbyists, and the results won't be pretty because the redistributions we end up with are unlikely to benefit the poor as much as they will benefit the middle class or even the rich.

16. Those governmental workers who strongly support redistributions act immorally when the voters make it clear that they want cutbacks in redistributions. Suddenly, these workers tell the voters that cuts will have to be made, not in the fluff jobs, but in basic governmental jobs such as those in the police or fire departments. It is very unlikely that these same governmental workers would react this way if they had to make cuts in their own household budgets because that is not how responsible households react when they have to make a cut. They do not make a drastic cut in their food budget so they can keep their art budget intact. They cut the luxuries first. The same goes

for companies. Yet it always seems as though governments make cuts in something basic and essential that the voters need, and never in those things that the voters don't need and so don't care about, such as people hired to be leadership coaches or consultants in choosing the art that will go on display in the lobbies of government buildings.

A recent episode, when the federal government was shut down for two weeks in October of 2013, was surreal in its immorality since the government decided that national parks and other public land owned by the federal government were now closed and that no one could be on that land. This required federal workers to keep off everyone, which of course used money for a totally unnecessary purpose, when the moral way to proceed was simply to let people onto the land but offer them no services. The stories of aging veterans unable to visit the Washington Monument, of foreign tourists prevented from seeing Old Faithful erupt, and of people evicted from their homes because their homes happened to sit on government land are about as close to fascism as I have ever seen in America, and I hope this never gets repeated.

17. What kind of government do we have if it takes money from some to give to others? I know that it sounds great if it means taking from the rich and giving to the poor, like the folk hero Robin Hood. Nevertheless, it means that the government is a thief, and that is not a good thing. Leftists who complain about capital punishment are basically complaining that the government murders people, but a similar complaint could be made about taking money from the rich and giving it to the poor: it means the government is stealing from people. If it is bad to have a government that murders people, it is also bad to have one that steals.

Incidentally, Robin Hood (as I heard about him when I was a child) was someone who was helping the poor deal with an increase in taxes; he was stealing from the rich government and giving the poor their money back. He wasn't stealing from rich individuals.

18. My preferred method of helping the poor is via private charity. Let's say that that isn't working very well because the rich are too stingy. But if the rich don't like giving voluntarily, they will not like giving involuntarily either, so those promoting redistributions should not count on getting much from them. On the other hand, if the rich are willing to give voluntarily, then there is less need for a government redistribution. Accordingly, redistributions are either ineffective or unnecessary.

19. Those who favor redistributions have no real answer for what to do when recipients simply squander what they received on something worthless, such as illegal drugs. When they come back begging for more money, what should we do? Most would say they should not receive another cent, but not leftists, who think they should be given money in perpetuity. Thatcher's slogan is true, because we definitely will run out of money if we keep giving away money to people who don't use it wisely. Needless to say, leftists in their personal lives would never keep giving. If a poor person kept demanding more money from them after having squandered what they had received in foolish ways, sooner or later even the most generous leftist would say no.

For all these reasons, redistributions are a bad idea. Pushing for them is nothing but "theater" from wealthy rich leftists who use it as cover to show that they are helping the poor, when instead they could give directly to the poor via a charity or an actual handout to a poor person. Saying they want higher taxes means nothing; it seems that what they really want is higher taxes on *other* rich people, but not on themselves. But those others (namely, the conservatives) look at rich leftists' lack of commitment, and ask, "Why should we pay if you aren't going to do the same?" They have a point.

One leftist who inadvertently pointed out the "theater" nature of leftists' calls for redistributions via higher taxes was G.A. Cohen in his book *If You're an Egalitarian, How Come You're So Rich?* This book has a great title, and he does identify the problem. For example, he tells of a wealthy Labour politician in Britain who was on a talk show during a time when the Labour party needed money. "Why not donate some of your own money?" one caller suggested. Both the politician and the moderator dismissed this suggestion as absurd and thought the caller impertinent.[2] But while Cohen thought the caller had a legitimate question, he ultimately is too trusting of rich leftists and allows certain excuses of theirs to pass. Here are the excuses he heard:

1. "Giving up my wealth won't bring the revolution any closer. It has its own mechanisms that are unaffected by my actions."[3] But there may never be a revolution. Besides, when one person starts doing something, it often inspires other people to do the same.

2. "Poor people know how to live in poverty with dignity, whereas we wouldn't know how."[4] I don't think that poor people know how to live in poverty with dignity any more than anyone else does. I lived in a poor neighborhood when I was a grad student and never saw any dignity in it.

3. Rich leftists prefer an egalitarian society, but that has no bearing on how they should behave in a non-egalitarian society.[5] Yet if someone prefers something, then they generally work to make it a reality. I prefer a soccer-loving society and have done what I can to turn America into that kind of society (not that I have much power to make changes). Alternatively, I could have left for a society that already is soccer-loving, but what seems strange to me is preferring a soccer-loving society and doing nothing either to make it happen here or else to move to such a society. The preference cannot be very strong if that is the case.

4. It is the state's job, and no one else's, to guarantee equality.[6] This again is a very low-level dedication to egalitarianism. Why would anyone hold such a crazy belief? It is basically the excuse of what I call Rich People's Leftism.

5. "A rich person's charity does nothing to eliminate unequal power."[7] Yes, it does, especially if enough rich people give. Or if it doesn't, then the government's charity won't work, either. Let me

note this is a particularly nefarious suggestion, given that leftists seldom concern themselves with equalizing power, but instead put all their efforts into equalizing wealth.

6. "Each person has a right to a private space into which social duty does not intrude."[8] Again, this represents a very low-level dedication to egalitarianism.

7. It's acceptable to demand automatic taxation, but unreasonable to expect charity.[9] As I've already argued, it is strange to think that someone dedicated to an egalitarian society would think this position is at all helpful. It doesn't inspire others, while saying "I want to give, but only if the strong arm of the law forces me to" is not what those who are desperate want to hear. They need help now, not when the government gets around to giving them some money. Is this any different from the position held by Ebenezer Scrooge in Charles Dickens' *A Christmas Carol*? Scrooge rejects giving to charity since he points out that he has already helped the poor via taxes (which built the workhouses for the poor).

8. Giving severely hurts the self-interest of a wealthy person when others like them won't give. It will hurt their children.[10] But what about the children of the poor, who will be hurt even more if the rich don't give? In addition, if one wealthy leftist makes a point of giving, the others might be shamed into it, too.

9. Giving would hurt the ability of the rich to influence society towards a more egalitarian one.[11] This is the last of the excuses, and it is basically the one excuse that Cohen accepts, but I think he is wrong to accept it. My cynical perspective is that the rich leftist wants to keep all the privileges for himself or herself that the rich have always had: going to the best schools, getting to do lots of traveling, getting the best jobs, and even on occasion getting government grants. When one adds up all they get from remaining rich and subtract what they're doing to make things better, it usually looks like they and not the poor are the winners. As I've said elsewhere, would these people be willing to have their children, who have gone to the best schools,

compete on equal terms with those who didn't go to the best schools? Almost certainly not. Their dedication to a society of equality simply isn't that strong, as far as I can see.

Incidentally, why did Cohen accept this as a legitimate excuse? He himself had come from a working-class background, but had managed to become a professor at Oxford. Unfortunately, this was enough to skew his view. Being successful in academia blinded him to the fact that not many people from his background get to reach such a lofty position. The fact that many others may have been thwarted from attaining such a position helps to show that the idea of keeping one's wealth to make society more egalitarian just isn't valid; it's nothing other than the rich keeping their wealth and influence.

One excuse not mentioned by Cohen is that leftists believe that the money of rich liberals and leftists was honestly obtained, while that of rich conservatives wasn't. Accordingly, rich conservatives should be willing to share what they have "stolen," while rich leftists ought to be allowed to keep their money. But this excuse is pathetic. To begin with, some on the left think that "others are poor because you are rich," and if that is the case, then no one who is rich is off the hook. As for the view that the money of rich leftists was honestly obtained, while that of rich conservatives was not, some rich leftists inherited their money from wealthy relatives who were conservative, so they would have no excuse for not giving up their money.

As for rich conservatives, it is certainly true that there are bankers today who have done illegal things, but who instead of going to jail were bailed out by the government. I agree that such people ought to give up their money. But when leftists complain about them and how they evaded jail, I point out there are plenty of libertarians who complain about them, too (such as Karl Denninger). I then add that these "banksters" could have been prosecuted in the first two years of the Obama administration when the presidency and both branches of Congress were controlled by the Democrats, yet they weren't. Leftists have no real response to this point.

But most rich conservatives made their money honestly. By that I mean that they offered a product that others wanted, that they produced it using labor that was not slave labor, and that those who bought it were not forced to buy it. Leftists will say that the profits from the company could have been distributed more equitably; I respond that money in academia could be distributed more equitably, too. For example, there is no justification for the comparatively large salaries (plus benefits) of tenured professors in comparison with the much smaller pay (without benefits) that adjuncts get, even though the difference in qualifications and experience can be negligible; nor is there any justification for the obscenely high endowments of elite schools. All of this is under the control of leftists, who refuse to make changes; so why should anyone else make changes?

Leftists may also say that while the labor was not slave labor in the formal sense, it was in effect slave labor since those working in that corporation had few other choices. The same can be said for adjuncts in academia today, yet somehow the wealth of tenured professors is thought by leftists to be legitimately obtained.

The lack of good choices is why job creation is so important for the poor, because it will give the poor more choices. But when leftists say that labor is in effect slave labor because the workers have so few other choices, it should be noted that leftists themselves could help create more choices for them. For example, for those leftists who think that Walmart doesn't treat its workers well, they could form their own company—similar to Walmart in all other ways (including offering low prices for the poor)—that does treat its workers well. However, starting new enterprises that would help the poor is not basically what the left is interested in. Or rather, the way that Rich People's Leftism operates is to attack existing enterprises while doing very little to begin better ones. A leftism run by the poor would be more interested in starting new enterprises so as to offer workers more choices.

Nor should anyone think that the left is too poor to start such an enterprise and go up against a powerful entity like Walmart. There are plenty of wealthy leftists around whose collective wealth is sufficient for this. As for Walmart's being a powerful entity, it is powerful only so long as it attracts customers, and a new enterprise that had prices just as good would easily flourish. After all, Walmart wasn't always powerful; it became powerful (as the right insists) by giving poor people what they wanted: low prices. No, any leftist version of Walmart would find that it couldn't match Walmart in terms of lower prices, and that would be because the higher wages of the workers would have to be offset by lower salaries of those higher up the ladder, and that wouldn't attract anyone. People from poorer backgrounds who had the choice of a management position at Walmart or at this leftist version of Walmart would choose Walmart because they would prefer to have the higher salaries. And wealthy leftists are not going to put up with the lower salaries from this leftist version, no matter how dedicated they say they are. (I could be wrong about this, but I don't see it happening, not after what I saw of the stinginess of leftist academics, and the fact that a leftist version of Walmart hasn't come into existence is a good reason to believe I am right.) Accordingly, there just isn't any way to make a leftist version of Walmart that would be better than the original.

Let me put it more bluntly: if leftists won't create a better Walmart, it shows they aren't really concerned about the plight of workers at Walmart; and if they can't create one, then why complain about Walmart?

To sum up, rich conservatives have usually obtained their money honestly.

Let me now consider socialized medicine as another example of a redistribution. Leftists are always pushing it as something "progressive" and "advanced" in comparison with a free market solution, the reason being that socialized medicine is better for the poor. Is it better for the poor? Isn't it really just more "theater" by wealthy leftists? In terms of what we have generally seen from those systems when they have been imposed, it is a familiar story. While the poor benefit because they don't have to pay, they lose out in terms of long waits for care (and probably in other ways as well). The middle class is the big loser because they, too, suffer from long waits. The big winners are, as usual, rich leftists because their health care remains the same (since they will be using private doctors) and because they get to feel good about themselves for imposing a "moral" system on the rest of society.

How is this system better for the poor compared with a free market system in which rich people are strongly encouraged to donate to local charities to help poor people pay medical bills? I cannot see that it is any better. Leftists will complain there is no guarantee that rich people will donate, and I agree. So long as rich leftists think they are excused from having to donate because they are leftists, rich conservatives will avoid donating, too. This is why rich leftists need to lead the way in donating, and once they do, conservatives are likely to join them. For those who are skeptical, let me remind them that conservatives do donate a lot already in comparison with leftists; it may not be to the charities leftists prefer, but they do donate.

A governmental system will not guarantee that costs will be met, either. Leftists always assume that the government can get more money from the rich, and they are almost always disappointed. Accordingly, taxes have to be raised—even on poor people—in order to make ends meet, shortfalls will exist in other areas because of society's medical bills, jobs won't be created because money for creating them is going to the wrong places, and so on. If there is a problem with rich people not giving enough voluntarily to help pay for the poor's medical bills, it won't be solved by getting the government involved.

A few more thoughts:

1. Any system that is halfway to socialism won't work very well, which means that leftists will put pressure on everyone to move toward total government involvement. That is what we are experiencing in the United States. The system that I grew up under was one that was a small step along the way to socialism because of government involvement in the process. During World War II, the government froze wages, so companies began adding benefits, including medical care, to help out their employees in lieu of a wage increase. Eventually, this system spread throughout most of society, making it very hard for those not employed by large corporations to get medical care or to get it cheaply. Obviously, the system was broken. The solution? More government involvement. So far nothing I have heard suggests that the new system will work any better or be any cheaper.

2. Once the government has total control, innovations will be few and far between since everything will be under government control. Using a new device or procedure will require that central planners give approval, and that will take forever.

3. We would all be better off if medical care was not given as part of a benefit of a job. It seems wonderful, if you have a job, but it also distorts the market. Poor people rarely get jobs with great medical benefits, self-employed people are cut out of the system, employers will be more reluctant to hire a person because they need to ensure that the person is worthy of not only the stated pay but also the extra benefits, some employees will stay in jobs they hate simply because the medical insurance is better than at other jobs, and so on.

4. Costs inevitably go up because of socialized medicine. The whole business needs an army of bureaucrats to run it, which adds to the costs of any actual care given. People will be inclined to take advantage of the situation because "it's free," so they will go to the doctor more often, thus guaranteeing not only that costs will go up, but also that there will be long waits. Moreover, in America, the land of frivolous lawsuits, little is being done to curtail medical

malpractice suits, so those suits can be expected to raise costs in the future, no matter how socialized the system gets.

5. Libertarians have pointed out that segments of medical care that are outside of government control, such as cosmetic surgery, have seen costs come down, exactly what proponents of the free market system expect will happen with our care generally once we get government out of the picture.

6. We have seen that once government gets involved, it demands that medical benefits include things that many of us regard as frivolous, such as help for sex addiction. In a free market system, most people would refuse to buy an insurance package that covered such items, and so insurance companies would offer cheaper packages that didn't have the frivolous items. But that apparently won't be true of our system, which means that costs for everyone will be higher than they need to be.

7. Socialized medicine works best when the population is expanding. That is, the people needing the most help with health care are the elderly, but when the population isn't expanding, the burden of taking care of those elderly people is put onto a smaller-than-normal cadre of young people. And who is pushing for a smaller population? The left, who thus undermine their own economic plans.

8. The Amish have managed to get themselves excluded from our new system because they have their own system in place. The community pays for medical bills on its own and has no need for government involvement, thus showing that a system of private charity can work. Likewise, in Japan a socialized system works because, as one economist has explained, social conformism encourages people to play by the rules, while in individualistic societies like England and America, people try to game the system; in Japan elderly parents live with their children, while in Britain "people were much more likely to leave elderly parents to the tender mercies of the National Health Service"; and finally in Japan firms are less likely to lay people off in a recession than they are in Britain and America.[12] The result is fewer costs for the system.

9. In a rich country like America, the percentage of people who are helped by socialized medicine is small, while the percentage whose healthcare becomes much more expensive is large. It is much better simply to encourage donations to help those at the bottom in need of assistance.

There is nothing about socialized medicine that indicates it is anything other than a scheme to make rich leftists feel good about themselves and to give them control over everyone else's healthcare while they opt out of the system. The basic truth is this: if rich people aren't willing to donate voluntarily to help pay the medical costs of the poor, it is very unlikely that a government system forcing them to do so will work very well, either.

Earlier I said that wealthy leftists don't really want redistributions, despite what they say. Probably the best reason to believe that about wealthy leftists comes from looking at academia. Tenured academics may bristle when they learn I regard them as rich; but when you're poor and unemployed anyone who has an income above average is rich, and nearly every tenured academic these days has an income above average. Let me repeat the simple solution to the adjunct problem that I mentioned in Chapter 8. That solution is to set up a voluntary fund, to which tenured professors could contribute, that would be redistributed to adjuncts. Let's say the expectation is that a tenured professor would give five percent of her income. This solution would also have the effect of making the job of professor somewhat less attractive (since the amount she was paid would be in reality five percent less than stated), so the supply side would be dealt with to some extent. In addition, by instituting such a program, leftist professors would be showing the world how wonderful they are and how wonderful redistributions are. It would be a showcase for redistributions in all their splendor and cause all the conservatives and libertarians no end of frustration.

So why hasn't this scheme been tried? The excuses given do not reflect well on the left.

One excuse, that academics are too busy dealing with their own narrow problems about Shakespeare or Emily Dickinson to notice what is going on, is absurd. Every leftist academic these days can give a long critique of America's foreign policy, and if they can do that, they must have the time to notice things beyond their own narrow professional concerns; accordingly, they could be noticing what is happening to adjuncts in academia.

A second excuse, that it would be thwarted by the conservatives, is not persuasive because the scheme I am suggesting is voluntary, and there are very few conservatives in academia these days anyway.

Another excuse, that it wouldn't do much, is basically what conservatives say about redistributions; conservatives are the ones saying that redistributions don't really do much. If leftists agree, then they have undercut their own reasoning promoting redistributions. A fourth excuse, that money to help adjuncts should come from some other source, just skirts the issue since the money is in fact *not* coming from any other source. We've had twenty plus years of money not coming from another source. Anyway, what other source would it be? From tuition? Tuition is already too high. From taxpayers? But why should they pay for a problem that is not their doing? From corporations or the military? The same answer: it's not their problem, so why should they give up their money for this? This problem is internal to academia, and it should be solved within academia and not by stealing money from outsiders. Moreover, there is plenty of money sloshing around in academia right now. It's just maldistributed. Anyone who doubts me should ponder the huge endowments of our most elite institutions. The adjunct problem could be solved (to a degree) by a redistribution; it's simply that those involved don't think along these lines when what is at stake is their own money.

Moreover, as I already pointed out in Chapter 8, if redistributions are wonderful, they could be done within the community of leftists, which includes some rich and some poor people. Since it would be a voluntary redistribution, conservative objections would not be obstructive, yet such a redistribution never happens. Why? Why aren't rich leftists giving their money to poor leftists? Isn't it the case that these rich leftists, who claim to want redistributions, in fact don't want them at all? Let's restrict the community just to those who are blogging. Some leftist bloggers make money at this activity while others don't. Why aren't those who are making money at it giving away some of their money to those who are not making money at it? There's just no real commitment among wealthy leftists to the idea of redistributions, in spite of how much they might claim to want them or to be genuine egalitarians.

Now let me consider the redistribution policies of John Rawls, perhaps the most famous redistributionist of our era. "Justice is the first virtue of social institutions," he writes near the beginning of his magnum opus, *A Theory of Justice*.[13] He then goes on to detail an elaborate scheme on how to generate principles of justice. This scheme imagines that what divides people on principles of justice are their particular situations, so that whites will choose principles favoring whites, blacks will choose principles favoring blacks, the rich will choose principles favoring the rich, the poor will choose principles favoring the poor, and so on. Accordingly, he suggests that we imagine that none of us knows what our particular situation is. This is called the Original Position, and the parties in the Original Position, although they know general facts about human life and human societies,[14] do not know particular facts about themselves. Given that people are behind this "veil of ignorance," and given that they are not likely to risk making a choice that could be to their disadvantage, what principles of justice would they choose? With respect to freedoms concerning, for example, religion and speech, Rawls believes they would choose the fullest freedom that is compatible with a similar freedom for others. But with respect to wealth, he believes they would allow for inequalities only if those inequalities are "to the greatest benefit of the least advantaged" and also that they are "attached to offices and positions open to all under conditions of fair equality of opportunity."[15]

Now whether any of this is plausible given his description of the Original Position, I leave to Chapter 16, but for now I want to ask simply, to what extent did Rawls, an academic, promote these principles for academia? As far as I know, *he did nothing along these lines.* Keep in mind that Rawls said explicitly that "justice is the first virtue of social institutions," so it is reasonable to ask, since he was a part of the social institution of academia, to what extent he worked to make it more just. His failure to do anything about the injustices within academia tells against his principles. Those injustices, as I have been explaining in previous chapters, are (1) the disparities in income between those who are tenured and those who are mere adjuncts, and (2) the vast advantage that those who are wealthy have over those who are poor when it comes to getting academic jobs, publications, and grants. Regarding the first injustice, the solution would be a redistribution of some sort, and regarding the second injustice, the solution would be simply including class background within affirmative action. Rawls wanted redistributions, and he wanted positions to be open to "fair equality of opportunity," so both sorts of injustice would seem to fall within the purview of Rawls' principles. Yet, to the best of my knowledge, Rawls never worked for reform in either of these areas of academia.

Naturally, if he were the only leftist academic who failed to apply his or her principles within academia, that would mean little, but what is significant is that almost none of them want to apply their principles in academia. Consider a parallel. If one or two fundamentalist preachers railing against "demon rum" are found to be secretly imbibing, that is a problem for them, their families, and congregations, but if *most* are secretly drinking, it becomes a problem for the message. If that were true, then most of us would stop thinking in terms of prohibition and total abstinence, and start thinking in terms of responsible drinking, harsh drunk driving laws, and so on. Likewise, when every academic who insists upon redistributionist or socialist principles for society fails to promote them within academia, it is high time that we stop thinking about their solutions and start looking for others.

I will say more about Rawls in Chapter 16, but for now let me conclude by noting that he, like so many other liberal and leftist thinkers, came from a wealthy background.

Let me now consider some general objections to my position against redistributions. Sometimes leftists try to shame people like me by pointing out how many redistributions we unwittingly take part in and would not want to part with, such as tax breaks on home mortgages. Since I come from the lower middle class, I doubt if I have participated in many redistributions, but I would gladly part with all my redistributions in exchange for some solid job creation. I remember the 1960s as a golden era of jobs, when workers had good jobs in manufacturing (that did not require a costly college degree), when corporations hired scientists to do basic research, and when it was easy to get jobs in academia. All that has vanished, and today young people worry not about whether they can get a good job that will be interesting but whether they will get a good job at all. If given a choice, then, I would give up whatever I have received from redistributions and take job creation instead. However, just to satisfy the curious, my wife and I took the tax break on our home mortgage during its first three years only. We were paying off the mortgage so fast that the tax break quickly became useless as a way to save money. Even when we did use it, we did not save much money.

Another objection by some leftists is that not only are redistributions moral, but also the economy goes haywire when inequality gets too out of line. People saying this wholly ignore the bad effects of the opposite, namely forced equality, under communism (such as the Cultural Revolution or the killing fields of Cambodia). It's a safe bet that the people saying this are themselves rich; would they really care to spend twenty years in an isolated rural region on a collective farm? I suspect that the economy goes haywire not so much because of increasing inequality, but because not enough jobs are being created. The same can be said about the results of those studies showing that inequality has bad effects on those at the bottom; again, if there is enough job creation so that those at the bottom can work their way out, those bad effects are unlikely to occur.

The most recent exponent of the view that society suffers when inequality gets too far out of line is Thomas Picketty in his book *Capital in the Twenty-First Century.* He claims that ever since World War II capital has been concentrating, but it was never clear to me why this was supposed to be bad. He discusses the economies of England and France in the nineteenth century, partly through the novels of Jane Austen and Honoré de Balzac. In Austen's novels, one couldn't live well without an income of at least £500 a year at a time when the average income was just £30 a year.[16] Only the very rich would have been able to afford carriages, for example, yet that isn't true today when even poor people here in America can own cars. Moreover, Picketty never argued in any detail that it was the concentration of wealth that was going to push us back to the conditions of two hundred years ago. On the contrary, the force in our society pushing us in that direction is *radical environmentalism.* It is the radical environmentalists who want to make having a car so expensive that only the very rich will be able to afford them. I am unpersuaded that a concentration of wealth today will be a horrible thing for the rest of us (even assuming it will happen).

In addition, Picketty like Rawls is in academia, and so we can ask to what extent he is working to reduce the inequality in academia. As far as I know, he is not working at all to reduce it.

Some will say that by going against redistributions, I am going against egalitarian principles. Anyone who has read my last two books will know how to answer this charge: the so-called egalitarians just aren't as committed to egalitarianism as they say they are. (I will say more about these books in Chapter 22.) The so-called egalitarians have shown that they really aren't that interested in equality, as seen by their resistance to adding class to gender and race as part of affirmative action, their preference for promoting environmentalism over egalitarianism, and their clinging to the power of elite schools for the rich. Anyway, I am abandoning redistributions not because I am abandoning egalitarian principles, but because I don't see them as working very well for the poor and because I don't see those demanding them as sincere in their demand. Any sincere egalitarians are perfectly free to promote one or more of the voluntary redistribution schemes I have already mentioned or to give away a lot of their money to the poor voluntarily, but they rarely do.

Moreover, consider the following reaction to Cohen's book on egalitarianism which appeared in a review by the philosopher Thomas Nagel:

> I could sign a standing banker's order giving away everything I earn above the national average, for example, and it wouldn't kill me.... I'm not about to do anything of the kind, but the equality-friendly justifications I can think of for not doing so all strike me as rationalizations.... One person to whom I presented Cohen's question replied, "I guess I'm not an egalitarian."[17]

Would that all "egalitarians" were honest enough to admit that they aren't really egalitarians. They aren't really interested in doing everything they could to help the poor, so the claim that *my* rejection of redistributions proves that I'm not egalitarian I regard as irrelevant. Nevertheless, in Chapter 20 I will explain how I would run a redistribution if it were absolutely necessary.

Let me conclude this chapter by challenging those leftists who believe in redistributions to do what Nagel cannot bring himself to do: give up any income or wealth they have that is in excess of what the average person has. Anything less than that is hypocrisy.

CHAPTER 15

LISTENING TO THE POOR AS THEY VOTE WITH THEIR FEET

Throughout the world, poor people (if they can) vote with their feet, and they almost always vote the same way: they head toward money. They may be indifferent about whether that money is a handout or a good job or something else (like the money found in a gold rush), but that is the direction toward which they move. They don't move in the direction of socialism or communism, unless there is money there as well. When my ancestors moved to America from northern Europe in the nineteenth century, they were all motivated to come here, as far as I can tell, by the endless opportunities America offered compared with the northern European countries from which they came. Today, tens of millions of people from Latin America have moved to America, while tens of millions of people from Africa and Asia have moved to Europe.

As Spanish-speaking people, Latinos could have migrated to Spanish-speaking countries like communist Cuba and, in recent years, socialist Venezuela, but they didn't. They came to America, where a foreign language (to them) is spoken and where capitalism reigns. The reason they have not gone to either Cuba or Venezuela is simply that there is no money there. The fact that the workers are supposedly treated better in those countries than in capitalistic countries like America didn't mean anything to them. What this shows is that alleged workers' paradises are not in fact what the workers want, unless there is money there; but typically in a workers' paradise there isn't much money.

Poor people from Africa and Asia do generally go to Europe, which is more socialistic than America and where they typically are given money outright rather than jobs. But again, the issue is money and not the socialism. Europe has money, and countries like Cuba and Venezuela don't. Moreover, many of those going to Europe have said they would rather come here. The main point is that the poor, when they can, will go toward the money, even if it is in a capitalistic country, and not to any workers' paradise that lacks money.

Leftists might protest by saying that all I am showing is that these poor people are exhibiting false consciousness. False consciousness, according to the left, is acting against one's own self-interest while thinking it is in one's interest. But how is going to a capitalist country to get a job a form of false consciousness? I have never heard anyone on the left berate our illegal immigrants for this sin; apparently, no one on the left has ever advised these immigrants to go to Cuba or Venezuela. That in itself should show the limitations of the concept of "false consciousness."

But why even invent such a concept? The concept was invented to show that poor people who didn't support communism or socialism were stupid, since obviously it was in their own self-interest to do so. Yet it isn't so obvious. The poor remain poor under communism, and they trade exploitation of their labor with exploitation of their time in the long lines that are typical of communist rule. Meanwhile, rich leftists stay rich. Why, then, is it in the poor's interest to prefer communism over capitalism, particularly a capitalist country with lots of good-paying jobs? Even if they should have preferred communism, it is not obvious that they should have done so; and now that communism is fading away, it seems obvious that they should *not* have done so. What is in a person's self-interest is not an easy concept to flesh out, and it is easy for people—yes, even leftists—to make mistakes about it.[1]

Leftists might also protest that the poor do other things besides vote with their feet. They will join the Communist party, for example, or vote socialist. However, not many join the Communist party these days, and in America it is unclear that many ever did (despite the claim by an old Communist who told me that at one time every worker in America was a Communist). Nor do many poor people in America vote socialist, even though they might do so in Europe. But what is striking is how many people in Latin America would rather come here than trust socialist or communist movements within their own country or other parts of Latin America. They prefer to rely on capitalism in a country where English rather than Spanish is spoken.

Now the question is, should all these poor people prefer America and other countries where they are offered jobs or countries such as those in Europe where they are simply given money? Even when lacking an educational background to make this decision, poor people often understand it is better to go to a country where they can get a job rather than one where they are simply given some money (which is why so many people in the Third World talk of going to America rather than Europe). In the former type of country, they bring value to those who hired them and so become integrated into society—it's wonderful to have a niche in society—and they can either get out of poverty themselves, or watch their children get out of poverty and get a good education. In countries where they are simply given a lump sum, they stay poor and their children stay poor, too. They do not become integrated into society, but remain isolated in immigrant enclaves. Moreover, they develop bad attitudes toward the society which is giving them money, while people in that society become resentful toward them, and the whole society moves in the direction of social breakdown or even civil war.

But the biggest problem is that as more and more immigrants move to such a society, the available money dwindles away. To repeat Margaret Thatcher's saying, the problem with socialism is that sooner or later you run out of other people's money. In fact, the immigrants represent an extra burden because not only must those who are taxed support the native poor, they must now support other poor people as well. The system will break down even sooner.

In a society where immigrants are given jobs (or can find them easily), however, they become integrated. Often, immigrants figure out ways to create new jobs serving their fellow immigrants, jobs that may even serve the natives. Here in America, for example, Mexican food has become a big hit in the last forty years, although it was completely unknown when I was a child in the 1950s, and so jobs have been created in restaurants that serve and in companies that manufacture Mexican food. As long as immigrants aren't taking jobs from citizens, most citizens won't be resentful of immigrants (unless they have high crime rates, which unfortunately can happen when leftists promote soft-on-crime policies). Giving jobs to immigrants seems to be a sustainable and healthy way to help the poor, while simply giving them a handout isn't sustainable since the money runs out sooner or later and since it creates big resentments on both sides.

The next question is what sort of jobs should poor people want. Consider the following passage:

> We have started including the question "What are your ambitions for your children?" in surveys given to poor people around the world. The results are striking. Everywhere we have asked, the most common dream of the poor is that their children become government workers.[2]

This is from a book surveying methods of helping the poor in the Third World and why seemingly obvious solutions didn't actually work. (For example, some poor people preferred to use loan sharks rather than microloans because loan sharks would offer a more flexible payment schedule.[3]) This passage comes near the end of the book in which many other methods of helping the poor were reviewed and were generally found to be wanting. It is quite clear that providing good-paying jobs to the poor is better than microloans and all the others ways of helping the poor that people in the First World dream up, and that having a job is moreover what the poor themselves want. I think they are wrong to want their children to have government jobs as opposed to jobs in the private sector, since if too many people have government jobs, they become a burden on society since they aren't actually producing anything. Nevertheless, it is perfectly clear why they want their children to have government jobs rather than private-sector jobs since in poor countries the number of private-sector jobs that are permanent and stable are few and far between. The only jobs they know of that are like that are government jobs. We have to be paternalistic here and say that their best bet is for private-sector jobs, if they are available.

My points in this chapter are that, first, the poor aren't ideological; they will simply go where the money is. It doesn't matter to them that the money is coming from a job gained in a capitalist society. My second point is that a society that offers jobs to immigrants is likely to be able to keep doing this as more and more immigrants come (though a huge number coming all at once could overwhelm even a robust capitalist society), while a society that simply hands out money will eventually run out of it. My third point is that private-sector jobs are better than government jobs since the private sector produces things or offers services and so is generally not a burden on society in the way that government jobs often are. There is a final point I haven't made but which is obvious: every country should do what it can to encourage job-creation in the private sector in order to help the poorest citizens, because then they won't need to emigrate.

CHAPTER 16

JOBS, JOBS, JOBS: WHAT POOR PEOPLE NEED AND WHAT RICH PEOPLE'S LEFTISM DOESN'T GIVE THEM

The best experience of my life, in terms of jobs, happened in East Asia a couple decades ago. My girlfriend (now my wife) wanted to go there to study the language as part of her project of writing a Ph.D. thesis in art history, and I tagged along to be with her and also because I generally enjoy foreign travel. We were there two months, and during that time I got several jobs teaching English. I didn't look for these jobs; they were simply given to me. The job situation was so wonderful that I actually gave away jobs I didn't want to other Americans. I had a great time there, at least as far as jobs were concerned. Not only was the work easy with reasonably good pay, but also the idea that so many jobs were available was delightful.

A situation not quite as good as that was when I spent three and a half years working as a computer programmer for a subsidiary (called Comten) of a large corporation (NCR). It took me a few months to find this job, but once I had it, I felt reasonably secure. I would even get the occasional call from headhunters trying to entice me away to other jobs. I would have stayed in the industry for the rest of my life if I hadn't found the work so uninteresting.

Finally, the worst job situation I've experienced has been in academia. I have spent a good deal of my adult life trying to squeeze out a living in the humanities, and it has been miserable. One job for which I applied (teaching philosophy at a small college) sent back a rejection letter saying they had received over five hundred applications. I will say that in certain areas, it can be easy. I took some Arabic classes and was able to get work in a college as a substitute on that basis, even though I did not even have a B.A. in the subject, much less an M.A. or a Ph.D. In fact, I was allowed to be a substitute in fourth semester Arabic, when I myself had only taken three semesters of formal study (though I had studied the fourth semester material on my own). This was because the number of people who had any knowledge of Arabic and who were available as substitutes was so small that the college was desperate. But this experience was a great exception because in general in the humanities, the jobs are few and far between, and the competition is fierce.

When I reflect on these experiences, I find it quite obvious what leftists should do to help the poor, namely create jobs for them. Creating jobs is the best thing to do to help the poor. In the last chapter, I argued that poor people go where the money is, and also that they should prefer to go where the jobs are rather than where money is simply handed out, because in the latter sort of society the money handed out is not enough to escape poverty and will eventually run out, while in the former sort creating jobs is a sustainable activity and in addition it allows an immigrant to create value for others and thus become integrated into society. Accordingly, it is creating jobs, and not forcing a redistribution, at which leftists should aim.

By creating jobs I don't mean make-work jobs that do nothing useful except absorb masses of the unemployed. Nor do I mean creating lots of government jobs (except possibly as an absolute last resort), because (as I argued in the last chapter) lots of government jobs mean a drain on the taxes of those not working in the government, and eventually that gets to be too much of a strain and the system collapses. In addition, as we saw with communism (in which everyone has a government job), the poor stayed poor, while the rich leftists stayed rich. So, creating lots of government jobs is generally worthless. Instead, leftists need to encourage job creation by entrepreneurs and private enterprises.

Unfortunately, encouraging job creation is not the way that leftists think. For them, the big idea is not to encourage job creation, thus enlarging the pie, but to push for redistributions, thus making sure the pie is cut fairly. To put this in other terms, they seldom think about creating new enterprises that would help the poor better than the existing ones, but instead they enjoy attacking the existing ones. Nor do they do what the CEO's of big corporations do, which is to brag about how many jobs they have created. Leftists are more likely to inadvertently *destroy* jobs than to create them, but in any case, they brag about having helped the workers get better wages or working conditions or about helping the poor via a redistribution. But as I have already argued, giving money to the poor via redistributions doesn't work very well, plus I'm not convinced that the rich people who run the left really want them.

Let me point out all the advantages of job creation. Note that some of these advantages are ones that leftists try to emulate in other, more difficult ways, when they could achieve them simply by pushing for job creation.

First, when many jobs are being created, wages go up. Employers will have to bid for workers, and they will give higher bids when many jobs have been created because workers will then be in shorter supply. Leftists try to gain this same advantage for workers in all sorts of other ways: using unions that engage in collective bargaining and even going on strike, nationalizing an industry, or simply mandating a minimum wage.[1] But the easiest way is simply to encourage job creation.

After all, mandating a minimum wage may help those who are already employed, but will discourage employers from hiring more workers because workers have become too expensive in their eyes. In response they will fire those who are too expensive (if they can get away with it), expect more from the workers they now have, hire temp workers who can be dumped as soon as they are no longer needed, hire illegal aliens willing to work for less than the minimum wage, or start replacing their workers with robots.

And this response applies only to those currently existing businesses; it does not apply to businesses which do not yet exist and which may never exist because those people contemplating starting a business may refrain from doing so because labor is too expensive to make a profit.

With job creation, not only do wages go up, there is also plenty of work for everyone. Besides, it is more satisfying. With job creation, the employer goes to the prospective worker and says, "Work for me, and I'll give you better pay than the other employers in town." But with a mandated minimum wage, the employer feels the employee is not worth the extra money and may withhold the extra pay, even though it is illegal, or else the employer will at the first opportunity fire those workers who are not seen as worth that extra pay. Obviously, it is better to be more appreciated than less appreciated.

Next, working conditions will be made as good as possible when jobs are plentiful. Why would a worker stay in a job with bad working conditions when other jobs are available with the same pay that have better working conditions? Accordingly, employers will do what they can to attract workers, and part of that is making working conditions as good as possible. Once again, the left's way of dealing with this situation is completely different and is much harder to achieve. Leftists often worry about workers being blacklisted by employers, but if jobs are plentiful, the shoe would be on the other foot. It would be companies that would be blacklisted; companies would have to worry about their reputation among the workers.

A third advantage is that job creation means that young workers, workers who have recently been laid off or fired, or those of any age who simply want to change jobs will have an easy time because plenty of other jobs will be available for them. Often, the methods that leftists use to help workers do a lot for current workers, but nothing for new workers. For example, making it hard to fire someone seems wonderful at first. Once that person gets hired, she has her job for life. The disadvantage is that companies trying to thrive under this system do not want to hire people they can't fire, so they have little incentive to hire new people. Accordingly, a regulation designed to help some, those who already have jobs, makes life difficult for others, those who do *not* already have jobs. Allowing workers to be fired can seem scary, but if job creation is emphasized, then a worker who is fired should be able to find another job easily.

Another advantage of job creation is that it avoids the situation which my parents' generation faced and which we are facing today: the destruction of young people's dreams because there are so few jobs. My father wanted to go into engineering, but because jobs were scarce in the early 1930s, he could not save up enough for college. Instead of getting to be an engineer, he wound up as a low-level accountant. Today, many young people are having a terrible time finding work, and it is destroying their dreams. The situation that I've been talking about with respect to adjuncts in academia seems to have spread over the entire economy. It is job creation that solves this problem.

Job creation would also help us with the problem of retirement. Currently, many people are worried whether our society will have enough funds in Social Security to be able to handle all the baby boomers retiring, with so few young people available to provide those funds. On the other hand, many baby boomers think they will never be able to retire because they can't afford it, whether Social Security is available or not. But then young people will not have access to the jobs that would be available if these baby boomers were to retire when older people usually do. Young people are in trouble either way, whether older people retire or not.

This whole situation could benefit from job creation. With lots of job creation, young people needn't worry if older people are going to retire. In addition, either their wages will be raised because of job creation, so that more funds will be available for Social Security, or foreigners will be imported, thus giving a larger pool of workers to support the baby boomers in their old age. Likewise, with lots of job creation, there will almost certainly be growth in the general economy, which means older people will see the investments they made when they were working bring in more money, which further means they will feel less angst about retiring. More of them will retire which means even more jobs will be available for young people.

Still another advantage of job creation is the reduction in racial tensions. Few will care about racial animosities when employers are desperate for workers and when nearly everyone has a good job. Few workers will think they are getting a raw deal because they are in the wrong racial group. When few jobs are created, on the other hand, then everyone is scrambling for the same small pool of jobs, and everyone will bicker over how those jobs are given out. Society easily becomes dysfunctional. The far right will experience an increase in numbers and will start demonizing anyone who has a job if others whom they favor don't have one. The left thinks the way to deal with the far right is with lots of propaganda and laws against them, while I think the way to deal with them is to have enough jobs created so that the far right never really gets going in the first place.

A further advantage of job creation relates to dysfunction in a different way, along class rather than racial lines. When there is job creation, instead of having a dysfunctional society where we push for redistributions, we have a partnership involving the rich and the poor. That is, with redistributions, the rich (and even the less rich) are resentful at having their money stolen from them, while the poor are resentful because they aren't getting enough from the redistribution, and they have no way to get out of poverty on their own. (They probably also feel resentful at having no real niche in society; they feel like nothing but society's garbage.) By contrast, with job creation rich and poor can both be happy. Rich people want a place to put their money that will give a better return on investment than a bank, because a bank account seldom keeps up with inflation (and even if it did, the interest rates still aren't anything special). Their choice is generally to invest in a company. At the other end, poor people count on companies to hire them. Few people, whether rich or poor, have the skills, inclination, and start-up funds to run their own business, and so the poor would rather be hired by a company than start their own. Accordingly, both rich and poor depend on companies, the one to get richer from getting a share of the profits, and the other to get a good job that will allow escape from poverty.

Unfortunately, this symbiotic relationship was nearly derailed from the start by leftists who insisted that workers were being exploited by the owners of these companies, even though without those companies the workers (of whom there was an oversupply) would have ended up, like India's poor, unemployed and living on a square of pavement. The result has been at best a long series of regulations that don't necessarily help the poor, even though that is their alleged intent, and at worst vicious dictatorships that murdered tens of millions of people.

Leftists don't seem to understand that companies are under no moral obligation to hire workers, any more than my wife and I are under a moral obligation to hire someone to mow our lawn or shovel the snow from our sidewalk. If a company wants workers, but too many regulations make hiring workers burdensome, the company will make do without workers. Just think what things would have been like if Walmart had all along used robots instead of human workers. Would that have helped those whom they actually did hire? Of course not. There would have been fewer jobs for them and for all the other people looking for work, so whatever jobs they did find would be even more exploitative than Walmart.

Another thing to note is that in this situation, rich people will still be happy investing in companies like Walmart since they don't care if the company uses people or robots. They simply want a place to park their money that will give them a good return. Accordingly, the push to "help" workers by imposing labor regulations on companies needn't hurt the rich investor, but it *can* hurt poor people who want work. The moral is that asking the rich for a job is much better than asking for money, because then there is an exchange of money for labor that the rich will respect rather than simply a payout for nothing that they will resent.

Finally, while leftists focus on inequality and think they can attack the problem directly by demanding higher taxes on the rich, it is better to focus on job creation and to attack the problem indirectly. When unemployment is widespread, those at the top and in the middle generally keep making money, while those at the bottom (including those who have sunk to the bottom via job loss) don't make money. Naturally, inequality increases in such a situation. The way to attack this is to create jobs so that those at the bottom can start making money again. Then inequality will diminish. Even if it doesn't diminish immediately, most people won't care because they will be too busy getting ahead. Leftists always want people to focus on the gap between the rich and the poor, while I want them to focus on whether rich people are helping to create more jobs and whether the government is helping in this endeavor or obstructing it.

Let me now make some comments on the basic idea of job creation.

1. During the Industrial Revolution, the left got off on the wrong foot. They focused on exploited workers when their priority should have been unemployed workers. By the time the Great Depression came along, this should have been clear, yet the left was still focusing on the wrong problem and offering solutions that weren't going to work. Their solution was to destroy capitalism, but what was needed to help the unemployed was to boost capitalism. (After all, of what use would it be for the unemployed if the government came to own the means of production when the economy was dead in the water?) By boosting capitalism, more jobs would have been created, but instead the left implemented solutions that kept unemployment high for a decade.

Leftists will argue that it was a breakdown in capitalism that led us to the Great Depression, but in response plenty of right-wing pundits have pointed to the recession of the early 1920s in which President Warren G. Harding refused to intervene. The result? The recession disappeared on its own quickly. The same could have happened in the early 1930s, and indeed, in the months immediately after the stock market crash of 1929, unemployment was actually not as bad as in 1921—9% versus 11.7%—and had actually gone down to 6.3% by June of 1930. But that's when federal intervention began, and unemployment hit double digits and remained at double digits for the rest of the decade.[2]

2. Many leftist theorists are from the ranks of the wealthy, and they all seem to have great jobs in government or in academia. Not many come from the bottom, and not many have actual work experience in corporate America or as entrepreneurs. I have had a share in all of these. I come from a lower-middle-class background and spent time in poverty as a grad student. As for work experience, as I explained earlier, I worked as a computer programmer for a corporation, and my wife and I have also engaged in small-scale entrepreneurial activities. A story circulating among people on the right is that George McGovern, after his failed run for the presidency, turned to running a hotel. He had had no experience doing that sort of thing, and so he failed miserably. But what he said was how irksome were all the regulations that leftists, including himself, had passed in order to "help" the workers or the consumers. It doesn't help them when they lose their jobs as a business goes under because it is regulated to death.

3. Detroit went bankrupt because of the left's ideas, not because of the right's ideas. (Almost no one on the left wants to admit that Detroit has had Democratic administrations for decades.) It went bankrupt because the left promotes strong government unions and redistributions, but never job creation. It went bankrupt because it tolerated a rise in crime, which led wealthier people to leave, which the left then blamed on racism rather than on the rise in crime. Leftists blame those who left for taking tax money and jobs with

them, but this wouldn't have happened if they had promoted job creation and curtailed crime.

4. Because leftists began by focusing on exploited workers rather than unemployed workers, they developed unhelpful ideas. As I have already mentioned, we often hear about some horrible situation in a factory in the Third World owned by some multinational giant, causing leftists to rail against it. But upon further investigation, we learn that in reality the factory treats its workers better than other employers in the region. At this point leftists are reduced to saying that the factory is still exploitative, which is clearly pathetic. Recall the comments of C.P. Snow from Chapter 11. His grandfather didn't mind the Industrial Revolution and thought it represented opportunities for people like him; he wanted changes to keep happening along those lines and not along leftist lines.

5. Some leftist economists today think they can do surveys of existing businesses to see if the recession is preventing them from offering jobs. They find (probably incorrectly) that it is not. But the real problem with the recession is the failure of many people to create new businesses. They look at all the regulations to be overcome and think, "Why bother?" (This is why real-world experience is important. I myself have several ideas for new businesses, but in the current climate, they don't seem worth the bother.) And since they don't bother, lots of young people simply cannot find jobs.

6. All the stimulus money provided by the government over the past few years has done almost nothing in terms of creating jobs, which simply shows it is better to let ordinary individuals create jobs on their own rather than trying to get the government to do it. Or if government needs to get involved, do it in this way: Have an annual contest for would-be entrepreneurs whose winner would get start-up funds from the government. The winner would be chosen based on which plan was best in terms of feasibility, least amount of funds needed to get started, and largest number of people who would potentially be employed. Here is another idea. Those who always

want to raise taxes on the rich should think about the following. Let the rich have an alternative, namely allowing them to use the money that would go to the government to fund a new company instead. They would then be allowed to get a share of the profits. Naturally, this would be less money for the government, but if it helped created jobs for the poor, why should we care?

7.   I live in a rural area where there are few good restaurants. My wife is a professor at a nearby college, and I know many of the professors at this college, most of whom are liberal or leftist. They all bemoan our area's dearth of good restaurants, especially good ethnic restaurants, but at the same time, they want strong regulations on business. It is useless to tell them that restaurants are small businesses and that strong regulations on business mean that small businesses will be hurt much more than larger ones, and so the restaurants we are likely to have in our area are the big chains rather than the smaller restaurants. These professors come from big cities (or at least big university towns), and in such areas ethnic restaurants can count on a large clientele which they cannot count on in a rural area, which is why reducing the regulations on them would help tremendously. This is a good (if non-standard) example of false consciousness!

8.   Most leftists think of big business as hostile to big government, but those on the right see the situation more clearly. They know perfectly well that big business likes big government because big government does so many things for it. For example, big government will institute regulations that force new competitors to fail because they don't have the funds to handle those regulations.

9.   It can happen, of course, that jobs are being created, but that the requirements for those jobs don't match up with what the unemployed have to offer. I suspect, however, that this happens when job creation seldom occurs. If jobs are seldom created, then a sudden spurt of job creation in one industry can mean that most people won't have the right background and training for those jobs. But if

job creation is happening constantly throughout the entire economy, then there should be a wide variety of jobs available so that most can find a job.

10. Am I talking pie-in-the-sky? Is all this talk nothing but idle dreams that can never happen in reality? Let me observe that when I was young there were plenty of jobs. My worry when I was growing up was that I'd be stuck in a job doing work I hated, so I tried as hard as I could to get into work that I liked doing. Nor do I think my experience was unusual. I grant that America at that time had a wonderful job situation partly because Europe was still recovering from World War II, while those countries of East Asia that are so impressive today had not yet begun their rise. But let me also note the long history of immigration to this country, which would not have happened if we had been bad at job creation.

11. Some leftists claim that not only does raising the minimum wage not cause layoffs or hurt job creation, it actually helps create more jobs due to the rise in demand as more people get more money. Fine, then, let's raise the minimum wage as high as possible. Make it $1,000 per hour instead of $10. The fact that leftists never push for much higher wages shows they know it would never work. It may be true that there is some minimal effect of the sort they believe in. But to put this in a larger context, the left is always fighting capitalism, and it never works very well. My suggestion is that we push in the opposite direction for more capitalism. As I have been arguing, the horrible exploitation that leftists associate with more capitalism is actually the result of the lack of jobs that allows companies to ignore bad pay and bad conditions. Accordingly, even if there is some minor amount of job creation associated with raising the minimum wage, doing so simply will not produce the enormous amount of job creation that is necessary if workers are to be treated as well as possible.

When we focus on job creation, we leftists find that we have to think along completely different lines. To begin with, rather than taxing the rich, we realize that we would rather have them create jobs, and that means making sure their money goes to private enterprise rather than to the government.

In addition, we want to have an environment where small businesses thrive, because job creation is most likely to occur in small businesses rather than big businesses (through not just the existing small businesses but through many new start-ups.) A small business is also what some of the unemployed try to start when they can't find work in any other way. Accordingly, we want an environment that is friendly to small businesses, and that means keeping regulations on businesses to a minimum.

Two groups like regulations on business, leftists and big businesses. Leftists like regulations because they think regulations help the little guy (whether as a worker or as a consumer), while big businesses like them because it keeps out new competitors while not raising their own costs too much. However, leftists are wrong to like regulations because although regulations might help the little guy in some ways, it hurts him in other ways, for example, by depressing the number of jobs available.

This observation leads to one of the most important points in this book: that helping the poor entails a number of tensions that leftists often don't notice. One such tension is that between currently employed workers and the unemployed. Whom should the left help more? Often, their priority is toward helping those who are currently employed, which skews things against the unemployed. Making it hard to fire people means that companies don't like to hire. Another tension concerns citizens and immigrants, for immigrants will in some circumstances be taking jobs away from citizens. Still another tension comes from the choice to help the poor versus helping the environment.

Here is what I believe the priorities should be from most important to least important:

1. Helping unemployed citizens.
2. Helping citizens who are already employed.
3. Helping immigrants.
4. Helping the environment.

Helping unemployed citizens should be the priority, because they are more desperate than citizens who are already employed; and we should help them by promoting job creation because, as I have been arguing, this will help with wages and working conditions. After that, the left should help those who are already employed, if they even need any help at this point. With jobs aplenty, it's not clear that they would need much help. It might be nice to push for a regulation to make it hard to fire people, but as I've been arguing, this makes employers reluctant to hire new people, and anyway if there are enough job opportunities available, then those fired will not be unemployed for long.

A lesser priority should be helping immigrants. As things now stand in America, the left wants to help all these different groups—immigrants (especially illegal immigrants), the unemployed, and those currently employed—but it hasn't thought much about how to prioritize and so it often helps one group at the expense of others. Currently, the left unconsciously gives priority to helping immigrants and those now employed over those unemployed. Leftist rhetoric would have one believe that the left is fully behind those who are unemployed, but the reality is that their own policies, as much as anything, have caused people to be unemployed. Helping immigrants doesn't do much to help unemployed citizens, since it cuts down on the number of jobs for them, and it depresses wages for the jobs that are available.

Exactly what particular policy should be chosen on immigrants, once leftists have their priorities straight, is beyond the scope of this book. But let me say that I'm not anti-immigrant. As an ardent soccer fan, for example, I appreciate the influx of so many soccer fans, and I've enjoyed watching many a game on the Univision television station, a station that wouldn't exist or be available without so many immigrants. Nevertheless, helping immigrants should be of lesser priority than helping our own citizens. Ideally, if each government in the world were to promote job creation, there would be less need for all the immigration of the last few decades. Immigration would be reduced to those looking for something new, those who like exploring other cultures, and those poor wretches who are forced to leave because of political persecution or some natural catastrophe.

Finally, the last priority should be helping the environment. I know that environmentalists will vehemently disagree, but it is the correct policy. When I confronted one leftist about which was more important, helping the poor or helping the environment, I could see he had never thought about this before. Eventually he chose helping the environment, because if we didn't do that, he said, the poor would be in even worse shape than they are now. But as I pointed out in Part I, the poor often bear costs imposed by the environmentalists that wealthier people don't have to bear, so this explanation for his preference just will not work. In addition, environmentalists have a bad track record because of their wild exaggerations of the threats they insist we are facing. The dire consequences have not in fact come to pass, and so we need to turn back to making the poor of more importance than the environment.

For those who can't tolerate this, let me put it somewhat differently. The environment should never be helped at the expense of the poor. For those who want all kinds of restrictions on various activities so that the environment won't be hurt, what I ask is that they personally be willing to contribute the money for these restrictions so the poor won't be hurt. To put it still differently, leftists love the concept of the environmental-impact statement because it has helped the environment so much. What I want, though, is something different:

a blue-collar impact statement. A blue-collar impact statement, as the name implies, is a statement declaring all the ways that poor people will be hurt by some environmental policy. Accordingly, whenever anyone suggests a restriction on our activities so as to help the environment, I would like to see a blue-collar impact statement that will show whether, or more likely how, the poor will be impacted by this restriction in comparison with people of other classes. Such a concept would greatly reduce the effects of the left's war against the poor that I talked about in Chapter 2.

I admit that in this list of priorities, I have not included the consumer. I do not see any obvious place where the consumer fits in this list, except that I think the unemployed deserve priority over the consumer. (Just ask most people who are unemployed.) Presumably, helping the consumer belongs higher than helping immigrants, since each country needs to help its own citizens first, and that includes the citizen as consumer as well as the citizen as worker. That means that helping the consumer is either right above or else right below helping citizens who are already employed. I leave it to others to make this determination.

This chapter's focus is on job creation as the best way to help the poor, but other things also should be done. One of these is lowering the costs that the poor face. Some of these are actual costs that they pay for in money, and some are simply conditions that hurt the poor.

To begin with, taxes should be lowered. Should anyone in the bottom half be paying more than 1% of their gross income? The current practice, as I have noted, is that those who are very poor don't have to pay taxes, but those who are somewhat poor do. It means that anyone who is single and making a mere $20,000 a year nevertheless gets taxed to the extent that over a thousand dollars of their pay is taken from them; people making as little as $20,000 need that money.

Another cost is that imposed by fuel, which environmentalists want to be even more expensive than it is now. When fuel costs go up, all sorts of other costs go up as well, such as food costs; so lowering fuel costs can mean that many other costs go down. That is why Poor People's Leftism wants fuel costs to go down rather than up, contrary to what the environmentalists prefer. That is also why I want blue-collar impact statements on all environmental policies, since these policies too often impose costs on the poor that they don't impose on others (especially on those making the policies).

Another cost from the left comes from the do-gooders who think that being soft on crime helps the poor, when in fact it hurts them. The same goes for those who wanted to improve public education but instead made it worse, and for those who have inadvertently pushed everyone into getting a college education, even for jobs that don't really require it. As for a college education, the heavy bureaucratic apparatus required by the New Left imposes burdensome costs on the poor as tuition keeps rising faster than inflation. All of these costs need to be contained in order to help the poor.

Containing costs for the poor is a lesser goal than creating jobs, but it is still important. It is important because, as some would argue, the days of creating good-paying jobs for the poor are over, and the only jobs we are going to create now are, say, service jobs in the fast-food industry. (I assume that if enough such jobs are created, then wages will go up because there will be a labor shortage.) If that is the case, then the best way to help the poor will be to keep their costs as low as possible, a goal with which Rich People's Leftism is unconcerned. Let's keep the necessary costs that the poor pay as low as possible, and let's eliminate the unnecessary ones.

One last goal of Poor People's Leftism is ensuring that the poor have the proper attitudes when they are looking for jobs. The attitudes instilled in the poor by Rich People's Leftism unfortunately makes them bad workers. The poor come to think that corporations are bad and that capitalism is evil, even though they expect corporations (which are part of capitalism) to give them a job. They think that rebelling is wonderful and that conforming is terrible, even though good jobs require that they be more conforming than rebelling. (As I said in an earlier chapter, I cringe when I think of the bad attitudes I had at some of my past jobs.) When they look for a job, they think in terms of what the employer can do for them rather than what they can do for the employer. If they haven't picked up such attitudes in school, they will pick them up in college, where few professors these days come from the lower class or even the lower middle class, which means they have very little understanding of what such students really need. These professors are part of what I am calling Rich People's Leftism, and they hate the 1950s because of the conformist attitudes encouraged in that decade and because schools back then were designed to churn out mindless automatons for the corporate world. In fact, these policies were good for the poor since they made the poor into good workers. That era was good for the poor in terms of job opportunities, but it was destroyed by rich leftists who thought the poor deserved something "better," which turned out to be something worse.

Now let me return to the topic of John Rawls' ideas on distributive justice. A basic question to ask at this point is, "Is it true that the parties in the Original Position would choose a redistribution over job creation as the way to help those at the bottom?" Recall that we are to imagine that people do not know particular facts about themselves while knowing general facts about history and humanity. They are required to choose principles of justice based on the knowledge they have, and Rawls believed that the parties in the Original Position would choose a redistributive policy. I disagree. Many poor people want to become rich. They have little use for redistributions because, first, redistributions won't help them become rich and indeed may even keep them poor, and second, they don't want their future wealth stolen from them. The woman I mentioned in Chapter 3 who came from a poor neighborhood whose denizens liked the police is one such person. She wanted to become rich and had no use for leftism.

When I pushed for socialism, she sneered that the slogan of the socialists is in reality "what's yours is mine and what's mine is mine." I don't know where she picked up such a cynical viewpoint at such a young age, but what struck me was that a person much poorer than I was would be saying it. In addition, it was years before I learned that her slogan was basically right in the sense that governmental redistributions don't work the way they should, partly because the rich have so many ways to avoid higher taxes that poor people instead of the rich end up with the higher taxes, and partly because some of that money goes to people other than the poor.

But even poor people who don't want to be rich often do want to get out of poverty, and redistributions are not the way to help them. What this means is that the parties in the Original Position would hesitate to prefer a system of redistribution over that of brisk and variegated job creation. After all, think about how Rawls wants white people to reason when in the Original Position. Since we whites won't know our skin color and ethnicity, we would not choose principles that favored whites over other groups. The same can be said for men: we men would not choose principles that favored men over women if we didn't know in advance if we were male or female. How does this reasoning work when it comes to wealth?

Wealthy leftists may think, when confronted with the ideas of Rawls' Original Position and its veil of ignorance, that if they didn't know they were wealthy, then they would want a system that redistributed wealth back to the poor, because that is what they imagine poor people want. *But given that plenty of actual poor people think differently*, that has to be a factor in choosing principles of justice. Yes, there are poor people who want redistributions. If you have heard about nothing all your life but the need for redistributions as necessary for helping the poor, and if jobs have been few and far between, then it is natural that you will choose redistributions; but it is an open question what you would choose if you were presented with the alternative of job creation. The many immigrants to America, for

CHAPTER 17
SOME DIFFERENCES BETWEEN RICH PEOPLE'S LEFTISM AND POOR PEOPLE'S LEFTISM

In previous chapters, I have referred to Rich People's Leftism (RPL) and Poor People's Leftism (PPL), but it is now time to spell out the many differences. The key difference between them, of course, is that RPL wants a redistribution of wealth (by the government), while PPL wants job creation. Both of these are designed to help the poor, but the likelihood is that job creation will help them more and will be more sustainable than a redistribution of wealth. However, there are many other differences. When I first began to think critically about the left a number of years ago, many things that had seemed sensible and wise before began to look ridiculous and stupid. In other words, my views on a number of issues were formerly adopted because other leftists adopted them and not because they helped the poor. With that in mind, let me enumerate the differences.

RPL originally came from rich people, who wanted (or said they wanted) to help the poor, while PPL comes from poor people. I come from a lower-middle-class background and have spent time being poor, and much of what I am saying was inspired by things said to me by poor people I have encountered down through the years and by relatives who had either been poor or whose parents had been poor.

RPL's basic effect is that everyone (except wealthy leftists) becomes poor, while PPL's basic effect is that poor people have a good chance of getting out of poverty.

RPL says it is trying to help the poor, but PPL thinks that mostly what RPL tries to do is to attack rich conservatives.

RPL thinks a redistribution of wealth is wonderful, while PPL thinks that the reason RPL thinks it is wonderful is not because it actually helps the poor, but because the members of RPL get to pose as friends of the poor and because a lot of that money gets diverted towards themselves.

RPL thinks that huge inequalities in income and wealth are bad, while PPL thinks that a lack of good job opportunities that would allow the poor to escape from poverty is bad.

RPL thinks that the Occupy Wall Street movement was wonderful and that their prescription to tax the 1% was a great way to sock it to the rich, while PPL thinks that the movement was pathetic and, though sympathizing with their situation, thinks that what they really needed was good-paying jobs and not an unearned share of some rich person's wealth.

RPL wants an egalitarian society (or at least it says it wants this), while PPL wants to provide poor people with opportunities to get out of poverty, after which its job is basically done. That is, whether some people make huge amounts and others merely end up in the middle class is not a matter that PPL cares about.

RPL respects wealthy leftists for wanting to help the poor. PPL observes that these wealthy leftists are reluctant to share their wealth, are well paid for what they do, and hog all the best jobs. PPL prefers to support wealthy conservatives, who at least are honest about where they are coming from and who may do a lot to help create jobs for the poor.

RPL likes high taxes so that the government can form a lot of agencies to help the poor. PPL thinks that all those agencies will be staffed by wealthy leftists and is tired of paying higher taxes so that wealthy leftists can get great jobs.

RPL wants to have higher taxes on the rich, while PPL wants to have lower taxes on the poor.

RPL wants to raise the price of gasoline, while PPL wants to lower it.

RPL likes minimum-wage laws, because they will help the poor receive a living wage, while PPL hates minimum-wage laws, because they inadvertently promote unemployment and because the goal of a living wage can be better produced by vigorous job creation.

RPL hates welfare for the rich, by which it means the ways that big corporations get help from the government, while PPL also hates welfare for the rich, by which it means the ways that wealthy leftists get help from the government (including the great jobs they get in government as well as grants they get in academia and the arts).

RPL sees government as the solution, while PPL sees government as sometimes helpful but mostly harmful.

RPL thinks regulation of the financial industry is good because it helps the little people. PPL thinks regulation does nothing since new tricks can be easily thought up by financiers, and the better solution is to educate people about finance.

RPL likes trial lawyers, because they go after corporations, and hates McDonalds and WalMart, because they exploit their workers. PPL likes McDonalds and WalMart, because they offer low prices which help most of the poor, and hates trial lawyers, since the increase in prices they inadvertently cause hurts most of the poor.

RPL thinks corporations should be socially responsible by not polluting, by supporting the arts, and so on. PPL thinks the most socially responsible thing a corporation can do is to offer good jobs to poor people.

RPL in general hates corporations and is always talking disparagingly of corporate interests and complaining if a corporation makes big profits. PPL likes corporations to the extent that they provide good jobs for poor people, and likes profits if it means there is more money available for job creation. In addition, PPL observes that RPL seldom complains about the huge endowments of elite colleges and universities, which mostly help the rich and not the poor. Finally, just about anything that RPL says against corporations—they're rich, they exploit people, and so on—can also be said against academia, even if RPL doesn't wish to acknowledge these parallels.

RPL thinks imposing taxes on corporations that outsource their work is a great idea, while PPL thinks corporations outsource when they are chased out by environmentalists or when the workers they find in their own country have picked up bad attitudes from leftists about working, about corporations, and about capitalism.

RPL thinks voting Republican is going over to the dark side. PPL thinks voting Republican is a useful way to keep RPL in line.

RPL favors equality and so implicitly rejects upward mobility (except as a rhetorical device to attack capitalists when capitalism's upward mobility isn't working). PPL favors upward mobility via capitalism, since it sees that "egalitarian" schemes never work and are really disguised hierarchies with wealthy leftists at the top.

RPL wants to destroy capitalism to help the poor, while PPL merely wants to make sure capitalism works for the poor—and capitalism can do this by creating enough jobs so the poor can escape from poverty.

RPL thinks capitalism is horrible, while socialism (or even communism) is best. PPL thinks capitalism is fine or at worst a necessary evil, while socialism and communism are horrible; and since the best jobs in such systems usually go to wealthy leftists, they are nothing but schemes that allow wealthy leftists to assuage their feelings of guilt about being wealthy while not actually doing anything for the poor. Basically, communism and socialism allow rich leftists to play at helping the poor; they are fantasies of Rich People's Leftism.

RPL thinks that when the government owns the means of production, the workers will fare best, while PPL thinks that what happens when the government owns the means of production is merely that ownership passes from the hands of one group of rich people to another and that the poor, on balance, aren't helped at all. Moreover, PPL thinks RPL is being naive in thinking that all poor people would be helped by this solution since it applies only to factory workers and not to other poor people.

RPL thinks it's a bad thing that America has never had a viable socialist party. PPL thinks it's a good thing, since socialism does little to help the poor and is nothing but a fantasy of Rich People's Leftism.

RPL thinks America is generally a terrible country for the poor, while PPL thinks it is generally a good country for the poor, which is why so many poor people in other countries want to move here.

RPL hates America and the West, while PPL likes America and the West.

RPL thinks poor countries are poor because America and other countries are rich, while PPL thinks poor countries are poor because they have made bad choices (in how they educate their young, in how they regulate businesses, and so on).

RPL likes the idea of a revolution that would throw out the wealthy capitalists. PPL doesn't like the idea of such a revolution because it would mean that (1) a lot of people would be murdered, (2) wealthy conservatives at the top would be replaced by wealthy leftists, while (3) the poor would remain poor.

RPL thinks poor people can be afflicted with false consciousness when they fail to see that RPL is the answer to their problems. PPL thinks the concept of false consciousness applies when poor people accept RPL instead of PPL.

RPL claims to be against private property, while PPL thinks that is hypocrisy since in the "egalitarian" schemes tried so far, those at the top got to enjoy luxurious private property while those lower down did not.

RPL thinks corporate heads are greedy, while PPL thinks many on the left are greedy, including rich leftists who refuse to share their wealth and leftist academics who don't want to redistribute the wealth of academia to poorly paid adjuncts.

RPL thinks the method used by Robert Mugabe in Zimbabwe (that is, confiscating the farmlands of whites) was a good thing, while PPL thinks it was a bad thing. It hasn't helped Zimbabwe, and the poor people there could have been helped instead by making an appeal to people in America and Europe to give money so that Zimbabweans could either start their own businesses or buy those farms.

RPL thinks socialism is the world's future and that capitalism is doomed to die. PPL thinks, as Margaret Thatcher has observed, that socialism will sooner or later run out of someone else's money, while capitalism will continue to thrive, as shown by its allowing for a constant influx of poor immigrants who can be integrated into the system.

RPL thinks socialized medicine is wonderful and should be adopted by all countries, while PPL thinks it is generally terrible and is promoted by wealthy leftists only because it makes them feel good about themselves while not actually doing much to help the poor.

RPL thinks unions are wonderful organizations that thwart the power of the capitalists, while PPL thinks what unions do can be better done by voting in politicians who truly represent the workers.

RPL is soft on crime, since it believes that crime represents an attack on an immoral system, while PPL is hard on crime, since it sees that crime generally just hurts the poor more than it hurts other classes or the system. RPL thinks crime has root causes such as poverty and racism that need to be addressed in order to get the crime rate down, while PPL thinks those are not the root causes, while being soft on crime might be a root cause.

RPL thinks "rebelling against the system" is wonderful. PPL thinks that is a wonderful game for rich kids, but it can severely hurt poor kids, making them unemployable and otherwise ruining their lives.

RPL complains about privileged white males, but PPL complains that the phrase "privileged white males" ignores important class differences among white males.

RPL constantly tells poor whites about privileges they have because they are white, while PPL tells poor whites about privileges they *don't* have because they are poor.

RPL hates the military, while PPL likes it, since it represents an opportunity for poor people.

RPL hates guns, while PPL respects them.

RPL thinks it's terrible that so many black men are in prison today and blames the situation on racism. PPL agrees that it's terrible, but blames the whole situation on mistakes leftists made in the Sixties (such as being soft on crime), which RPL is reluctant to acknowledge.

RPL thinks the changes made in the schools since the Sixties are wonderful. PPL thinks these changes are awful and have made it harder for poor people to escape poverty.

RPL thinks the Fifties were awful, while PPL thinks that as far as the job situation was concerned, they were pretty good. RPL does acknowledge that the high taxes on the rich in that decade were good, while PPL thinks that the high taxes on the poor in that decade (around 20%) were bad.

RPL blames the high cost of college on the right, while PPL blames it on RPL because the inevitable increase in bureaucracy needed to implement their vision adds to the costs of college, plus the strong leftward drift in the professoriate meant a decline in donations from conservatives.

RPL thinks the strong leftism of the professors is good for society, while PPL thinks it turns off donations from conservatives, which in turn makes college much less affordable for the poor.

RPL wants affirmative action for race and gender, but not economic background. PPL thinks there should be affirmative action for economic background as well as race and gender. PPL further thinks that RPL's resistance to including economic background for affirmative action shows its true anti-poor colors.

RPL loves newspapers like *The New York Times*, while PPL thinks they cater too much to wealthy leftists (and what they think about the poor) and not enough to the actual poor.

RPL loves the idea of tenure in academia, while PPL thinks it's just another way that RPL guarantees that wealthy leftists will get great jobs.

RPL hates conservatives who think that blacks have lower IQs than whites, while PPL hates leftist elites who think that anyone who didn't get into an elite school (which is just about every poor person) is less intelligent than those who did.

RPL thinks being green is important and good, while PPL thinks that green policies usually entail small sacrifices for rich people but big sacrifices for poor people.

RPL thinks the EPA (Environmental Protection Agency) is a great agency for keeping polluters in check, while PPL thinks it's the enemy of the people. RPL also thinks environmental impact statements are a great way to stop corporations from polluting, while PPL wants blue-collar impact statements on all environmental policies in order to see how much more they hurt the poor than the wealthy.

RPL thinks growth is a terrible thing, since it caters to greedy capitalists, destroys the environment, and so on, while PPL thinks shrinkage is a terrible thing, since it has ruined Social Security, makes it harder for the poor to get out of poverty, and generally puts a country's economy in the doldrums.

RPL likes mass transit, because it's better for the environment. PPL thinks RPL is constantly scaring people about the environment and prefers to help poor people escape mass transit by promoting cheap and affordable cars and fuel. Moreover, to the extent that poor people have to ride buses, PPL thinks the people who should be in control of the bus schedules and routes are poor people and not elites who never ride the bus.

RPL loves graffiti, since it thinks it's a way for poor people to get to voice their viewpoints, while PPL hates graffiti, since it thinks the existence of graffiti on buildings shows that the neighborhood is on the way down and so encourages criminals to do as they wish.

RPL hates offshore drilling, new pipelines, fracking, and so on, because of the potential environmental problems. PPL likes all these because they help the poor by keeping the price of gas low while at the same time providing jobs for poor people.

RPL hates America's foreign policy, while PPL hates RPL's foreign policy.

RPL thinks foreign aid to poor countries is good. PPL thinks foreign aid is bad because (as the saying goes) it takes money from poor people in the First World and gives it to rich people in the Third World. In addition, PPL thinks that there are plenty of rich people in poor countries who should be encouraged to give to the poorer people around them.

RPL slams everyone in the West with guilt for actions done by the ancestors of the wealthy, while PPL refuses to do this. Let those whose ancestors actually did these things feel guilty instead.

RPL's first instinct when it sees an environmental problem is to restrict people's freedom, while PPL's first instinct is to look for a technological solution.

Finally, RPL thinks the type of poor person who represents all the other poor people is the exploited factory worker, while PPL thinks it is the unemployed worker.

PPL is like the main character in the 1967 movie *Bedazzled*. After selling his soul to the devil and getting a lot of wishes that don't turn out well, he manages to escape from the devil's clutches, and when the devil comes calling again, he basically says, "Thanks, but no thanks." PPL says to RPL, "Thanks, but no thanks. We'll do things our own way."

CHAPTER 18
A CLOSER LOOK AT SOME OF THESE DIFFERENCES

In this chapter, I want to take a closer look at some of the differences mentioned in the last chapter, specifically guns, unions, foreign policy, environmentalism, and which type of poor person represents all other poor people.

Guns

While RPL hates guns and wants them banned, PPL favors them for the following reasons:

1. Guns allow poor people to supplement a meager income by hunting, which can bring in some extra food.

2. Guns give poor people some security. Since poor people cannot afford to live in gated communities and are likely to live in crime-infested neighborhoods or else in rural areas where police presence is minimal, guns allow poor people to protect themselves.

3. In rural areas, the deer population is a problem. They can be kept in check either by hunting them or by accidentally running into them with one's car. The latter, if it happens to a poor person, means a great deal of bother and expense, while the former means extra food.

4. The poor are much more likely than rich leftists to end up in the military, where having some prior experience with guns can be helpful. That includes so-called assault weapons, about which the left claims there can be no reason why a civilian would need one. But allowing them to be legal does give poor people a chance to use such weapons before needing them when they get into the armed forces.

I know that every time there is a mass shooting at a school or a mall, every leftist will complain about guns and how we need to ban them, but there were no such shootings when I was a child, even though there were plenty of guns around. Why? The reason is our culture was different at that time. One big change is that the mentally ill were locked up, whereas now they aren't. This leads to two problems: homelessness and shootings.

Not only are guns helpful to the poor, but the anti-gun culture of the left is fostered by rich people who don't themselves need guns (although as many conservatives have pointed out, they sometimes have bodyguards who have guns). They live in gated communities, or in communities that are relatively crime-free. They usually live in urban areas, where running into a deer is not a problem; they seldom end up in the military where knowledge of guns is useful; and of course they are wealthy enough not to need to go hunting. It's easy under these circumstances to think that not only are guns unnecessary, but also that their use is morally repellent and that those who want them and like them are moral monsters.

Unions

The next difference I want to address is unions. RPL is all for unions, while PPL takes a more nuanced view of them.

To begin with, PPL is against government unions. The idea of a government union doesn't make any sense in current leftist ideology since the government is supposed to be the good guy against the corporate bad guy. Accordingly, how could the government mistreat its workers? That is what corporations do. And if government can mistreat its workers, that calls into question the leftist idea that government is the solution. One can't have it both ways. If government is the solution, then there is no reason to expect that government will mistreat its workers, and so there is no reason for government unions.

But if there is a reason for government unions, then leftists should give up on the idea that government is the solution.

Beyond this theoretical problem, there are others. When workers in a corporation demand a raise, management is a strong force on the other side that can and will say no. It is a strong force because it knows that if it caves in too much, the company will go under. But a government manager is much weaker; if that manager caves in to union demands, the government is unlikely to go under, at least not immediately. The government is going to stay there through thick and thin. But this eventually leads to what we are seeing today, namely that at some point the pay and benefits of government workers exceed those of the average non-government worker. When those who work in the private sphere look at those who work in the government, they see higher salaries, better benefits, and often lifetime tenure, all of which are things that they don't have. Their response is hardly to feel solidarity with such privileged people, especially when their taxes have to pay for those goodies.

If the government manager does somehow manage to resist giving raises to the workers, trouble can still happen if the manager creates too many jobs. The problem of too many jobs can be created in the private sector as well, but the feedback on this action happens sooner rather than later. If a company has hired too many people during good times, it will have to lay them off during bad times, or else go under. But with government workers, it may be impossible for legal reasons to lay them off, and the bad times may not be so obvious when the government is involved. It can be decades before people realize that way too many workers are on the payroll and that many of them should not have been hired. Accordingly, whether government managers give raises that are too big or hire too many workers, we have to reject government unions.

But private unions must be rejected as well, though less vociferously. While I acknowledge the contribution that unions have made for workers, my rejection of them is based on the idea that a better way to help the workers is through electing congenial politicians and promoting job creation. That is, congenial politicians can make as good a work environment as a union can. And when lots of jobs are being created, the workers get treated better automatically as employers fight to retain them. Either or both of these together negate the need for unions.

The biggest problem of private unions is that they help current workers, but do nothing for future workers or for the unemployed. As I mentioned in Chapter 16, the left's top priority in helping people at the bottom should be to help unemployed citizens, after which one helps those who are employed. Unions do nothing for the unemployed and may even make things harder for them, if they have imposed enough arduous conditions on the employers. Such conditions (such as making it hard to fire a worker) make employers reluctant to hire new workers.

Another problem is that when a union wants to take action, its basic tactic is to go on strike. But strikes require a great deal of co-operation with others, so they often fizzle. In addition, a strike inconveniences the general public, so one requires a lot of good will from them to proceed, and anything can turn them against the strikers. Moreover, a strike can easily be undercut, morally, when the company hires people even more unfortunate than the current workers.

Now think of how things can be dealt with either by using politicians or job creation. With politicians, one doesn't need the enormous percentages of support required for a successful strike. Getting the right politicians elected requires only that one's candidate get more votes than all the others, and so the general public isn't inconvenienced by a strike. Likewise, with job creation the conditions at any job are likely to be much better, simply because employers will compete for workers, which means they will make conditions as good as possible. Accordingly, there is no need for a strike.

There are also the silly rules that one hears about with respect to unions: this worker can't lift a box and put it on a truck because that is a job for a worker in a different union. Such rules add to costs, which makes the company less efficient, which makes it more likely that it will eventually go out of business. A lack of flexibility doesn't help the workers, if the company goes under.

In recent years as political winds have shifted, some workers have complained the unions support political candidates that they themselves do not support. Thus they find themselves inadvertently giving money to their political opponents via their union fees. When corporations give to the "wrong" political candidate, leftists scream bloody murder on behalf of the workers in those corporations; but if so, it can't be permissible for a union to do it as well. More broadly, unions often have a large percentage of union dues going to the bureaucracy rather than to worker interests. When that happens, the unions make decisions based more on what the bureaucracy wants than on what is good for workers.

Unions were most useful before workers gained the right to vote, after which they became less useful. Once workers began voting, they could vote in congenial politicians (since the workers usually outnumber the bosses and owners), who could then enact legislation to help the workers.

Foreign Policy

RPL hates America's foreign policy, while PPL hates RPL's foreign policy. RPL not only hates America's foreign policy, it has done its best to get the entire world to hate America and its foreign policy.

Much of the hatred America has attracted to itself due to its foreign policy is the result of its fight against communism, which was mistakenly promoted heavily by RPL. Had communism not been present in the twentieth century, then America's foreign policy would have been vastly different. There would have been no Cold

War. There would have been no Vietnam War (the U.S., after all, took over for the French in that country, yet it had no inclination to help the French in Algeria, for the simple reason that Communists weren't involved). There would have been no need to overthrow the Iranian government back in 1953. There would have been no need to topple the Allende government in Chile in 1973. The list is endless.

America did not just have to fight communist regimes; it also had to deal with the fallout from its having fought against communist regimes. Its current bad relations with Iran are part of this; another part is its having inadvertently strengthened Al-Qaeda by helping its future members fight the Soviets in Afghanistan.

Instead of fighting communists during this time, America could have spent its time helping people in the Third World escape imperialism by other Western countries (or for that matter, by any other country) and helping them escape poverty (not by adopting the methods of RPL, but by adopting the methods of PPL).

Another reason America has a bad reputation is simply because much of the media worldwide has adopted the RPL position that America is bad. Having never heard much of anything except RPL propaganda, most people repeat the party line. In spite of this, many poor people still want to come to America in order to escape poverty.

An important theme in the left's anti-American propaganda is that of Western imperialism, which for the left has now become American imperialism. Never mind that American "imperialism" is hardly worthy of that name. In Iraq, for example, our "imperialism" didn't lead to an imposition of heavy taxes on the locals, but instead led them to have their first elections. But even if one wishes to call this imperialism, it's a simple fact that many parts of the world have been imperialistic down through the centuries. RPL tends to ignore the sins of non-Westerners, while exaggerating the sins of Westerners. It was in the West that the idea of slavery was condemned for the first time, but one would never know this based on what RPL propaganda is saying these days. The heavy dose of guilt that RPL lays on us in the West is never laid on people from countries like Turkey, which historically speaking is occupying Greek territory, or on Muslims in India, who are living in a land that historically speaking belongs to Hindus. Why is no guilt laid on any of these people? Likewise, the slave trade involved more than just Westerners; it involved Muslims, too, and in fact some white Americans were entrapped by it (which is what our first foreign wars, the Barbary Wars, were about). Yet no guilt is laid on them, either.

With respect to Islam, RPL propaganda locates the problem with the West, and it even looks back to the Crusades to blame the West for bad relations with Muslims. But Muslims were imperialistic before the Crusades. They conquered Spain and tried to conquer France, though they were turned back in the year 732 by Charles Martel.

RPL is very reluctant to call Muslims imperialists, but when they actually do, they tend to say that (1) it was justified because others had tried to conquer them, and (2) it led to the wonderfully enlightened society in Muslim Spain. Regarding the first, it makes some sense to say that Muslims had the right to conquer the Persians or the Byzantines, but that hardly justifies their conquest of India or Spain or the attempted conquest of France. What had these regions done to the Muslims that they deserved to be conquered? As for Muslim Spain, I believe its degree of enlightenment has been very much exaggerated—consider, for example, the massacre of Jews at Granada in 1066—but this is not the place to get into such a subject.

As for the problems with RPL's own foreign policy, RPL generally looks out into the world in order to see American malfeasance (or else Israeli malfeasance or, when considering the past, Western malfeasance), but nothing else. Accordingly, it tends to be oblivious to horrible things that non-Westerners do to each other, because those episodes have no political payoff for the left. The situation in Darfur a few years ago befuddled leftists when they were asked to think of a solution, because they really wanted to think only about the harm caused by the United States, and the Darfur situation had nothing to do with the United States since it was one ethnic group in the Third World attacking another. Since the left tends to think of the entire Third World as victim, they had a terrible time dealing with it and as far as I know, never did conjure up any solution to it.

Anyway, the situation in Syria today exhibits a variety of flaws in the left's foreign policy. Let me enumerate:

1. The current regime in Syria was one that, prior to the current troubles, RPL wanted us to reach out to. The idea seemed to be that since it was hostile to America, it must therefore somehow be worth pursuing, perhaps in the belief that since it was not ruled by an American puppet, it must be genuinely loved by the people. No one would think that now.

2. RPL's earlier support for the Syrian regime shows that the foreigners it supports are worse than the ones the U.S. supports. The U.S. supported Egypt's Mubarak, who (although a dictator) was gone fairly quickly once the Arab spring began, while RPL has supported Muammar Gadhafi in Libya and Bashar Assad in Syria, both of whom were far more brutal towards their own people when trying to keep power during the uprisings than Mubarak was.

3. Syria's many massacres of its own people make the RPL's fixation on Israeli oppression look wholly absurd and biased against Israel. Despite the oppression that Israel engages in, Israel has never treated the Palestinians as badly as the Assad regime has treated the opposition (nor has the Assad regime treated its opposition in the terrible way that the new Islamic State in Iraq and Syria, also known as ISIS or ISIL or just IS, has treated its opponents). Syria's actions confirm the response made by Israeli Prime Minister Benjamin Netanyahu that Israel acts the way it does because it lives in a tough neighborhood. It's just hard to take Palestinian complaining very seriously after this.

4. The longer the massacres go on, the more that RPL looks bad for not demanding intervention. The left always complains when

those on the right want to intervene. They talk about the horrors of war, the slaughter of innocents, the children killed, and so on. What they *don't* do is talk about how these things can happen even if we don't intervene. Not intervening in a war in the Third World seems similar to not intervening in cases of domestic violence.

5. The ineffectuality of RPL's preferred solutions, such as diplomacy and going through the United Nations, isn't to the left's credit, either. Those solutions simply haven't worked. Whatever the outcome in Syria, it most likely will occur through the use of force.

6. The call for a new beginning of relations between America and the Muslim world by President Obama looks pathetic and out of touch with reality when one part of it is massacring another part. The implication of that call was that America was at fault for bad things happening to Muslims, so we should be nice to them; but when one sees the brutality of Muslim killing Muslim, our own share of the blame should be re-assessed. We were merely doing the best we could in a region fraught with high passions that easily breaks out into vicious sectarianism.

7. RPL's refusal, as a result of its belief in cultural relativism, to push non-Western cultures to become more Western didn't help with this situation. Encouraging these countries to adopt Western values might have prevented the massacres.

8. The fact that the Syrian rebels wanted us to intervene shows that the world doesn't hate us for interventions as much as RPL thinks it does. Foreigners expect us to rescue them, despite that being an intervention.

In connection with the situation in Syria, there is one other mistake the left makes that is so colossal in its incomprehensibility and so staggering in its stupidity that it may be suicidal. But first let me digress a little. I have talked about the left's war against the poor in this book, but of course I am using the word "war" metaphorically. However, that war is not the only war the left is waging against its own would-be supporters, and the other war it is waging has led to people being murdered. I am talking about the left's war against liberals and leftists in the Middle East (a war that has spilled over into the West wherever Muslims are concentrated). Contrary to what liberals and leftists here in the West seem to think, some people in the Middle East grow up eschewing the traditional cultures that surround them. They include women who want to go to college, gays who want to live openly, and secularists who want to live in a culture whose religion doesn't suffocate them. Nevertheless, they get no support from liberals and leftists in the West these days, who prefer to support their mortal enemies, the Islamic right. Although for a long time I was oblivious to the left's war against the poor, I never wanted to have anything to do with this other war. One victim of this war, a young Algerian woman named Amel Zenoune-Zouani, was abducted from a bus and had her throat slit by Muslim extremists. Her crime was simply wanting to go to law school. Her murder was described by Karima Bennoune in her book *Your Fatwa Does Not Apply Here*,[1] a book that also describes many similar murders and threats to women and secularists in the Middle East. Bennoune's complaint is that the left is supporting not the Middle East's liberals and leftists, but their murderers and would-be murderers. As I said above, I find this policy completely incomprehensible. However, I have already talked about this topic elsewhere, so I won't repeat it here.[2]

I could detail various other failings of the left's foreign policy, but these should suffice.

Environmentalism

Perhaps the biggest difference between PPL and RPL (other than the main one concerning job creation vs. redistributions) concerns environmentalism. Today, environmentalism trumps egalitarianism for RPL; that is, for today's leftists helping the environment always trumps helping the poor. PPL reverses that ordering: egalitarianism trumps environmentalism. This is for two reasons.

The first is that environmentalists do not have a good track record of helping the poor. In fact, they generally hurt the poor. At the very least PPL wants (as I have already argued) what I call *blue-collar impact statements* on all environmental policies. Environmentalists won a huge battle when they managed to force society to accept environmental impact statements on all projects, but it has given them far too much power; when that power hurts the poor, it needs to be countered. For every policy or restriction environmentalists want to impose on society, we need to see how it impacts the poor first. If it hurts the poor (and not other classes) or hurts the poor too much, then we need to stop or modify its implementation.

The second reason for preferring that egalitarianism trump environmentalism is that the environmentalists do not have a good track record when it comes to making predictions. They have made predictions of dangers that in fact haven't come or are unlikely to come to pass, but we are all forced by them to take steps to avert these dangers, steps that needlessly turn our lives upside down. For example, in the early 1970s we were warned that pollution was so bad that we would soon all have to wear gas masks. This of course didn't happen. We were also warned that certain natural resources were being used up so quickly that we would run out of them. That didn't happen, either. We have also been warned about the dangers of growth, and there are still people today who talk about this danger. Yet these people have never warned us about the dangers of the opposite of growth, namely shrinkage.

Shrinkage has a potentially large impact on our future because of the looming Social Security problem. Since Social Security here in America is set up as a pay-as-you-go system, the younger workers are paying for the older retirees, and in the near future there just won't be enough younger workers to support the older ones who will be retiring and going on Social Security. This is a problem of shrinkage and not of growth; if the population had grown, then Social Security wouldn't be threatened. Likewise, certain professions such as teaching have become less needed, while other professions such as in health become more needed as the average age of society gets older and older. Many other issues could be mentioned in connection with shrinkage, but environmentalists never want to acknowledge their existence.

The biggest boondoggle of the environmentalists has been the global warming scare. That is nothing but Rich People's Leftism in action, despite claims that science is behind it. I've already argued that those pushing for changes because of this perceived warming have not taken into account how their changes will affect the poor. I could spend a great deal of time arguing in favor of skepticism and caution, but it would take me far astray, so I'm going to limit my remarks to just a few points.

First, let me give an analogy. Suppose that instead of leftists dominating academia, conservatives did so, and suppose that conservative scientists had shown that women who get abortions are likely to die at a comparatively young age and that they justified this conclusion with peer-reviewed science. Claims by leftists to know of many women who had abortions who lived beyond this age were dismissed as mere statistical quirks of no value in determining the truth of the matter. Then a scandal erupts when emails are revealed similar to those of the ClimateGate emails. I ask leftists, "Would you still trust the science in this case?" I assume not. But if a scandal similar to the ClimateGate scandal is one that would ruin your trust in the science, why not in the case of global warming as well?

The second point is that there has been a "pause" in the warming for the last decade and a half at least. The pause was not predicted by those who have been warning us about global warming, and it has lasted through a significant percentage of the period in which we have been hearing about global warming. That is, we first heard about global warming in the summer of 1988, which means that over half of the time period since the prediction was made turns out to be wrong. That is hardly persuasive.

The third point relates to peer review. We are frequently told that we ought to accept global warming because it is guaranteed by "peer-reviewed science." I am the last person who would ever be persuaded by such an appeal, given the shabby way I was treated by the peer-review system. (Just as blacks do not trust the police when told what happened when a black has been shot by them, I do not trust the science just because it has been peer-reviewed.) In fact, I think that instead of appealing to peer review to show that global warming is happening, leftists ought to be *reforming* peer review so that it doesn't hurt those of us from modest backgrounds.

But let me ask, Exactly why are we supposed to trust peer review? The left trusts peer review because they have been listening to those at the top only, even though they claim that they listen to those at the bottom. Listening to those of us at the bottom would give a completely different perspective on the matter.

Moreover, those at the top tend to manipulate things. Alexander Cockburn, one of the few leftists who has expressed skepticism about global warming and also about peer review, mentions a story from a scientist, Martin Hertzberg, who tells of how some distinguished German scientists in Nazi Germany formed an "Anti-Relativity Society" that published papers trying to debunk Einstein's theories, which they found repugnant; no doubt these papers were peer-reviewed.[3] Is peer review in this instance to be relied upon? Of course not. Today in climate science we have journals run by people who think that humans are destroying the planet, and as far as I can tell, "peer review" involves these people but not people who don't accept that premise. Isn't it likely they are going to be biased in favor of articles that show global warming and against those that say nothing is wrong? I'm not accusing these people of being in other respects like the Nazis; I'm simply saying that when a group of like-minded people are doing all the reviewing, when everyone running the journals thinks alike, a lot will be published that would not be published were a more diverse group involved in the reviewing. This is not exactly science, and no one should be surprised that there is a "consensus" on global warming.

Despite what environmentalists insist, it's not about science, but trust. Those who believe in global warming typically sneer at science done by those working for oil companies, and they are right to be cautious about such science since scientists in the employ of any company are likely to be advocates for their companies first and scientists second. But likewise, the rest of us are right to be cautious about science done by people who are environmentalists, since they are likely to be environmental activists first and scientists second. Or else peer review itself could be the problem, for it could be thwarted by a few people at the top who believe in global warming and who ensure that all articles that do not accept that premise never get published.

For leftists to have tied their fortunes to the idea of global warming was one of the more foolish things the left has done in my lifetime. Such a program could go wrong in many ways, either because the science was bad, or because it was good enough in a limited way but didn't take into account all possible variables, or because the warming effect was caused by the sun, or because a few large volcanic eruptions could wildly skew all predictions, and so on. The best way for the left to handle new claims in science is simply to say, "Let's wait a bit and see if this result holds." The fact that there has been a fifteen-year pause in the warming, a phenomenon not predicted by those who were screaming that we must believe or be considered the equivalent of flat-earthers, would not then have fueled so much skepticism and mistrust in science. A similar thing can be said about all the dietary claims that have been made in my lifetime. We were told that saturated fats were bad for us and that we ought to avoid them for the sake of a healthy heart, but now we are being told that they aren't so bad after all and that it is sugar and processed foods that are bad. A lot of leftist preaching was predicated on the idea that saturated fats were bad for us.

Before concluding this topic, I want to emphasize that I am not irrational, a liar, like either a flat-earther or a Holocaust denier, or in the pay of the oil companies (though if they want to send some money my way, I won't refuse). I can be persuaded that there is significant warming in one of three ways: (1) actual warming that everyone can actually experience on their own when they step out of their front door, (2) accurate predictions, or (3) solid science.

The first of these hasn't worked. Let me take my own hometown of Minneapolis, Minnesota, as an example. The current all-time high was set in the 1930s when the temperature reached 108° F, and that decade also produced a number of days when the temperature was up to 105°. Yet throughout my childhood the high temperatures never even made it past 100°, and even during the more recent warm period, the temperature still never came close to setting a new record. Anyone who believes in global warming has to take these facts into account, but they almost never do. I simply don't see anything in the temperatures of the last few years that indicates that anything has changed. It is not as though Minneapolis now has snow-free winters. If anything has changed, it is a statistical change that is barely detectable and may be outside the limits of experimental error. I will be told that at the poles, it is a different matter, but not many live in polar regions, and so anyone can say anything they like about what is happening there without fear of being contradicted.

The second way of convincing me is to make accurate predictions, and that hasn't been done. No one predicting global warming predicted the pause of the last fifteen years or so, and as a result, a number of specific predictions have not panned out. For example, in 2007 the BBC reported a prediction that in the arctic summers would be ice-free by 2013.[4] That simply didn't happen. Those who look at sunspots seem to have a better record of making predictions of future weather than climate scientists do.

Finally, there is solid science. If science – done by the best scientists, subjected to intense scrutiny by other scientists posing as devil's advocates, and with all scientists allowed to get their say in – shows that there is global warming, then we ought to believe it. However, the left has foolishly identified solid science not with the cautious process I have just described, but with peer review, which is at best only the first step in such a process and at worst not even that. In addition, the fact that we were being told about global *cooling* back in the mid-1970s does not inspire any confidence that scientists have gotten things right this time. It leads one to predict that soon enough they will change their minds again. Moreover, if global warming is such a dire and urgent problem, how is it that scientists were so wrong about it back then? Presumably, they had solid data for their claims, yet we are now being told that we have had continuous global warming for decades.

Given that those who believe in global warming have a program that entails a lot of back-breaking labor for the poor, I think I am perfectly justified in being skeptical and cautious.

The Representatives of the Poor

For one hundred seventy-five years and longer, RPL has seen the exploited factory worker as the representative of all poor people. Accordingly, whatever perspective the exploited factory has should be the perspective of all poor people, and whatever helps the exploited factory worker is assumed to help all other poor people. From the perspective of the exploited factory worker, a number of familiar conclusions were drawn. Profits were seen as evil since profits constituted money that had been stolen from the worker. In addition, owners—and later on corporations, when they emerged—were seen as evil, along with the entire capitalist system, simply because their existence allowed for the exploitation of the factory worker and encouraged the greed of those at the top. Helping the factory worker therefore entailed owning the means of production, nationalizing industries, and in general using big government, especially central planning, to run the economy.

However, other poor people will see things from their own perspective, which may differ drastically from that of the exploited factory worker. (That is, they will see these things if they are acting rationally and have not been influenced by propaganda from RPL.) Let me consider the possibilities:

- **Exploited servants**. Exploited servants will not see profits as a problem since the entity for which they are working, a household, is not typically engaged in seeking profits, and to the extent that it is (from tenant farmers, for example, living on the household's estate), it is not exploiting the servants by seeking those profits. Nor do exploited servants have any reason to think that corporations or capitalism are evil since their jobs have nothing to do with either because the use of servants predates the arrival of both. Owning the means of production is irrelevant since some of the servants are not engaged in production, and those who are so engaged are producing clean floors and dishes, both of which can be produced by cheap means. (A broom doesn't cost that much.) Accordingly, even if those servants did own the means of production, their situation would change very little. Finally, exploited servants have little reason to see central planning or big government as any kind of solution to their problems.

- **Peasants**. The situation of peasants has little in common with that of exploited factory workers. It has varied tremendously down through the centuries, but since their situation predates capitalism, peasants have no reason to hate capitalism. Nor did anyone prior to the Industrial Revolution ever suggest that the plight of peasants would be improved by government control of the whole economy. Indeed, when leftists did get control of the government in Russia, the peasants were often hurt by the government's edicts.

- **Exploited adjuncts in academia**. Once again, this group has no reason to hate profits. Since they are working in the non-profit sector, profits are irrelevant to their exploitation. Likewise, they have no reason to hate either corporations or capitalism because their institutions have no strong connection with either. Furthermore, some are employed by governments (since they are employed by public universities) and so they have good reason to hate big government as an exploiter. Owning the means of production is nearly unintelligible since they are not producing anything tangible (but having control over the administration would be helpful).

- **Unemployed workers.** The unemployed worker has no reason to hate profits since, not being employed, profits do not represent the theft of part of their pay the way it does for exploited factory workers. Profits can even be seen as a source of good since a company that is profitable may be able to hire people, which is good for the unemployed. Likewise, the unemployed worker sees corporations as the source of future employment, so there is no reason to hate them; and if there is no reason to hate corporations, then there is no reason to hate capitalism. Capitalism does have periodic recessions, which make life hard for the unemployed, but today we can see that the 1920 recession was brief and that perhaps the same thing would have happened in the 1930s if there had been no government tinkering. Moreover, countries in which the government takes full control of the economy have not thrived, and so there is no good reason for the unemployed to prefer them to a capitalist system.

The only commonality among all these groups is perhaps the belief in the greed of those at the top. However, notice that while the exploited factory worker thinks that those at the top are not just greedy but that they have stolen his money as well, the unemployed person can make no such accusation. For the unemployed worker, the greed of those at the top is manifested in their failing to hire new workers at their corporation and instead keeping their profits to buy luxuries. That is a considerably weaker accusation than what the exploited factory worker is making.

CHAPTER 19
A New Role
for the Rich Leftist

My plan for helping the poor via job creation can, I admit, go astray for some poor people if they experience a major setback such as an illness or the death of a spouse or even a broken refrigerator. Since the poor, unlike the middle class, often have no other resources to turn to in situations like this, they can be devastated by such an event. RPL insists that the government step in, but PPL says that rich leftists need to step in. Ideally, those in the upper half should be voluntarily helping those in the bottom half.

In short, we need a new role for rich leftists. Their current role seems to consist mostly in demanding that the rich pay higher taxes, under the proviso that the rich in question do not include themselves, but includes rich conservatives only. In fact, much of what rich leftists do seems to consist in verbally attacking rich conservatives rather than actually helping the poor. We need a new role for rich leftists, one that is more directly activist for the poor.

What this role is can be stated quite simply: it is to give to the poor in one's region, either directly or via a local charity. Giving in this way is more personally satisfying because one can see the results. It allows one more control over where that money is going than when one gives money to the government in the form of higher taxes, because one is more likely to see to whom it goes. Moreover, for rich leftists to do a lot of giving means that rich conservatives would then have less of an excuse to avoid giving to the poor.

In my community growing numbers of families are using a local charity. If I were very rich, I would first find out which of those families were there simply because of something like a broken refrigerator or a utility bill that was unexpectedly high. Paying for these would reduce the number of families using that charity. Next, I would look for those who had high medical bills and pay them off. Next, I would find out which ones would be amenable to retraining, and I would pay for retraining. Finally, I would look for ways to start new businesses (such as restaurants) that would hire those without jobs who weren't amenable to retraining. Doing all that would allow many of the families using this charity to break free and live on their own. That would leave just those whose problems are so severe that a cash infusion wouldn't help them get back on their feet, such as alcoholics, compulsive gamblers, or the mentally ill.

At this point, I would be out at most a few million dollars. No one using a charity is likely to have a medical bill much higher than $100,000, and in my rural location there are unlikely to be more than twenty such people. That would be at most two million dollars, and the retraining costs would hardly add up to more than another half million. For someone who is a millionaire many times over, this would be nothing. Since there are one or two people in my county who are this rich, there should be a nice sum of money flowing into that charity.

In addition, while those who are "rich" only in the sense that they are in the upper half and not the bottom half won't be able to give as much as the multi-millionaires, they would be able to give something, and it all contributes to helping the poor. (A few years ago my wife and I finally escaped from the bottom half, and we now give to the local charity, usually in the form of grocery items, but occasionally in the form of checks to help people pay utility bills.) All that money given voluntarily would greatly reduce the number of people needing to use it. Instead of a flood of people coming in for help, there would only be a trickle. Besides, once the numbers are reduced, those remaining would get a greater share of the charity's resources. The point is to get as many people off the charity rolls as possible. The point is also to use local knowledge regarding who is actually deserving of help, who is just a layabout, who is so hooked on drugs that ordinary help won't suffice, and so on.

Now suppose this practice were instituted everywhere in the world. One of the biggest changes would occur in Africa. Africa is filled with rich elites who stash their money elsewhere when they should be donating it to their neighbors. Instead, we in the West are called upon to give money to them, and it simply disappears into thin air and is never seen again. Cynical observers in the area say that aid money is stolen by the first, second, or third person to lay their hands on it. If it doesn't reach the poor anyway, why should outsiders like us bother giving? I've been to the Third World, and I've seen both the poverty *and the wealth*. Why aren't those wealthy people being urged to give to their neighbors?

In any case, the rich leftists who see their role as merely urging conservatives to pay higher taxes, while they themselves either avoid them or never give anything voluntarily, have to be swept aside. If there are homeless people in an area, their presence should not be seen as an indictment of the local government or any other government, of local corporations or any other corporations, or of capitalism, but instead should be seen as an indictment of the local rich leftists and their stinginess. The question should be, "Why aren't they stepping up and giving money to help those people?" For too long we've heard about how heartless conservatives are and how greedy the corporate bosses are when in fact it is often the other way around: conservatives and corporations are giving, while rich leftists merely shame them into giving while giving nothing themselves. It's time for a new role for the rich leftists, one that involves them giving up some of their money voluntarily.

CHAPTER 20

How to Do
a Redistribution
If It Is Needed

Some critic is certain to say, "Your solution is basically to grow the pie and not to worry about dividing it, in the hope that if the pie grows, then people at the bottom will get plenty. But what happens if the pie doesn't grow, and what happens if rich leftists are not in a position to give as much to charity as you'd like and if rich conservatives won't give? Won't you have to have a redistribution then?"

Let me begin by observing that if your big answer for all time in political economy is that we should focus not on how to grow pies, but on how to divide them; that the way to divide a pie is not to give larger slices to some and tiny ones to others, but is instead to give all equal slices; and that those who don't agree with your answer are not just wrong, but are also immoral, disgusting vermin; then the absolute worst advertisement for your answer is to say and do nothing about an unequally divided pie when it is fully within your power to do something about it. That is the situation today in academia, and as I have already observed in previous chapters, tenured leftists have done nothing about the horrible situation of the adjuncts (involving pay and benefits, among other things). That is the reason I switched from thinking that how pies are divided is the most important thing to thinking that growing them is the most important. It became as clear as could be that many of those who talked of nothing but dividing pies into equal slices were merely engaged in "theater" and didn't really mean it.

But since I've already talked about all that, let me answer the question. Let's say we do need a redistribution. What this entails is higher taxes on the wealthy, so let me spell out the conditions under which I would accept such a policy.

The first condition is that taxes on those in the bottom half should not be raised and, if anything, should be lowered. If we are trying to help people at the bottom, then it makes no sense to tax any of those people at higher rates. Higher taxes on the upper half should not entail higher taxes on the bottom half.

The second condition is that the extra money taken in should not find its way back to the rich, whether in the form of grants or in any other way. Leftists complain about corporate welfare, while I complain about grants to wealthy academics and artists, but in a redistribution neither should be allowed.

A third condition is a simple corollary of the second, that the bureaucracy dealing with this extra tax money should be populated by those from the bottom half. If we are trying to help the poor, then none of that money should be going to the rich. The second condition prohibited that money going to the rich in the form of grants, gifts, or bailouts. But it should not be going to the rich even as compensation for work done, that is, even in the form of salaries. Obviously a bureaucracy will be required to run this redistribution, but those in this particular bureaucracy should themselves come from modest backgrounds.

This is one of the differences between RPL and PPL. Consider how RPL handles this situation. What can we say about the heads of the bureaucracies that deal with redistributions to the poor?

1. They will come from a rich family.
2. They will have been educated at an elite school.
3. They will have a big, fat salary.
4. They will have the job until they retire.
5. The job will last forever.
6. The job will be part of the national government rather than a local government.

PPL declines to accept any of these requirements. There is no reason why someone from a poor family who was educated at the local university can't do this kind of thing, and there is no reason to give them a fat salary. After all, a redistribution takes hard-earned money from other people, so it needs to be spent wisely, cautiously, and prudently.

Nor does it even need to be done by a single person over a long period of time. Consider how the assembly in ancient Athens was run. Citizens were part of this on a rotating basis and not as people who had membership as a permanent job. (And one fine day in 406 B.C. it was Socrates' turn to run things, and he stood firmly against those who wanted to do something illegal.) The head of the agency for redistribution should be someone who was chosen by lot and who has it for a comparatively short period of time before someone else is chosen for the job. There really is no need for someone to have this job permanently. (As an aside, I have to wonder how many of the intellectuals who like central planning would have endorsed it if it had been done in this way.)

Moreover, the agency also ought to be restricted in time. That is, such an agency would ideally be needed only for a limited time, until the rich could afford or be encouraged to give again, or until job creation was creating opportunities again. As such, this agency should never be granted a charter in perpetuity. Its charter should be granted for a limited amount of time, after which it would go out of existence, unless an extension were granted by lawmakers.

Finally, when at all possible the bureaucracy involved in a redistribution to the poor should be run by local governments and not the federal government. Local people are better placed to understand who in their community needs help and what sort of help to give than people in a distant city, who have no idea what is going on. Local people are likely to do this sort of thing better than the federal government.

That is the best way to run a redistribution.

CHAPTER 21
DISPELLING SOME MYTHS ABOUT CAPITALISM

Rich People's Leftism promulgates various myths about capitalism that are necessary to dispel before I conclude.

Myth Number 1: "Republicans help the rich, while Democrats help the poor." I hope that in Part I of this book I have dispelled the idea that Democrats do nothing but help the poor. In some ways they help the poor, and in other ways they don't. (The same can be said about Republicans.) In addition, Democrats help the rich, by giving rich leftists a chance to remain rich while looking like they care about the poor, and also by expanding the government, thus giving them access to good jobs and power.

A more accurate claim is that there are two parties of the rich, and a rough characterization of them would be that the Democrats are the party of rich professionals and the Republicans are the party of rich businesspeople. If you're poor, you have no real party of your own, so you must choose which rich people to follow. One party will help you by trying to raise your pay, while the other party will help you by trying to cut unnecessary costs.

Myth Number 2: "They are poor because we are rich." The "they" in this instance is the Third World, but that is just another way that Rich People's Leftism imposes guilt on people. An obvious counterexample is the old South as it existed when I was young in the 1950s and 1960s. It was poorer than the North, but was that really the North's fault? I think even the most hardened of leftists will say no. The South managed to cripple its economy on its own with no interference from the North. What did they do wrong? They treated a substantial part of the population (blacks) as second-class citizens, they did not emphasize education to the extent that the North did, they were too dependent on agriculture, and so on.

One of the amazing things in my life is seeing how many countries in East Asia managed to rise out of poverty to become prosperous, even though other countries of the Third World languished. For example, South Korea was equal in prosperity to Brazil when I was young, but it leaped ahead because of its superior schooling.[1] Inferior schooling is what one usually finds when a country is poor. They have lousy educational systems. But that is just the beginning of their problems. They are riven by ethnic strife. They have civil servants who demand bribes, which leads people to think that honest work is worthless. They have so many restrictions on opening a business that most people believe that it's pointless (which means they have little in the way of job creation). They have a culture that doesn't value innovation. When they are lucky enough to get some money, they squander it instead of investing in the future. The possibilities are endless.

The worst possibility is that they adopted the ideas of socialists and communists, ideas guaranteed to keep a country in poverty for many years. Redistributions together with lots of regulations don't work very well. Encouraging job creation works much better.

Look at it this way. Individual people can be poor for many reasons, some of which the rich can do little or nothing about. People who gamble away their earnings are likely to end up poor, for example, and if individual people can make stupid decisions, why can't countries do the same?

Finally, let me apply this same idea to academia: "Others have few publications because you have so many." How many academics who are both successful and lean left would agree that the reason they managed to get a lot articles and books published was because many of the rest of us were unjustly prevented from doing so? Not many, I suspect. And how many would want a forced equality scheme in which each academic who wanted to get published would get a certain guaranteed number each decade which they were not allowed to exceed? Again, not many, though that is the logical consequence of their socialist views.

Myth Number 3: "Prior to their exploitation in the factories, the workers of two hundred years ago lived happy lives as peasants." Even during the period when I was closest to accepting Marxism, when I subscribed to *The Nation* and *In These Times* and considered myself to be to some extent a fellow traveler, I did not believe this. My father had been a liberal, but he turned conservative before I was born, so when I was in my socialist phase we had many bitter arguments. But when some of my contemporaries took off to form communes, and he responded by declaring that they would have to work hard to make them succeed, I never felt the slightest urge to disagree. He had grown up on a farm, so I figured he knew what he was talking about, and I myself had been to camps when I was a young teenager where we worked hard (for example, at fetching water). Since then, I've always assumed that the life of the poor has been hard, though with technological improvements, things have gotten better. I would need to see a lot of historical evidence to believe that peasants led wonderful lives, something which I believe no one has yet provided.

Myth Number 4: "Profits are evil." As I suggested back in Chapter 18, that idea comes from the perspective of exploited factory workers, who believe that profits represent money that the owners stole from them. But other poor people have different perspectives on the matter. For example, anyone exploited in an entity other than a for-profit venture, such as a household or a non-profit organization, has no good reason to hate profits. Moreover, the unemployed see profits as potentially good if they lead to job creation. There is no good reason to think of profits as evil just because exploited factory workers think so. If we have to give preference to one of these perspectives, it would be to that of the unemployed, who are in a more desperate situation than that of people who are exploited but are still employed.

Myth Number 5: "People before profits." The same considerations apply to this myth. Let me just say that if the slogan "people before profits" leads to policies that entail that jobs will be scarce, why should I support it? Why should I support high unemployment? Why would that be thought of as a way of helping people?

Myth Number 6: "Non-profit enterprises are moral." Colleges and universities are non-profit enterprises, yet they are the ones engaged in the exploitation of adjuncts.

Myth Number 7: "When profits go up, that entails that workers are being exploited more than before." This myth ignores the likelihood that profits go up when a company is selling to more customers.

Myth Number 8: "Industry X is making obscene profits." That is often said these days about the oil industry, but it has no doubt been said in the past about other industries. I don't know if the expression "obscene profits" means that modest profits are permissible while large ones are not, or if it means that all profits are evil, but large ones are especially evil. Anyway, since there is nothing really wrong with profits, there is nothing wrong with large profits. Typically, what happens when a company is making "obscene" profits is that they are then in a position to offer jobs to more people; is that obscene? This can even include jobs not usually thought of as part of the corporate world, such as a corporate gifts officer. Or else they can offer raises to their workers.

Another point is that those complaining about obscene profits seldom complain about the "obscene" endowments of certain elite colleges and universities, even though obscene profits could lead to good jobs for the poor, while obscene endowments at elite schools seldom do anything for the poor.

Myth Number 9: "More capitalism (i.e., unregulated capitalism) leads to more exploitation." I have already dealt with this in Chapter 11, but it's worth repeating. The exploitation of the Industrial Revolution was the result not of capitalism but of a population expansion (as well as some political factors). The capitalists were creating jobs, but the population pressure was such that even they couldn't produce enough jobs for the growing population; and if they hadn't been around to produce the jobs they did, those people would have been unemployed and living on the streets. Also, with an oversupply of potential professors, tenured leftists in academia haven't dealt with this situation any better than the capitalists of old did, even though they are not capitalists. Capitalism per se has nothing to do with exploitation.

Myth Number 10: "Cooperation is wonderful, but competition is harmful." This sounds wonderful in theory, but in practice it didn't work out so well, as the experience in the communist countries has shown. Also, I have not seen it much in another leftist-dominated area, namely academia.

In Ursula K. Le Guin's novel *The Dispossessed* the main character responds to someone who champions the law of evolution and survival of the strongest in this way:

> Yes, and the strongest, in the existence of any social species, are those who are most social. In human terms, most ethical.[2]

That is one way of looking at how survival of the strongest works among social species (and correspondingly at how important cooperation is), but it is not the only way. A more pessimistic way would be to say that the strongest are the best at manipulating social situations to their advantage. That is not ethical, even if those at the top are good at arguing that it is ethical. Those lower down may not be able to out-argue those at the top, but that doesn't mean they are wrong.

Myth Number 11: "Capitalists are greedy." I used to accept this without question when I was younger until I saw how stingy leftist academics could be. Greed is widespread throughout the population, and saying that capitalists as a group are greedy isn't especially informative, since one could just as well say that workers and other groups are greedy. One could also say that big government is greedy for tax money.

Myth Number 12: "Property is theft." It is fun to say this kind of thing, but the reality is different. If it is supposed to result in the government's owning the means of production, the fact is that the government in the communist countries was in the hands of rich leftists. In other words, some person had control over that property, even if they didn't formally own it, and that person was likely to be a rich leftist and not one of the workers.

Those who argue in journals and books that property is theft—generally, they are professors—certainly don't act like they believe it. Nor are they as egalitarian as they'd like to believe. If they were, then they would be willing to apply their egalitarian principles in academia, but they aren't. Maybe there are some people saying this sort of thing who live their lives as if they actually believed this. It would entail living in voluntary poverty so as to keep one's possessions to the bare minimum. It would also entail being willing to allow anyone to poach whatever they have bought, since they have no real claim to it. Such people are few and far between.

Living this way in our society is hard, but leftists could respond that it might be easy to do if society were structured in a completely different way. Yet, that was tried in the New Harmony colony established by the industrialist Robert Owen, and it failed. It failed partly because skilled laborers had no incentive to join such a colony, since it offered them nothing beyond what it offered unskilled laborers, and partly because obviously there would never be any reason for anyone within the colony to become a skilled laborer for the same reason.

But the biggest objection to the idea that property is theft is that the poor don't like it. The poor don't want everyone dragged down to their level. Instead, they often want to become rich themselves. They are interested in *gaining* the property that they see others getting to enjoy. Dragging everyone else down to the level of the poor is the idea of rich leftists, who as I have argued generally retain their wealth while arguing that property is theft.

Myth Number 13: "Property really belongs to the government." The people who say this sort of thing (generally wealthy leftist intellectuals) never act as though they believe it, and until they do, we can ignore what they are saying. Moreover, since the sort of government they want is a government run by the rich, we have to decline to accept such a theory of property since it will be rich people who will in effect own everything. More useful for the poor in terms of job creation and more in line with what the poor actually want is the libertarian view of property, which says that property belongs to the individual and not to the government or to society as a whole.

Myth Number 14: "Alleged job creation is nothing but the discredited trickle-down theory." If there is job creation, and if the jobs being created are generally ones that poor people will be successful in landing, then it doesn't matter whether the policy that caused those jobs to be created was entailed by a "discredited" policy or not. The point is that they have been created, and they will help the poor. Moreover, while I have opinions on the best ways to create jobs, I am open to anything that works. So far, however, what seems to work best is fewer regulations and lower taxes on the rich (so that they will invest in start-ups). What seems to discourage job creation is the various policies promoted by liberals and leftists: minimum wages, making it hard to fire workers, raising corporate taxes, and so on. In addition, pushing for lots of immigration at a time when unemployment is high is not something that will help the unemployed, even if it doesn't do anything to discourage job creation.

As for the trickle-down theory, what it is and whether it has been discredited I leave to others to explain.[3]

Myth Number 15: "Inequality is bad for society." We've seen how awful "equality" can be by observing the communist countries, with many murdered, many shortages, and so much oppression. But the claim that inequality is bad for society misses the problem. Lack of job opportunities, especially for young people, is the problem. When plenty of jobs are available, most people don't even think about inequality, so it is wrong to talk about inequality as the problem. To the extent that inequality leads to problems, it is still the lack of job opportunities that (to some extent) leads to inequality.

Myth Number 16: "The value of an object produced by a worker is related to the amount of labor by that worker that went into making it (and to nothing else)." This is the labor theory of value, and Marx used it to show that the workers were being exploited because they were getting less for their labor than they should.

Aside from the fact that this theory is devoted to improving just one group at the bottom, the exploited factory worker, while ignoring all the others at the bottom, it can be refuted by a simple counterexample. Consider a skilled craftsman who works on his own. He makes things that he then sells, like artistic coffee mugs. He puts a certain amount of time into making those mugs, and according to the Marxist, that time multiplied by the value of his labor should be the price of the mug. Except that to sell the mug, the craftsman must engage in a lot of other activities. He must somehow attract customers, transport it to where customers are likely to be, or sell it to a middleman who will find customers. All of these activities are time away from his "real" work, which is making mugs. These activities, whether he does them himself or hires someone else to do them, cuts into the money he would ideally get. That is, ideally, an eager customer would show up at his door the instant he finished making his mug, but since that doesn't always or even usually happen, he must engage in these other activities instead of just making mugs. The result is exactly the same as what happens to an exploited worker in a factory, that what should be the wages of the craftsman turn out to be less than what he "deserves." But in this case it wasn't a capitalist exploiting him. In this case, we can see clearly that what depresses his income is rather the exigencies of the situation. He must somehow get the mugs sold if he wants to make a living, and he might not be able to count on eager customers appearing right when he finishes making them.

In other words, we could imagine this craftsman wearing two hats, his productive hat (when he is making mugs) and his nonproductive hat (when he is doing the other things required to keep his business going). We can further imagine dividing that pay between the two hats, and when we do, we see that the productive hat is going to get less than what it deserves according to Marxism, because the other hat deserves some of that money. It is sad, of course, that this means workers will get paid less, but I don't see any way around this situation. (By contrast, while it is sad that adjuncts get so little in academia these days, that situation is something that could easily be changed simply by giving some others doing much the same work less money so that adjuncts could get more.) That is, I don't see any way around this situation that would be effective.

Moreover, any free marketer will point out that the value of the craftsman's labor isn't going to be fixed, but will vary according to the demand for that labor. The craftsman may start out making mugs that people love, but others will train themselves to do the same thing, so his labor won't be as valued as it was before. Or else people will tire of his sort of mugs and want something new, which means he must either continue to produce the old mugs, even though it means a downwards spiral for his income, or he must take the time to come up with a new design that the public likes, and the time required to do that will not produce any actual income.

Now let me consider a somewhat more complicated example. Suppose someone buys a factory from the owners and gives it to the workers collectively, after which they fire all the managers. Will this mean that they finally get the wages they deserve? Let's say they do.

As our world is constantly changing, these worker-owners are going to have to keep on top of things in order to maintain their new high wages. Maybe they will be able to do this, and maybe they won't. Nothing is guaranteed, so their owning the factory doesn't mean anything by itself. (Some will say this is why everything needs to be owned by the government, but there is nothing intrinsically different about that from what I am now considering.)

Moreover, simply owning the factory collectively leaves open a lot of questions about how it is to be run. If the workers decide they should be allowed to work at a relaxed pace, then profits may fall as customers in a hurry decide to go to other producers. Maybe the workers want high wages and lots of vacation, but the same problem may arise. Owning the factory collectively also doesn't entail that squabbles *between* workers will be easier to deal with. If some workers want a relaxed atmosphere and others don't, how will that be decided? What if some of the workers are stealing from the company? How will they be dealt with? Idealists may assume that such thefts won't happen, but it's hard to imagine why not. And what if some workers want their friends to be hired, except that these friends have less of a work ethic than the people wanting them to be hired? Decisions must be made if the price of raw materials goes up, if a competitor drops her prices, if one of the workers comes up with a new but unproven way of doing things, and so on. All these decisions, which are currently decided by managers, will have to be decided on by the workers, and that will take time. Accordingly, even if they contrive to get the wages they deserve, they will find themselves spending extra hours at the factory in order to hold meetings to decide these things, and those extra hours will not increase their pay.

That is to say, suppose they made $10 per hour before ownership, but once they got control of their factory, they fired the managers and divvied up all that money so their pay is now $20 per hour. But now they have to do the managers' work, and this means staying after hours to hold meetings to make decisions. Since they are doing nothing "productive" in those meetings, their pay can't be increased since no products are being produced that would bring in more money. So their overall pay stays the same while the number of hours spent at the factory increases. This means their actual pay per hour will go down. If they are lucky, it will go down only a little bit (say, to $19 per hour), but since they have no experience or education in dealing with these extraneous, managerial issues (such as how to advertise, deal with changing consumer tastes, resolve squabbles, investigate employee theft, and so on), their pay may go down a lot. They could hire experts to deal with these issues, but their first act was to fire the experts they already had, so bringing them back is tantamount to saying that the Marxist theory of labor is worthless. Nor does holding meetings *during* working hours instead of afterwards change anything since this will cut into the time they are actually making things.

There just isn't any guarantee that a worker-owned enterprise will help the workers more than would one owned by a "greedy" capitalist. In fact, not only is there no guarantee that the workers will get more pay, there is no guarantee that the company won't go out of business. Similarly, other schemes, such as having workers take part in corporate meetings, do not guarantee anything, either. And demanding a thirty-hour workweek in order to create more jobs either means that those currently working will take home less each week or that they will somehow get a raise to cover that loss, which means there will be no funds to create any more jobs.

Some leftists will dismiss some of these problems. For example, the mug-maker who has to design a new mug is the victim of consumerism, which is one of the consequences of capitalism. In a Marxist economy, consumers won't be interested in the latest fashion in mugs, and so the mug-maker won't need to design a new mug. That, at any rate, is the theory, though whether it is true in practice is another matter. But there are two important points to make here. The first is that designing a new mug in line with the latest styles may be frivolous, but how about designing a new mug made out of a cheaper material or using cheaper tools? The profit motive in capitalism guarantees that new materials and new tools will emerge all the time, whereas in Marxism, the workers are stuck using the same materials, the same methods, and the same type of tools forever. Possibly, innovations would lead to greater worker safety, but innovations aren't likely to occur because there is little incentive for creating them compared with the incentives in a capitalistic economy.

The other point is that even in a non-consumerist society, the mug-maker will still have to do various other non-productive jobs, such as acquiring the raw materials, repairing broken tools, getting the finished mugs to the customer, doing some bookkeeping, and so on. These are costs that eat into the workers' pay. As Thomas Sowell has pointed out, when Lenin was on the verge of getting power, he thought that all the nonproductive activities in a business could be done easily, but once he gained power and the economy deteriorated, he was forced to change his mind.[4] There just isn't any way to instantiate Marx's theory of value.

Myth Number 17: "We taxed the rich at high rates in the 1950s and 1960s, and it worked in terms of job creation." The 1950s and 1960s were a special time for our country. Europe was devastated by World War II, while the East Asian countries had not yet begun their rise, so America could produce goods for the world without much competition. Moreover, the environmental movement had not yet begun chasing factories overseas, which meant there were many good jobs for Americans in manufacturing. But while the rich were taxed at high rates, *so were the poor*, which actually made things worse for them. Also, I remember the leftist rhetoric of that era, which included the complaint that the rich were wriggling out of those high taxes. There is nothing to suggest that bringing back high taxes on the rich will be anything other than an exercise in futility.

Myth Number 18: "Socialism will work, if only given a chance." This ignores a big question: why should poor people want socialism if they will still be poor? If "socialism" means the poor will stay poor, the middle class will become poor, and the wealthy leftists will get to keep their wealth and control society, poor people will have no reason to care if such a society works or not. As for a genuine egalitarian society, leftists have had many opportunities to create, if not an entire egalitarian society, some egalitarian subset of a society. As I have pointed out, there is nothing stopping tenured leftist academics from sharing their wealth with lowly adjuncts. There is nothing stopping wealthy leftist bloggers from sharing their wealth with poorer leftist bloggers. And there is nothing preventing wealthy leftists from sharing their wealth with poorer leftists. The fact that none of these redistributions ever happens goes a long way toward showing what socialism is really about, and it is *not* actually about redistributing wealth to the poor.

Myth Number 19: "Cuba's problems are the result of the American embargo." That is awfully far-fetched. There are many countries in the world, and all can trade with Cuba. Just because one doesn't do so will hardly affect that country's economy. In fact, when America and other countries band together to slap sanctions on other countries (Iran, for example), the effect isn't as great as they hoped for. Anyway, there is no embargo on Venezuela, and they have still contrived to mismanage their economy.

Myth Number 20: "Fascism is late capitalism." I tended to believe this until I started looking at how fascism actually got started. It was pretty surprising. I hadn't realized that Benito Mussolini had originally been a militant leftist. Moreover, fascism started in Italy, which was only starting to industrialize at the time, so capitalism there was hardly in its *late* stage. Why, then, believe that fascism was closely connected with capitalism? The idea promoted by Rich People's Leftism that fascism represents late capitalism has nothing going for it. On the contrary, some non-leftists have argued that fascism is some kind of variant leftism. Mussolini adopted the idea (that obviously originally came from leftists) that Italy, not just its poor but all of it, represented the proletariat in comparison with the more industrialized countries of Europe. This was why he and other fascists decided that socialism in their situation needed to be national and not international. Moreover, it was the leftist Soviet Union that had a formal alliance with Nazi Germany, not capitalist countries like the U.S. and Britain. Leftists seldom want to advertise this fact, but it happened. Also, the Soviet Union and China each called the other "fascist" in the early Sixties, though neither in fact was capitalist. So much for the claim that fascism is nothing but late capitalism.

It is true that not all on the right believe fascism is a movement of the left. Stephen R.C. Hicks believes fascism is a movement of the right, but he also believes it was strongly anti-capitalistic.[5] He also believes there was a period when those on the right who considered themselves socialist (such as Oswald Spengler) were trying to wrest the socialist label from the left, but as a result of the horrors of Nazi Germany, the socialist right has vanished so completely that not many now are aware of or acknowledge that it ever existed.

Anyway, there is no historical evidence that capitalism leads to fascism. America has been capitalist now for centuries and has never been fascist, despite the predictions, and maybe even the hopes, of leftists that this will happen. As conservatives like to say, leftists always declare America is becoming more fascist, but it is always in Europe that fascism actually erupts.

Moreover, this myth about fascism should be considered together with the possibility of an unsavory beginning to leftism as we know it. How many early "leftists"—and recall that I have argued they were mostly from the upper classes—were motivated not by concerns for the workers, but by hatred of capitalism, the reason being that it threatened their own status? Such people may have championed the workers as a cover for their anti-capitalistic activities, and as I have argued, their concern for the workers has been much less than one would expect, given their rhetoric, while their hatred of capitalism has been much greater than one would expect, given that capitalism actually did help the poor in some ways. (One of the ways capitalism improved the lives of the poor was by making clothing much cheaper than it had been before. We today are used to cheap clothing, but that wasn't true before the Industrial Revolution.) We need to consider to what extent the anti-capitalism movement of the nineteenth century was helped by aristocrats who were unwilling to give up their power and privileges and by conservatives of that era who were unwilling to countenance the changes that capitalism promised. The science fiction writer Sarah A. Hoyt has stated that "in its end stage, communism is a complete reversal of the anti-nobility revolutions of the eighteenth century,"[6] which is why she believes so many rich people have supported it; that is the result they wanted. If so, then communism, far from being a movement for the poor, is really not for the poor at all. It is neo-feudalism. I will not go further into this question, but it needs to be considered against fictional claims about the relationship between capitalism and fascism.

Finally, one could argue that communism, at least as it existed in countries like Russia and China, ended up being nothing but proto-fascism. Neither Russia nor China were industrial powers when they turned to communism, and fascist theorists predicted that a revolution of the proletariat would not work for them.[7] And it didn't.

Myth Number 21: "The lower middle class brought on fascism through their fear of the proletariat." Again, that is very unlikely. One source says that in Italy, the number of members of the proletariat supporting fascism when it gained power exceeded the number in Russia when Lenin took over.[8] Another source says the fascists had an easy time converting workers from communism to fascism, and in addition, fascism was strongly supported by students and even professors.[9] Singling out the lower middle class is not warranted.

Myth Number 22: "There ain't no clean way to make a hundred million bucks." So says a police detective in a Raymond Chandler mystery,[10] but though this is an odd source, it sums up very nicely a Rich People's Leftist attitude that says that anyone who is rich, particularly a rich businessman, must have made his money in immoral ways. I have already discussed this idea in Chapter 14, but let me remind the reader of what I have been saying about academia, namely that just about any criticism of capitalism can be applied equally to academia. Is there a clean way to publish, say, thirty or more scholarly articles and books? I ask this as someone who has spent almost all of his life in the bottom half economically and who also has nary an academic publication to his name. Making a hundred million bucks and having a large number of academic publications look equally unattainable to me, and if one is unclean, the other is likely to be unclean as well. My assumption about those who have many publications is that they had soft referees, unlike the unremittingly hostile referees I was saddled with during twenty years of trying (and failing) to get published, or else that they had connections that I didn't have, or some other easy road to the top. Why should I respect authors whose publications didn't go through the gauntlet that I went through?

Myth Number 23: "You didn't build that." This claim, from President Obama, expresses the general leftist view that big government is helpful to people, even those who are hostile to it, and that cooperation is better than competition. Let me respond by comparing it to academia. Suppose leftist professors were told: "You didn't publish that." How many would agree? Not many, I suspect, even though many of them get federal grants that supplement their salaries. And while leftists like to talk about all the help the government gave to businesses as those businesses rose to success, those who did the building will also talk about the *obstacles* they had to overcome on their way to success. And, yes, some of those obstacles came from the government.

Myth Number 24: "You've made too much money." Leftists love it when this is said to rich conservatives, though I suspect not many rich leftists would like it if it were said to them. But this statement, just like the one in the last myth, points to a huge misunderstanding of how the world of jobs works. Restricting the amount of money that people make can also restrict the number of jobs created, if would-be entrepreneurs decide there is too much resistance to becoming wealthy. Poor people should not care how much money a rich person has, but should care instead how many jobs a rich person is creating.

Myth Number 25: "There's a finite and constant amount of wealth." If so, this myth implies, then anyone who takes more than they need is impoverishing someone else. This myth is no different from Myth Number 2, that others are poor because we are rich. It is odd that people who thought we could raise the social and economic status of blacks *without anyone else being pushed down* would adhere to this particular economic myth, but that is for them to sort out. The point allegedly is that money represents a zero-sum game, with some winning, but others inevitably losing out. This myth is behind the left's intense interest in how the pie is divided as opposed to how we can grow the pie.

Yet the whole business is silly. We can grow more food now not only because we have more areas that we can cultivate than in the past, but because scientific advances ensure that yields are higher, so as far as food is concerned, there is more of it than in the past. And if there is more food, then farmers are getting wealthier, without anyone else losing money. The same can be said about the mining of minerals or producing electricity via hydroelectric, solar, or wind power. Moreover, if I engage in some kind of exchange where I believe I have gained, it often happens that the other party believes they have gained, too, which shows that money needn't represent a zero-sum game.

Myth Number 26: "Socialism is more democratic than capitalism." As I argued earlier, socialism was never conceived in a democratic fashion by those who originally called for it, so historically it never had any connection with democracy, until perhaps the last fifty years when socialist-leaning countries like Sweden also had democracy. Democracy was added on, but there is no reason to say that socialism per se was democratic.

However, on the website of the Socialist Party USA, the statement of principles entitled "Socialism as Radical Democracy" represents an advance over the socialism of the past. The authors of this statement recognize that in the communist countries, ordinary people did not have a lot of control over their lives, which they rightly deplore, and that decisions were made by Communist Party officials, which they also rightly deplore. So they have devised something new:

> Socialism is not about government ownership, a welfare state, or a repressive bureaucracy. Socialism is a new social and economic order in which workers and consumers determine their own needs as well as how they are met, and community residents control their neighborhoods, homes, and schools. The economy is democratically managed by and for the benefit of all humanity, not for the private profit of a few.

This statement sounds nice, but it screams out for details, which are not forthcoming in the rest of the statement. For example, the quote says that as a worker and consumer I get to determine my own needs, but also that the economy will be democratically managed. What is this supposed to mean? If it just means that in the workplace, managers will be elected rather than simply appointed, that might not be so bad. Unfortunately, it may mean that all kinds of rules would be set up regarding work and many other aspects of our lives. For example, let's say that a vote is taken and it is agreed that only a thirty-five-hour workweek will be allowed. No one would be allowed to work less or more than thirty-five hours in any week. Yet obviously this is going to be a big problem because some will want to work more hours in order to buy more things, while others will want to work fewer hours in order to have more free time. Sticking with this law is an example of what is called the tyranny of the majority.

Moreover, once the idea that everything will be up for a vote takes hold, there is no stopping this sort of thing. If anything is clear about the nature of elections, it is that some people lose and don't get their wishes fulfilled. If that's the case, then it should be quite clear that the extent to which I get to determine my own needs will be much more limited than it might seem at first. What sort of products I get to eat, what sort of housing I have, how I get around town, what type and style of clothing I can wear, the kind of music I will get to listen to or the books I will get to read will all be vulnerable to the majority's will, and those who are inconvenienced by that will be ignored. Right now in American society, it seems that the latest dietary information (whatever it may be) brings out the fascist in some people as they want to restrict other people's eating habits, even though individual differences might mandate different types of diet. Or to put it all more starkly, would you approve of your neighbors telling you what television shows to watch and what music to listen to? That is a possible consequence of this kind of democracy.

By contrast, in a capitalist society with free markets, if enough people want something then someone might decide to produce that thing, even if most people don't want it. Their reasoning would be that just so long as some people want it and that they can make money from it, it is worthwhile doing. Maybe I have misinterpreted what these socialists mean when they say that the economy will be democratically managed and that community residents will control their neighborhoods, homes, and schools, but without details it is hard to say.

We have to conclude that either socialism is not democratic, or if it is made democratic, it can become an undesirable sort of democracy in which people become busybodies who get to control what others are allowed to buy and do.

Myth Number 27: "Conservatives want to privatize gains and socialize losses." This is one of the problems facing those who want big government that the rest of us find amusing: the wrong people sometimes get welfare. But let me point out that those who want this are not necessarily conservative theorists, but big corporations, and while leftists identify big corporations with conservatism, conservatives tend to see big corporations as to the left of them.

But let me also point out that leftists are not above wanting to socialize undesirable things, for they want to socialize guilt. They want everyone in the West to feel guilty about slavery and imperialism. On the other hand, they often want to privatize responsibility for helping the poor by limiting it to the particular companies that poor people happen to be working for. "Raise their pay" is the constant cry of the left directed at the owners of some company (such as Walmart), but why not make every rich person (including rich leftists) responsible for helping those workers?

Myth Number 28: "Capitalism destroys as many jobs as it creates." If so, then why have so many immigrants poured into our country in search of jobs? Yes, capitalism destroys some jobs, and that is a problem. (It is why I deviate from what might seem like a completely libertarian position by advocating a safety net in the form of grants for retraining, which I will discuss in the next chapter.) But while capitalism destroys jobs, its record of destruction is nothing compared with that of leftist policies, which destroy jobs at a much higher rate. Leftist policies are generally focused on those already employed, while ignoring the unemployed. Policies that promote a minimum wage, for example, do nothing for the unemployed and discourage job creation, especially by those who are contemplating starting a company.

Myth Number 29: "The current malaise in the world's economy is the result of capitalism." In fact, there were a number of problems that have caused America's malaise. On the left, there was the problem of demanding that poor people be approved for mortgages which they were unlikely ever to pay back. On the right, there was the problem of selling off mortgages whose risks weren't calculated properly. (When a bank sells a mortgage, there is little incentive on their part to ensure that the buyers of the home can pay.) There was the problem of the rating agencies' having given high ratings to bad bonds. The biggest problem seems to have been that the housing industry didn't expect that all housing prices everywhere would all go down at the same time.

As for Europe's problems, even if America's problems are the result of capitalism, Europe's (especially Greece's) are the result of something closer to socialism. Too many people are retiring way too early for the small number of younger workers to be able to pay for their lavish retirement benefits.

Myth Number 30: "The pay of the average American has stagnated for the last forty years, and it is capitalism's fault." Given the large number of changes we have undergone over that time period, it is unfair to blame capitalism while not considering other factors. For example, in the early 1970s the feminist movement encouraged many young women to opt for careers rather than staying home and doing housework. That entailed a large increase in the number of workers, and whenever the number of workers relative to the number of jobs goes up, the power of workers to get higher wages goes down. In addition, the environmentalists added so many new regulations to our factories that many corporations decided it was better to move them overseas, so the number of jobs went down as well. Finally, leftists to the extent that they could have pushed for anti-growth policies, but it is very hard for the poor to maintain their wage levels when the pie is shrinking.

Myth Number 31: "So-and-so was speaking truth to power." This myth is somewhat off the main topic, but I have gotten sick of hearing it. This phrase is often used by leftists these days when an individual (like Cindy Sheehan) without any power says something that goes against what conservative politicians believe. That person, they claim, is speaking truth to power. Yet the truth is that they were not doing anything of the sort because the individual in question has a number of powerful allies (in Sheehan's case, the mainstream media and most people in the Democratic Party) who ensure that their truth is heard by those in power. People who genuinely have no power are seldom heard by those in power, and for a couple of genuine instances of speaking truth to power, take a look at my last two books.[11]

CHAPTER 22
How Is Poor People's Leftism Different from Conservatism or Libertarianism?

Most leftists will be wondering how what I am saying is different from conservatism or libertarianism. First, let me observe that both conservatism and libertarianism suffer from bad press or public relations. Consider the conservatives. It is perfectly true they are reluctant to move to the left, as many leftists have complained. But they are just as reluctant to move to the right, as some of us on the left have found. What I mean is that those of us on the left (such as Bruce Bawer, Phyllis Chesler, Nick Cohen, Paul Berman, and others) who have reacted, not just with disapproval, but with outright horror to the alliance between Western leftists and the Muslim right, an alliance we fear will drag us back to the seventh century, have found that conservatives have no interest in moving to the right either and are just as horror-struck as we are.

As for libertarians, they tend to talk in terms that do not suggest they are interested in helping the poor, even though their policies often help the poor more than leftist policies do. Instead of talking about job creation, for example, they talk about growth, which doesn't sound helpful at all, even though the two often go hand-in-hand.

Anyway, my starting point is vastly different from the starting points of conservatives and libertarians. The conservatives' basic impulse is caution, while the libertarians' basic political value is liberty. My basic goal is helping the poor. That goal is entailed by my holding the political value of equality as higher than other political values, except that I am willing to reject those types of egalitarianism which aren't genuine or which haven't done the poor any good. Let me add that initially I was taken in by leftist rhetoric about helping the poor, until I got into academia and saw how wealthier leftists stomped all over academics like me from poorer backgrounds, after which I realized that much of what they were saying was either unhelpful or else motivated by merely looking good since it was not accompanied by action.

Moreover, while leftists claim to be egalitarian, there have been too many times when I saw them fail to pursue egalitarian goals. As I pointed out in my book on soccer, our schools privilege certain athletes, the big and the tall, because they emphasize certain sports (football and basketball) and not other sports that are more inclusive (like soccer). Yet, when I point this out to "egalitarians," they immediately say that it is not important to make any changes of that sort. Since I am the one who wants to make a change (and yes, it is a progressive change), my wanting that change shows that at least on that issue I am to the left of everyone else. Likewise, in my last book I observed that feminists claim to be in favor of gender equality, but when I point out to them that traditional roles on dating and getting married favor women since men are expected to beg for sex, feminists insist that it is not important to make any changes in that area. Once again, in demanding that those roles be dumped, I am to the left of everyone else. More recently I have been pushing for the idea that affirmative action should include class background, but the support for this among liberals and leftists is weak. Eventually, after watching all this behavior, I concluded that *while the right doesn't like making changes in society, the left doesn't like making changes in its agenda.*

Leftists have principles, but their current agenda (whatever it may be) is always more important than those principles, and pointing out that they aren't acting true to their principles does not cause them to change. I have to go so far as to say that libertarians are more principled than leftists are. That is a harsh judgment, but libertarians generally move in whatever direction their principles push them, while leftists don't. Leftists may dispute the first part of this claim, but they have an image of libertarians constructed by the liberal media, which highlights the occasional unprincipled libertarian, while ignoring all the others. Leftists, meanwhile, constantly make excuses for not following their principles.

In addition to the examples mentioned elsewhere, there are many others. Most leftists who consider themselves anti-war refused to oppose the invasion of Kuwait by Saddam Hussein, and they will keep refusing to do this until the sun stops shining. Leftists also have focused an enormous amount of energy getting America and other Western countries to treat minorities well, but they are unconcerned when majorities in the Third World treat their own minorities harshly. I also earlier mentioned the leftist principle of listening to people at the bottom and how leftists refused to listen to people like me at the bottom of the hierarchy in academia when it came to peer review. There is also the reluctance on the part of rich leftists to engage in voluntary redistributions, to acknowledge that an egalitarian society would not have elite schools, to acknowledge certain harsh truths about academia (that adjuncts in academia are exploited and people from poorer backgrounds are not treated well), to acknowledge that fundamentalist Muslims are sexist and homophobic to a degree completely unknown in the West, and, most importantly, to be critical of themselves and their movement. I don't know of any principled leftists, while there seem to be many principled libertarians.

As for my particular brand of leftism, I believe that where one comes from ideologically means more than where one ends up. If what I am saying looks like something other than leftism, that doesn't mean it can't be leftism or that it must be something else. I started from egalitarianism and saw that redistributions didn't work very well, so reckoning that the point of egalitarianism is to help the poor, I thought about how to do that in the best way possible. What I ended up with is somewhat closer to conservatism and libertarianism, but that doesn't mean I agree with everything they say or with their starting points. Here are some differences:

- I make a major point of lowering taxes on the poor. Leftists want to raise taxes on the rich, and those on the right want to lower taxes generally, which I agree with; but I don't know of anyone who is specifically saying, "Let's lower taxes on the poor." Leftists, for some reason, are not interested.

- I want affirmative action to include class background. Leftists want it to include race and gender, while those on the right want it eliminated. Not many on the left are pushing for affirmative action to include class background.

- I have talked as much as anyone about the plight of adjuncts in academia. People on the right are not too interested, except as a way to show how atrocious academia is; but people on the left are not too interested either. To the extent that they are interested, they point the finger of blame in every direction except where it ought to be pointed: at tenured leftists.

- I don't know of anyone who has pointed out that poor people fall into different groups that have different perspectives and needs and that the left continues to cling to the exploited factory worker as the model for dealing with all poor people. The right could conceivably have done that—and for all I know someone on the right has talked about this matter—but it is not an idea I got from anyone on the right, except in a fragmentary way. That is, many on the right will promote growth as the way to help the unemployed, but I don't know of anyone on the right who has systematically looked at a variety of groups of poor people and argued, as forcefully as possible, that they have different needs and that the left isn't helping the poor by not acknowledging that.

- I don't know of anyone, whether on the right or the left, who has made my distinction between Rich People's Leftism and Poor People's Leftism.[1] I admit I was inspired to make this distinction because of the hints dropped by many on the right who, when discussing some leftist leader of the past, would note they had come from a wealthy or at least a comfortable middle class background. That eventually led me to realize that the left has mostly been run by the wealthy and to suspect that their ideas on helping the poor may not actually be what the poor either need or want.

• I talk a lot about job creation, while people on the right talk more about growth. Job creation may rise with growth, but it needn't do so, so simply pushing for growth in an economy may not help those who are unemployed.

• I have no particular commitment to free trade, which every libertarian wants. When libertarians justify free trade, they point out the advantages this gives to consumers; but as I observed back in Chapter 16, leftists ought to place a higher priority on helping the unemployed than on helping consumers, and if free trade hurts the unemployed, then it needs to go (hopefully temporarily).

In addition, those who advocate free trade sometimes advocate it in circumstances that make no sense. For example, if some other country (like Japan in the 1980s) refuses to buy our products while flooding our country with their own products, free traders will insist that we ought not to put tariffs on their products because then the whole system would break down. But keep in mind that the usual argument of the free traders is that (1) when one country puts up barriers, then (2) the system will break down because other countries will respond in kind. At that point, (3) the original country, having seen what it is like to have barriers put up against its own products, might be persuaded to lower their own barriers. But the free traders never let us get to (3) since they insist that we ought not respond as in (2) by putting up our own barriers in response to another country's doing so. So, we are permanently stuck at (1), which means we have to endure their barriers while having none of our own. It's like having another person punch you constantly and your refusing to punch back because it might lead to a fight.

Japan is involved in another free trade problem in that it refuses to import rice and prefers to grow its own. Free traders think this is insane because there might be cheaper rice on the international market, but it should be pretty clear what Japan's reasoning is. Japan reasons that there may be a day when international markets aren't working—because of, for example, a war—and so it is better to be safe than sorry. It is better to grow one's own rice even if it is more expensive today than to depend on others and find their rice is unavailable tomorrow.

• Another difference also relates to tariffs. America relied a lot on tariffs before the income tax was instituted, and I see nothing wrong with going back to that system. But the libertarians wouldn't like it because it would restrict free trade.

• Yet another difference relates to foreigners as workers. Once again, the priority should be helping our own unemployed citizens before bringing in foreigners, while libertarians will say that companies ought to be able to hire the best available workers and that those may be people from outside the country. (Here is a possible point of difference between libertarians and conservatives, since conservatives worry that too many immigrants will change the character of our society, while libertarians don't care.) Yes, if they really were the best available, that would be a good idea, though too often one finds that foreigners are being hired when there are plenty of Americans who could have been hired. (Those Americans have no voice in policy making and so have no leverage to prevent foreigners from coming in and taking their jobs.) Adding foreigners to the job-applicant pool just makes life harder for Americans.

• I also see nothing wrong with bank deposits being guaranteed by the federal government. Thomas Sowell has pointed out that the reason banks failed in America in the 1930s was because of onerous regulations on banks and that those regulations didn't exist in Canada, which meant that none of Canada's banks failed.[2] Despite knowing that, I still like the security of having deposits guaranteed by the federal government because banks can fail even when they aren't regulated.

• Another difference between me and libertarians is that I am not averse to having a bit of a safety net in the form of a sturdy job retraining program. That is, in spite of my pushing for a new role for rich leftists that consists of giving to locals who need help, what these rich leftists give may not be enough, and so the government may need to step in to help. That doesn't bother me, but it does bother libertarians.

Libertarians have always been far too casual about people losing their jobs. Their point of view is that if capitalism is working properly, other jobs will eventually be created, and those displaced will have new job opportunities. I am impressed by their claim that the recession of 1920 was short-lived precisely because, despite pressure to act, President Harding did nothing at all. The economy righted itself and began working properly again. Had the recession that began in 1929 been handled the same way, it is possible the Great Depression would have been just as forgotten as the 1920 episode has been. But even if a recession is short-lived, that still doesn't mean that people won't experience a lot of pain as they struggle to adjust to new conditions. As I said, libertarians are far too casual about this business; they seem to be looking at the forest and not the trees. (To be fair to libertarians, some environmentalists have been just as casual with their talk of green jobs that will supposedly help those who lose their jobs as traditional sources of energy give way to greener sources.) That is why money that is available for retraining would be a godsend for many.

Sometimes, it is true, retraining isn't the problem, but relocating to a new location, and funds should be available for that, too. What is needed is just something to tide people over until they can adjust to new conditions.

However, the retraining funds shouldn't be the sort I encountered in recent years when I wanted to learn Arabic. After the attacks of

9/11, I thought there might be need for our government to have people with knowledge of Arabic, so I looked for grants that would help me learn it. I found that grants were being given to either teachers of Arabic (who didn't really need them because suddenly they were in demand and could write their own ticket) or else full-time students. But people interested in retraining are uninterested in becoming full-time college students, which requires taking many extraneous classes unrelated to learning a new discipline. Instead, these grants should have gone to anyone willing to learn Arabic, whether they were full-time students or not. People like me, who were unemployed, were ideal since we had the time and the inclination to do so. Full-time students may have been interested only to the extent that they could satisfy a distribution requirement, after which they might have lost all interest (as most of my fellow students in fact did). Forcing people to become full-time students when all they need is to study one subject is not the way to do job re-training.

Of course, allowing governmental funds to be used for job retraining should be implemented only if the money wealthy people are donating does not cover such costs for the poor and unemployed (and if companies themselves are not offering to retrain). If that were the case, then as I argued back in Chapter 14, a governmental safety net of this sort would not likely work very well, so the better policy would be to ramp up efforts to get the rich to donate more.

• Libertarians are fearful of big government, but they are not fearful of big corporations. Leftists are fearful of big corporations, but not of big government. The truth is that there is reason for an individual to be fearful of both. Nor does it stop there. An individual should be fearful of big media (if it tells mostly lies), big schools (that is, the system of schools if it is engaged in propaganda), big unions (if they get too much power and force companies to go bankrupt with their demands), and in fact anything big that can crush an individual who gets in a big entity's way.

- Finally, the most extreme libertarians reject government projects many of us take for granted, like public roads. I have no interest in having all roads be private.

These are the main differences, but there are also problems with libertarianism that I myself encountered. When my wife and I lived in Britain for a couple months back in 1992, we found that ordinary lamps were not sold with plugs; the cord for the lamp ended with bare wires. Either one had to attach a plug oneself (and while I can do this sort of electrical do-it-yourself task here in the U.S., I don't know that I'd want to try it in another country), or one had to hire an electrician. Since we were planning to be there for only two months and since paying an electrician to do this seemed expensive and onerous, we put up with the dingy lighting of our apartment. It was pretty obvious what was going on. No company wanted to be the first to attach a plug to a light because it would raise the price, and the do-it-yourselfers in Britain would have howled. Not until the government stepped in and mandated that all lamps have plugs did the situation change. This was a problem that required government intervention, and it is not the only such situation, though I leave it to others to talk about them.[3]

Let me also point out that liking capitalism doesn't mean liking everything that emerges under capitalism. These days the heads of corporations get raises when their company is failing. This seems about as wrongheaded as can be, and as a leftist I am against it because it means the corporation is probably not fulfilling its primary social responsibility, namely providing good jobs for the poor. Another example is the way that banks were bailed out at the beginning of the current recession, which many leftists hated. However, they don't seem to believe me when I tell them that there were plenty of libertarians who didn't like it, either. Leftists associate the bailout with capitalism, when it was really more politics with both some on the right and some on the left supporting it.

So far I have been enumerating my differences with conservatives and libertarians, but I also share some things with the mainstream left. Unions have been helpful at times, even though I think voting is a better way to deal with labor issues and that job creation is even better than voting is. I also like Minnesota's rent-credit program, which gave me as a renter some nice refunds. Also, since I am pushing for class-based affirmative action and funds for retraining (though only if rich people aren't contributing enough voluntarily), I am to some extent relying on the government. It should be clear by now that I don't really trust the government very much, so some will ask why I bother. However, it is something to try. We tried redistributions, but they didn't work, and if these other possibilities don't work, we can abandon them as well.

Some will insist I am not a leftist, despite what I said at the beginning of this chapter. I doubt they are very leftist, either, but let that go for now. I think I am a leftist, but let's say I'm actually on the right. All I insist is that I am neither a conservative nor a libertarian. Over the last twenty years, I have come to have more respect for those positions than I formerly did, but ultimately I am neither. So if I am on the right, what am I? Taking a hint from those leftists who call themselves left libertarians, I would call myself a right egalitarian. My goal is to help the poor, and there are so many flaws in the way that leftists are currently doing this that they really ought to be embarrassed by their policies.

One last point on the subject: if I am on the right, it was the left's inaction on the problems of academia that drove me there. Who was sticking up for adjuncts? Who was sticking up for me when I got nothing but rejections for perfectly satisfactory articles? Not tenured leftists. (I wrote plenty of letters to them complaining about the situation.) Nor were outsiders offering any help. Where were the communists? Where were the socialists? Nowhere. I used to enjoy reading Anthony Lewis's column in *The New York Times*, but as the 1990s wore on, and as the adjunct situation got worse,

I found he never had anything to say about it, and so I got tired of reading yet another column of his on the mistreatment of some foreign traveler or immigrant by our Immigration and Naturalization Services department. I thought that the book *Manifesto of a Tenured Radical* by leftist Cary Nelson, in which (as I mentioned in Chapter 8) Nelson talked about the reactionary response of tenured leftists to a strike by teaching assistants at Yale, had all the makings of a strong wake-up call for the left, but it turned out not to be, and there was no soul-searching about why tenured leftists would stomp all over members of a union. It was always so much easier for tenured leftists to denounce America's foreign policy than to deal with a terrible problem in academia.

This is the background against which I abandoned the left as it now exists. Accordingly, I began, as I like to think, not so much turning to the right as becoming more willing to read people who didn't like leftists. I learned a lot from the right, but I still don't think of myself as being on the right.

CHAPTER 23
A WHOLE NEW LEFTISM

It should be evident from what I have said that a leftism run by and for the poor will be quite different from leftism as we now have it. To begin with, the priority of such a leftism would be the poor and not some other issue or group. Those who think the left should give equal weight to other issues or groups should think about what I explained in an earlier chapter, namely that it is impossible to have two top priorities. Situations will always crop up that force one to make a decision about which issue will be favored on that occasion. One could try to randomize these decisions so they could go either way, but I've never heard of this being done. The reality is that one of the two is favored over the other, and during the last forty years or so the poor have suffered because leftists gave priority to other causes.

Environmentalists will take issue with this, but as I have already argued, they do not have a good track record on helping the poor. It would be different if there were, say, vouchers given to everyone in the bottom half to compensate for the high price of gasoline and for other environmental policies, but there are not. Instead, environmentalism is in effect a regressive tax on the poor. In addition, environmentalists do not have a good track record in making predictions. They predict horrible outcomes from this or that activity, but those horrible outcomes do not happen, or else new technology comes along and makes the whole issue irrelevant.

Next, although the preferred method of helping the poor today is via redistributions funded by high taxes, I have argued that those don't work very well for the poor. The money coming in to be redistributed is never enough, some of the money collected actually goes to the rich, and worst of all, redistributions are not usually what the poor want. What the poor usually want are job opportunities that allow them to escape poverty. Accordingly, the various systems that dominated the last century such as communism and socialism can be dismissed as nothing but Rich People's Leftism.

To further strengthen this conclusion, the adjunct situation in academia shows that all the rhetoric associated with those systems can be junked. There simply isn't a good reason any more to talk disparagingly about profits, corporate interests, private property, free markets, capitalism, or any of the other related concepts that leftists rail against. Adjuncts have been exploited in non-profit institutions that are obviously not corporations and do not try to be capitalistic. Moreover, the preferred solution to this problem so far by everyone on the left has been the free market solution. Anyone who finds these conclusions altogether beyond the pale is invited to apply socialist principles within academia, where they will be resisted despite the fact that leftists dominate.

One of the elements of leftist rhetoric was the prediction that capitalism was going to die, but that hasn't happened. The best time for it to have happened was in the 1930s, but it didn't die. It was still around when I was young, and in addition, was working quite well for the workers. But then various things ruined the situation, such as the leftist emphasis on environmentalism, which put more costs on corporations that in turn hurt the workers. (Either they lost their jobs as factories were shut down, or they had to take pay cuts, or their jobs were sent overseas). In addition, schools deteriorated so that workers weren't as well prepared for the jobs their parents had had, and rebellious attitudes were instilled in students that did nothing for them in terms of getting employment.

Where does this leave the poor? The fact is that the poor are going to have to make an alliance with some rich people in order to thrive. Rich leftists want the poor to ally themselves with them (rich leftists), but that hasn't worked so well. It is better when the poor become allies with rich conservatives. Rich conservatives are the people who run the corporations that the poor hope to be employed by. If the poor hate corporations, whom do they think is going to employ them? They can of course run their own little companies, but not enough of them have the talents to do this; or they can hope to be employed by the government, but we have seen what happens when everyone is employed by the government: it just doesn't work very well and does nothing to get the poor out of poverty. It is better, then, to avoid hating corporations if you hope to get a good job.

In addition, at least some of the leftist rhetoric on corporations is suspect. Those who say that corporations run the government but who then turn around and say we need more government to help the poor are not making any sense.

Thus the poor are better off siding with rich conservatives than with rich leftists. I have called the former Poor People's Leftism and the latter Rich People's Leftism. A variety of differences exist between these two approaches to helping the poor, which I recounted in Chapter 17. Perhaps the most important is that government, so beloved by today's leftists, fades in importance. It is not wholly unimportant, but it should not be seen as some magical factor in society that automatically will help the poor. Sometimes it helps the poor, and sometimes it hurts them. That is the sum of the experience I and others have had with government.

Where does this leave leftism? It doesn't seem to have a distinct message for economic policy anymore. I cited some differences between me and people on the right in the last chapter, but I will admit they are rather small. What message, then, remains for leftism? In terms of economic policy, there is almost none, but there is a problem looming that the left should be dealing with, and that is what Megan McArdle has called the mandarinization of America.[1] The mandarins in China, she explains, became mandarins by doing well on a test, and we are fast approaching the same kind of system here in America. There are strengths to such a system, she acknowledges. The mandarin elite "really are very bright and hardworking." However, they are also "prone to be conformist, risk averse, obedient, and good at echoing the opinions of authority, because that is what this sort of examination system selects for." Moreover, "the even greater danger is that they become more and more removed from the people they are supposed to serve." She goes on to argue that too many younger people rising through the ranks in academia, government, and journalism don't have a lot of variety of work experience: "The road to a job as a public intellectual now increasingly runs through a few elite schools, often followed by a series of very-low-paid internships that have to be subsidized by well-heeled parents, or at least a free bedroom in a major city." A century ago, for example, journalists were often people who had worked their way up from the lowest jobs at a newspaper, but now people come out of the best schools and get good jobs as reporters right away. People who try working their way up from the bottom don't get very far. They generally stay at the bottom.

But the biggest problem—one she doesn't dwell on too much—is that the poor are mostly shut out of such a system. This is what I experienced in academia where I ran into the "class" ceiling.

We see this same idea at work when the Democrats nominate a presidential candidate. The last time the Democrats nominated a candidate who hadn't gone to Harvard or Yale was way back in 1984. The argument Democrats give me in support of this practice is that this way they know they are getting the best. But supporting alumni from elite colleges over everyone else, whether as presidential candidates or for other jobs that are intellectually challenging, is in effect to create an aristocracy, for it entails that no poor person who didn't do well on standardized tests when they were young adults will ever be allowed to get one of those jobs in preference to those who did. Even when they show superior abilities later on in life, they will still be excluded.

This is the kind of class discrimination that the left needs to be fighting. It is a fight I thought was won in the early nineteenth century, but apparently we still need to fight it. It is a fight to ensure that upward mobility remains an important feature in American life, the way it used to be. It is true that leftists these days often complain about the lack of upward mobility here in America. They think this is a complaint against capitalism, but it is just as much a complaint against a system that leftist elites themselves like and promote. Moreover, while people on the right may believe that some *races* are less intelligent than others, elites on the left seem to believe the same thing about different *classes*. They have put implicit faith in standardized tests, even though such tests greatly favor the wealthy since those who do well on tests are likely to come from wealth. Even when the wealthy don't initially do well on tests, they have many resources for improving their scores, such as high-priced tutors and extremely good private schools, resources that are out of reach for the poor. In addition, they marry each other, making it likely that their children will stay in the same niche as they, while the poor are almost completely shut out.

Tests don't test everything. They don't test for creativity and originality. They also don't indicate the trajectory a person is on. That is, the implication behind the test score is that everyone with a similar score is improving at the same rate; but what if they aren't? I was on a steep trajectory when I first took a philosophy class as a sophomore in college. I got only a C in that class, and even that was probably a gift. (Robert Nozick claimed he failed three classes in philosophy as an undergraduate,[2] yet he still ended up as a professor of philosophy at Harvard.) The next term I did better, and I kept improving until I was a graduate student in the subject. I kept going until I had a Ph.D, and then I still kept going. Even when I had had my Ph.D. for just four years, I remember feeling mildly insulted when I was at a job interview and one of the interviewers asked me about my thesis. I had moved well beyond my thesis at that point, so why ask me about that and not my current work? I kept moving beyond my thesis for a number of years afterwards until I had done as much as I wanted to do. The book that I finally produced—and had to self-publish—incorporated the findings of my Ph.D. thesis, but that material took up perhaps a paragraph or two at most. The rest of that book was all done afterwards.[3] As I said, I was on a steep trajectory, but tests wouldn't show that. Nor would looking at what I had done on my thesis, which I admit was mediocre.

Lest you think I'm bragging, let's not make it about me. Let's just say someone was on a steep trajectory, steeper than everyone else around them. How would you know this by looking at what they did on a test at age eighteen or twenty-one? At that point, they might still be level with everyone else, or even below them. Yet at some time in the future, they are going to be far ahead of all the people who tested better than they did. This point was made by the artist Susan Rothenberg. She had risen to the top, enough to be written up in *The New York Times Magazine*, but here's what she said: "Growth is more important to me than talent. I was not the best kid at art school, by any means. I'd love to know what that best kid is doing right now."[4] Her unspoken implication is that the best kid in art school hadn't ended up at the top, no matter how much promise he or she had shown.

Another person who could not easily be tracked and who was on a steep trajectory is the printmaker Steven Andersen. According to an account of him in a newspaper,[5] in high school he hung around with juvenile delinquents until he got into trouble and a judge told him to find some new friends, after which he began hanging around with the "hot-rodders." After high school, he joined the Navy and was put on a ship headed to Vietnam. After that, he tried to enroll at my own alma mater, the University of Minnesota, but his grades in high school weren't good enough, and they told him to try what we now call community colleges. Once there, he got straight A's and was finally allowed to enroll at the University of Minnesota. He was taking art classes and doing well when he happened to sign up for a lithography class. He said he thought it had something to do with "contour mapmaking," which he knew about from his time in the service, but instead it was about printmaking, about which he knew nothing. But Andersen quickly became the best student in the class. The professor, Zigmunds Priede, commuted between Minneapolis and a print shop in New York reputed to be the best in the country. "During that first semester, Jasper Johns, sometimes called the greatest American print artist, asked Priede to do a print and Priede asked Andersen to help. Before long he, too, was commuting to [the print shop in New York]." It turned out Andersen was not just the best student in the class, but maybe one of the best in the entire country; at any rate, by the time he graduated he had already established himself as a printmaker in New York. Not many people rise that far and that fast, but it can happen.

Relying on tests means believing tracking works, that is, believing we can make accurate predictions about what sort of futures people are likely to have. I do not trust such predictions. Even if they are mostly right, they are not always right. As I have already observed, several people I knew in high school who seemed to show little academic promise were nevertheless allowed into college where they came alive intellectually. Using tests to track people will mean missing out on people who are late bloomers, on steep trajectories, taking unusual paths of intellectual development, or simply brilliant without doing well on standardized tests. Leftists often attack some policy of conservatives by complaining about the small percentage of people whom the policy mistreats, but it is the same with tracking that uses these tests. Some people who deserve to be at the top will fall through the cracks, and it should be the left's job to see they aren't prevented from reaching the top.

This, then, is the new role for the left. It should be the left's role to ensure that upward mobility can still happen for the poor and that people aren't judged simply by how well they did on a test when they were young adults. They should be judged on actual accomplishments later in life and not just on test scores. Another way to say all this is that we ought to use sports rather than academia as a model for helping the poor. Sports do a very good job of helping poor people make it to the top, while academia does a terrible job. Or to put all of this in a still different way, supposedly only 20% of the jobs in our economy require a college education. From an egalitarian standpoint, what is the best way of deciding which 20% of the population will get these jobs? So far, the left's answer is that society will use tests given to young adults and that those who do best on those tests ought to have first crack at these jobs, an answer that basically favors the rich over the poor. Perhaps some leftists would disagree with this answer, but this is the answer given by leftist elites. Nor am I the only one thinking this about leftist elites. McArdle says:

> Even many quite left-wing folks do not fundamentally question the idea that the world should be run by highly verbal people who test well and turn their work in on time. They may think that machine operators should have more power and money in the workplace, and salesmen and accountants should have less. But if they think there's anything wrong with the balance of power in the system we all live under, it is that clever mandarins do not have enough power to bend that system to their will. For the good of everyone else, of course. Not that they spend much time with everyone else, but they have excellent imaginations.[6]

Destroying aristocratic privilege was what the left, when it first emerged during the French Revolution, aimed at. It is what the left should have aimed at in the Russian Revolution, except that by that time the left had gotten pointlessly distracted by socialism. Today, the left's goal ought to be to destroy any emergent aristocracy, and it can help to do that by accepting affirmative action based on class background.

I have no doubt this idea would split the left. Those leftists in my poorer position will be with me, while those on top will be against me. As I remarked earlier, I doubt that those who spent so much money on their children's education want them to have to compete on level terms with the likes of me. They expect to get their money's worth, no matter how much this goes against the egalitarianism they think they accept. But these people often say they want a class war. Well, let this be the class war that they get.

Let me conclude with this thought. Karl Marx said the point of philosophy wasn't to understand the world, but to change it. It turns out that to help the poor we don't need to go so far as doing what Marx thought we should do, namely destroying capitalism. What we need to do instead is to ensure that capitalism works for the poor, and capitalism works for the poor when it is creating lots of jobs. Let us create a plethora of good jobs for the poor so they can easily escape poverty and in so doing find a satisfactory niche in society that suits them.

NOTES

Introduction

1. When I was in the last stages of preparing this book, Joel Kotkin published a book with related themes, *The New Class Conflict* (Telos, 2014). While his book appeared too late for me to make much use of it, let me note that his term "gentry liberalism" (p. 8) seems to correspond to my term "Rich People's Leftism."

2. When I speak of the middle class, I mean people in the middle between the very rich and the very poor. This is not the way that Thomas Picketty defines it in his recent book *Capital in the Twenty-First Century* (Belknap Press of Harvard, 2014). On pp. 250-251 he defines the middle class as those between the rich and the bulk of the population, so that they are in the 50th percentile up through the 90th. I doubt if most Americans think of the middle class in this way, and I assume Picketty's definition is something accepted by the French, but not by Americans.

3. *The New York Times*, November 15, 1987, section F, p. 18.

4. *Soccer, the Left, and the Farce of Multiculturalism* (AuthorHouse, 2010) and *Begging for Sex: Gender Equality from the Other Side* (AuthorHouse, 2012).

Chapter 1

1. Garrison Keillor, *Homegrown Democrat* (Viking, 2004).

2. Thomas Frank, *What's the Matter with Kansas?* (Metropolitan/ Owl, 2004).

Chapter 2

1. Reserve Mining Company vs. Environmental Protection Agency, overturned on appeal 1974, to RMC's favor.
2. *Washington Post*, Jan. 16, 2005, p. W12.
3. *Wall Street Journal*, Dec. 1, 1994, p. A18.
4. *The New York Times*, Nov. 3, 2004, via the Internet.
5. *Columbus Dispatch*, Sept. 30, 2005, A8.
6. *Los Angeles Times*, "A Vicious Cycle in the Used-Car Business," Oct. 30, 2011, via the Internet
7. Victor Davis Hanson, "Liberal Indulgences," October 28, 2011, from the Internet site *Pajamas Media*: http://pjmedia. com/victordavishanson/liberal indulgences/?singlepage=true.

Chapter 3

1. *Columbus Dispatch*, Oct. 10, 2002, p. G7.
2. For example, *Wall Street Journal*, May 12, 2000, p. A18.
3. I am relying on information from Bill Buford, author of *Among the Thugs* (Norton, 1991), which he gave at a talk at the Hungry Mind Bookstore in St. Paul, June 3, 1993.

Chapter 4

1. *Wall Street Journal*, May 9, 2003, p. A10.
2. *CBS News* for March 7, 2013.
3. Specifically, Richard Vedder, an economist at Ohio University, has argued for this claim. For a brief statement of his views, see Mark Steyn, "Gaudeamus Janitor," *National Review*, August 25, 2013, from the Internet.
4. *The New Yorker*, Nov. 28, 1977, p. 49.

5. Christopher Lasch, *The True and Only Heaven* (Norton, 1991), note on p. 499.
6. Jonah Goldberg, "You Can't Say That," column for July 7, 2007, via the Internet.

Chapter 5

1. See Bryan O'Keefe and Richard Vedder, "Griggs vs. Duke Power: Implications for College Credentialing," an article from the John William Pope Center for Higher Education Policy (via the Internet).

Chapter 6

1. John C. Goodman, "Keeping Poor People Poor, on townhall. com, October 22, 2011.

Chapter 8

1. For example, *The New York Times*, March 14, 1990, p. B7.
2. Robert J. Sternberg, "What Should We Ask About Intelligence?" *American Scholar* vol. 65, Spring, 1996, 205-6.
3. See also Malcolm Gladwell, *Outliers: The Story of Success* (Back Bay, 2008), chapters 3 and 4. He makes many similar points: that those who are smart but poor are often hampered by lack of opportunities, and that those who win Nobel Prizes come from a variety of schools and not just the elite ones since winning such a prize probably depends on more than just doing well on a standardized test.
4. According to James D. Watson, *The Double Helix* (Mentor, 1968), pp. 102-4.
5. João Magueijo, *Faster than the Speed of Light: The Story of a Scientific Speculation* (Penguin, 2003), p. 217.

6. Cary Nelson, *Manifesto of a Tenured Radical* (New York University Press, 1997) p. 143.
7. Jane Austen, *Persuasion* (Oxford Edition), p. 19.
8. Simon Winchester, *The Map That Changed the World; William Smith and the Birth of Modern Geology* (Perennial, 2002).

Chapter 9

1. Hedrick Smith, *The Russians* (Ballantine, 1976), p. 211.
2. Richard Pipes, *Communism: A History* (Modern Library, 2001), pp. 43 and 149-150.
3. Smith, *The Russians*, p. 272.
4. Smith, *The Russians*, p. 276.
5. David Ramsay Steele, "The Mystery of Fascism," from the Internet.

Chapter 10

1. Smith, *The Russians*, p. 622.
2. Smith, *The Russians*, pp. 33 and 652.
3. Smith, *The Russians*, pp. 461-2.

Chapter 11

1. C.P. Snow, *The Two Cultures* (Cambridge, 1969), p. 27.
2. Snow, *Two Cultures*, p. 26.
3. Snow, *Two Cultures*, p. 27.
4. See, for example, Thomas Sowell, "Third World Sweatshops," Jan. 27, 2004, and "Third World Sweatshops, Part II," Jan. 28, 2004, both from the Internet.

Chapter 12

1. See, for example, "Wealth by Degrees," *Economist*, June 28, 2014, p. 66. The chart displayed on this page shows the percentage of people in various countries aged 55 to 64 years old who have a university degree. For the U.S., it is about 41%, while for Britain it is about 31%. In fact, the percentage for the U.S. is not only higher than it is for Britain, it is also higher than it is for every other country on the chart (South Korea, Japan, France, Sweden, Greece, and Germany). It is true that it also shows the percentage of people aged 25 to 34 who have a university degree, and three of those countries now do better than the U.S: South Korea, Japan, and Britain. But this doesn't invalidate my point, which is that poor people when I was young were more likely to get a college degree in capitalist America than in many countries that were more socialist. Even if conditions have changed, that still represents a demerit for socialism, as does the fact that the U.S. even today does better than Sweden or Germany.

2. Sarah A. Hoyt, "Of Books, Compassion, and Cruelty," from her blog entitled *According to Hoyt*, June 6, 2013; my italics.

3. "We can't afford it," said one of them as quoted in the *Economist* magazine, Feb. 2, 2013, special report p. 4.

4. See also Megan McArdle, "The New Mandarins," Feb. 21, 2013, on the Internet at *The Daily Beast*. I will be talking about this essay in more detail in my last chapter.

Chapter 13

1. George Walden, *The New Elites: Making a Career in the Masses* (Allen Lane, 2000) pp. 22-3.

2. Whittaker Chambers, *Witness* (Random House, 1952), p. 616.

3. Joshua Muravchik, *Heaven on Earth: The Rise and Fall of Socialism* (Encounter, 2002), pp. 230-243 on Gompers, and 229-230 and 244-257 on Meany.

4. Muravchik, *Heaven on Earth*, p. 261.

5. See, for example, Sarah A. Hoyt, "And Shame the Devil," on her blog *According to Hoyt*, Feb. 2, 2014:

> The rich are more likely to be extreme left. And it's not guilt. It's that they know what is the end result of communism: a sort of techno feudalism. They want that. In its end stage, communism is a complete reversal of the anti-nobility revolutions of the eighteenth century.

6. *Economist*, March 12, 2005, p. 49.

7. The first one I found was from Xan Smiley, "Misunderstanding Africa," *The Atlantic Monthly*, September 1982, p. 72: "An eccentric Frenchman traveling downstream by raft from the distant headwaters of the Zaire River was recently greeted by joyful villagers as the harbinger of a returning Belgian administration." See also the *Economist*, Aug. 30, 2003, p. 62, which briefly mentions the wish of some Africans for recolonization. There is also Ibn Warraq's *Defending the West: A Critique of Edward Said's Orientalism* (Prometheus, 2007), pp. 171ff., which argues that Hindus owe to the British knowledge of their own past, which they had forgotten and the British had managed to retrieve.

8. He said this on his blog, but I now can no longer find it.

9. *Economist*, Sept. 10, 2005, special section, p. 8.

Chapter 14

1. *Economist*, Feb.2, 2013, special report page 4.

2. G.A. Cohen, *If You're an Egalitarian, How Come You're So Rich?* (Harvard, 2000), p. 152.

3. Cohen, *Egalitarian*, p. 153.
4. Cohen, *Egalitarian*, pp. 153 and 176.
5. Cohen, *Egalitarian*, p. 158.
6. Cohen, *Egalitarian*, p. 164.
7. Cohen, *Egalitarian*, p. 166.
8. Cohen, *Egalitarian*, p. 167.
9. Cohen, *Egalitarian*, p. 169.
10. Cohen, *Egalitarian*, p. 175.
11. Cohen, *Egalitarian*, p. 178-9.
12. Niall Ferguson, *Money: A Financial History of the World* (Penguin, 2009), p. 211.
13. John Rawls, *A Theory of Justice* (Belknap Press of Harvard, 1971), p. 3.
14. Rawls, *Theory*, p. 137.
15. Rawls, *Theory*, p. 83.
16. Picketty, *Capital in the Twenty-First Century*, pp. 105-6.
17. *Times Literary Supplement*, June 23, 2000, p. 6.

Chapter 15

1. In my book on soccer (*Soccer, the Left, and the Farce of Multiculturalism*, pp. 215-6), I observe that it is obviously against the self-interest of blacks in America who are of average or less than average height to prefer basketball to soccer, yet no one on the left seems interested in telling them this.
2. Abhijit V. Banerjee and Esther Duflo, *Poor Economics* (Penguin, 2011), p. 226.
3. Banerjee and Duflo, *Poor Economics*, p. 167.

Chapter 16

1. Incidentally, see the column by black conservative Walter E. Williams, "Race and Economics," (Aug. 31, 2011, on the Internet), where he observes that the minimum wage was originally used to curtail black employment.
2. See Thomas Sowell, "A Return to Keynes?" from the Internet, Oct. 15, 2013. I admit that other factors may have been at work that would render Sowell's analysis worthless. For example, the level of household debt in the earlier recession was minimal compared with what it became by the later one.

Chapter 18

1. Karima Bennoune, *Your Fatwa Does Not Apply Here* (Norton, 2013), pp. 178ff.
2. See my blog, *I Want a New Left*, and my book *Begging for Sex*, ch. 12. In that book, I recommended a book by Hege Storhaug, *But the Greatest of These Is Freedom*, in which she points out the brutal way that Muslim women are treated in Muslim enclaves in Norway. (I apologize to her for getting the name of it wrong in that book.) In other words, not only does RPL's policy hurt women, gays, and secularists in the Middle East, it can hurt them here in the West, also.
3. Alexander Cockburn, "The Psychopathology of Shrinks," *Counterpunch*, weekend edition, June 16-18, 2007, from the Internet.
4. "Arctic Summers Ice-Free by 2013," Wednesday, 12 December 2007, *BBC News*, by Jonathan Amos, http://news.bbc.co.uk/2/hi/7139797.stm.

Chapter 21

1. *Economist*, June 6, 2009, p. 36.
2. Ursula K. Le Guin, *The Dispossessed* (Avon, 1974), p. 177.
3. See, for example, Thomas Sowell, *Basic Economics* (Basic Books, 2004), pp. 388-9.
4. Sowell, *Basic Economics*, p. 126.
5. Stephen R.C. Hicks, *Explaining Postmodernism: Skepticism and Socialism from Rousseau to Foucault* (Ockham's Razor Publishing, 2004), pp. 130-4.
6. From the entry entitled "And Shame the Devil" on her blog *According to Hoyt*, Feb. 13, 2014.
7. See A. James Gregor, *The Faces of Janus: Marxism and Fascism in the Twentieth Century* (Yale, 2000). On the emergence of fascist thinkers in Russia as the Soviet Union was dying, pp. 97ff. On the critique of communism in Russia by Italian fascists, pp. 133ff. Some of those giving this critique were Italian Marxists.
8. Gregor, *Janus*, p. 25.
9. F.A. Hayek, *The Road to Serfdom* ed. Bruce Caldwell (University of Chicago, 2007), pp. 80-81: "The relative ease with which a young communist could be converted into a Nazi or vice versa was generally known in Germany, best of all to the propagandists of the two parties. Many a university teacher during the 1930s has seen English and American students return from the Continent uncertain whether they were communists or Nazis and certain only that they hated Western liberal civilization." Also, p. 182: "From 1914 onward there arose from the ranks of Marxist socialism one teacher after another who led, not the conservatives and reactionaries, but the hard-working laborer and idealist youth into the National Socialist fold."
10. Raymond Chandler, *The Long Goodbye* (Ballantine, 1953), p. 227.

11. *Soccer, the Left, and the Farce of Multiculturalism* (AuthorHouse, 2010) and *Begging for Sex: Gender Equality from the Other Side* (AuthorHouse, 2012).

Chapter 22

1. Joel Kotkin has recently published a book in which he uses the phrase "gentry liberalism" in a way that seems to correspond to my "Rich People's Leftism." See note 1 above in the Introduction.
2. Thomas Sowell, *The Housing Boom and Bust* (Basic Books, 2009), p. 125.
3. Scott Alexander talks about this topic extensively in an Internet article called "The Non-Libertarian FAQ (aka Why I Hate Your Freedom)," at his blog raikoth.net: http://raikoth. net/libertarian.html.

Chapter 23

1. Megan McArdle, "America's New Mandarins," at *The Daily Beast* on the Internet: http://www.thedailybeast.com/articles/2013/02/21/america-s-new-mandarins.html.
2. Robert Nozick, *Philosophical Explanations* (Belknap Press of Harvard, 1981), p. viii.
3. *Forgotten Debates: The Hidden Story of Ancient Greek Philosophy* (AuthorHouse, 2006).
4. Grace Glueck, "Susan Rothenberg," *The New York Times Magazine*, July 22, 1984, p. 20.
5. *The Minneapolis Tribune*, December 26, 1980, p. 1C. No doubt this account comes from Andersen himself, but I have no reason to doubt its general point.
6. Megan McArdle, "America's New Mandarins."

INDEX